INTERNATIONAL DEVELOPMENT IN FOCUS

Scaling Up Nutrition in the Arab Republic of Egypt

Investing in a Healthy Future

CHRISTOPHER H. HERBST, AMR ELSHALAKANI,
JAKUB KAKIETEK, ALIA HAFIZ, AND OLIVER PETROVIC, EDITORS

 WORLD BANK GROUP

Contents

Boxes

Figures

Tables

Foreword

Maximizing the nutrition status of women and children is not just a moral obligation but also critical from an economic perspective to increase the well-being of the individuals and ensure a more inclusive and just society. Nutrition is an essential component of strengthening human capital—the knowledge, skills, and health that people accumulate so they can become productive members of society. Moreover, investments in nutrition interventions, in particular those that target women and children, pay off not only in economic terms but also in supporting the success of other development interventions.

The Middle East and North Africa Health, Nutrition, and Population Team of the World Bank is working across the region to maximize rapid progress toward a world in which mothers are healthy and all children arrive in school well-nourished and ready to learn, can expect to attain real learning in the classroom, and are able to enter the job market as healthy, skilled, and productive adults. This is closely aligned with the broader efforts by the World Bank of supporting countries in the Middle East and North Africa region move from stabilization to transformation, unlock the vast economic potential of youth and women, and ease the constraints that hamper their creative energies.

This report, *Scaling Up Nutrition in the Arab Republic of Egypt: Investing in a Healthy Future*, was produced in close collaboration with UNICEF Egypt. It generates new important evidence on the nutrition situation in Egypt, including evidence to help policy makers understand the potential benefits of scaling up key interventions and to identify and prioritize the most cost-effective package of interventions. The findings of the report will be of interest to researchers and policy makers involved in developing and implementing nutrition interventions and all those who are working toward the goal of maximizing human capital in Egypt and beyond.

Rekha Menon
Practice Manager
Health, Nutrition and Population
Middle East and North Africa Region
World Bank Group

Foreword

This investment case in nutrition shows that the faces of malnutrition in Egypt are changing, revealing a triple health burden: persistent stunting, increasing wasting, and rapidly rising overweight among children, a rate that is now one of the highest in the world. Far too many children are not getting the diets they need. This deprivation undermines their capacity to grow, develop, and learn to their full potential.

UNICEF recently launched *The State of the World's Children* report, underscoring its commitment to improving the nutrition of children and highlighting UNICEF's new nutrition strategy, setting out the plan to improve the nutrition of children and women. We know what actions are needed to prevent malnutrition. A positive change needs the political determination of the government across the sectors of health, education, water and sanitation, and education and food systems. It needs the right amount of funding, including investment from the private sector. By working together, we can ensure that every child, young person, and woman has affordable access to the nutritious, safe, and sustainable diets they need.

I want to express our commitment to work for better nutrition for every child, especially in the crucial first 1,000 days—from conception to the age of two years—and during adolescence, two unparalleled windows of opportunity for child development.

Bruno Maes
UNICEF Representative in Egypt

Acknowledgments

This report was prepared under the overall guidance of Ernest Massiah (practice manager, World Bank) and Asad Alam (director, World Bank). It was led by a team composed of Christopher H. Herbst (senior health specialist, World Bank) and Amr Elshalakani (senior health specialist, World Bank). The team worked closely with Alia Hafiz (senior nutrition officer, UNICEF Egypt), Jakub Kakietek (economist, World Bank), and Oliver Petrovic (chief of Child Survival and Early Development Section, UNICEF Egypt), who provided guidance and support on development of the report. Matthew Robinson (consultant, World Bank) provided invaluable advice and input on editorial and structural matters.

Editors of the overall report are Christopher H. Herbst, Amr Elshalakani, Jakub Kakietek, Alia Hafiz, and Oliver Petrovic. Chapters were authored by a combination of World Bank staff and consultants. Chapter 1 was written by Jonathan Kweku Akuoku (World Bank); chapter 2 by Frank Hu and Yanping Li (Harvard University); and chapter 3 by Fayrouz Sakr-Ashour (University of Maryland), Bjorn Ljungqvist, and Matthew Robinson (independent nutrition consultants). Rania Abdelnaeem and Nahla Zeitoun (World Bank) provided critical input for the chapters on social protection–related issues and interventions. Chapter 4 was authored by Davide de Beni (United Nations Population Fund) and chapter 5 by Helen C. Connolly (American Institutes for Research).

The team would like to extend particular thanks to the following World Bank staff (in alphabetical order) for their valuable advice and support throughout the development of the report: Hanzada Aboudoh, Gustavo Demarco, Mariam Ghaly, Poonam Gupta, Sherif Hamdy, Aliya Husain, Fatima Mansouri, Layla Mohamed-Kotb, Rekha Menon, and Mariam William Guirguis.

The team would also like to sincerely thank the minister and staff of Egypt's Ministry of Health and Population and other key agencies and development partners for their guidance, assistance, and contributions during this study.

Last but not least, the team would like to thank Meera Shekar (global lead on nutrition, World Bank) and the Scaling up Nutrition (SUN) Trust Fund donors for the financial contribution that made the production of this report possible. Financial support for this work was provided by the government of Japan through the Japan Trust Fund for Scaling Up Nutrition.

Executive Summary

The Arab Republic of Egypt has achieved significant improvements in key health indicators over the last 30 years, particularly maternal and infant mortality. However, Egypt has been identified as one of the 36 countries in which 90 percent of the global burden of malnutrition falls (Horton et al. 2010). It is, then, facing the growing challenge of a "double burden" because overweight and obesity among children and women of reproductive age are rising, along with the incidence of wasting, whereas the level of stunting has plateaued. As a result, Egypt is currently on track to meet only one of the six nutrition targets established by the World Health Assembly (WHA) for 2025 (WHO 2017).

Malnutrition is a huge burden on Egypt's economy. According to the study *The Cost of Hunger in Egypt* (IDSC 2014), undernutrition, as manifested in poor linear growth (stunting), wasting and micronutrient deficiencies in children, and anemia in women of reproductive age, will sap an estimated 1.9 percent of Egypt's annual gross domestic product (GDP) through productivity foregone and costs to the health system. Altogether the economic hemorrhaging will amount to about $3.6 billion a year. At the same time, as noted, Egypt is facing a further challenge from the coexistence of overweight and obesity with undernutrition among children, leading to a double burden of malnutrition.

The government of Egypt (GoE) has shown a strong political commitment to assessing and addressing malnutrition. A nutrition "landscape analysis," the first in Arab countries, was carried out by the Ministry of Health and Population (MOHP) and the United Nations Children's Fund (UNICEF) in 2011 (MOHP 2012) to complement the ministry's 10-year National Food and Nutrition Policy and Strategy 2007–2017 (NFNPS). The landscape analysis described the extent of the malnutrition problem (including rising obesity rates) in Egypt and provided possible solutions to optimize outcomes with the available resources. It provided clear immediate, medium-term, and long-term recommendations to guide investments in nutrition. Two more recent policy reports, the *Nutrition Agenda for Action* (MOHP, NNI, and UNICEF 2017) and the *Nutrition Stakeholder and Action Mapping Report* (MOHP and UNICEF 2017) further specified the key challenges and corresponding priority actions needed to strengthen nutrition governance, coordination, and accountability mechanisms, as well as mobilize the available resources to improve the targeting and coordination of nutrition interventions in the most vulnerable areas.

The objective of this report, developed at the request of the government of Egypt in close collaboration with UNICEF, is to help inform the development of an updated nutrition policy and strategy and to guide nutrition investments over the next five years. The report provides an updated overview of Egypt's nutrition situation, the nutrition-specific and nutrition-sensitive interventions currently in place, opportunities to scale up the response to alleviate the burden of malnutrition, estimates of the costs and benefits of scaling up key interventions, and analyses of the fiscal space required to implement these key interventions at scale. Although the overnutrition situation in Egypt is discussed in chapter 2, in the remainder of the chapters in this book the emphasis is on undernutrition. Additional considerations and analyses will be needed to address overnutrition challenges and the rising obesity rates.

Nutrition status and determinants among children and women in Egypt

This assessment of nutrition status uses the UNICEF conceptual framework of malnutrition and analyses data from the Egypt Demographic and Health Survey (EDHS) to understand the status and trends of key indicators and identify the immediate, underlying, and basic determinants of malnutrition in Egypt.

Stunting remains at a high level of public health significance in Egypt, with the prevalence among children under 5 higher than the average in the Middle East and North Africa region. Although there are less discernible differences in the levels across wealth quintiles, the reduced disparity has been due in part to the greater downward trends among the poorest wealth quintiles and in part to a significant upward trend among children from the richest wealth quintiles. There is a general downward trend across the regions of Egypt, but prevalence has sharply increased in urban Upper Egypt in more recent years. The declining trend is significant for both boys and girls, as well as in rural but not urban areas. Key determinants of stunting include being a boy, maternal education, size at birth, urban residence, and residence in urban Upper Egypt.

Wasting has increased significantly since 2000, rising from a low to a medium level of public health significance after 2005 and steadily climbing since. The increasing trend is significantly higher for the frontier governorates (versus urban governorates) and among girls. The increasing trend in wasting prevalence is also significant across urban and rural areas. Similarly, there is an increasing trend across all wealth quintiles. Key determinants of wasting include residence in the frontier governorates, younger age, birth order, and maternal body mass index (BMI).

Egypt is facing the challenge of the double burden of malnutrition, with almost 15 percent of children under 5 overweight. Overweight is a significant and increasing public health problem in Egypt, with rates increasing steadily since the 1990s among children under 5, and particularly among those living in urban areas. Children who are overweight or obese are at an increased risk of obesity in adulthood (Black et al. 2013) and are at a higher risk of developing serious health problems, including type 2 diabetes, high blood pressure, and liver disease (WHO 2014). Meanwhile, among the 14.9 percent of overweight children in Egypt in 2014, 7.6 percent were also stunted. This double burden should be considered in any strategy or intervention designed to tackle malnutrition.

High levels of overnutrition are affecting women of reproductive age, with more than 80 percent overweight or obese. The prevalence of obesity among women is alarmingly high across all wealth groups and education levels. Diet quality in Egypt is heavily influenced by long-standing food subsidy policies that focus on energy-dense foods. This may have resulted in the overconsumption of calories by Egyptians, especially poor and rural populations. Rising food prices and food inaccessibility have led more families to revert to calorie-dense foods rather than consume nutrient-rich foods (WFP 2013), resulting in a higher likelihood of being overweight. EDHS data and the literature reveal that maternal obesity is a critical factor in the development of childhood obesity, and thus the time period of pregnancy and childbirth is an important window for the prevention of maternal obesity.

Although the recent data on micronutrient status and deficiency are limited, the available data indicate high levels of anemia among both children and women and reduced consumption of iron and vitamin A–rich foods among children under 5. In 2014 almost one-third of children between 6 and 59 months of age were anemic, which was an improvement since 2008, but still detrimentally high. The anemia prevalence among children has been especially high in the frontier governorates and rural areas and in children from poorer households. Fewer than one in seven children 6–59 months of age received a vitamin A supplement in the short term. However, this low rate is likely due to vitamin A capsule (VAC) supplementation being provided only in conjunction with the immunization visits at 9 and 18 months.

Only about one in three women of reproductive age in Egypt report receiving vitamin A supplements after their delivery, although it can prevent night blindness and support the immune function. The level of supplementation is showing a declining trend and also varies significantly across regions of Egypt. Anemia in pregnancy is related to higher maternal mortality, low birthweight, and increased perinatal mortality. Iron deficiency can result from inadequate consumption of iron-rich foods and, among women of reproductive age, the depletion of iron stores during menstruation. Iron supplementation during pregnancy is a key intervention to reduce levels of anemia. In 2014 a majority of women (67 percent) reported receiving iron supplements during their last pregnancy—a significant increase over 2008 (42.5 percent).

Undernutrition interventions in Egypt: status, gaps, and opportunities

Compared with many other countries affected by a large and detrimental burden of malnutrition, Egypt, as a lower-middle-income country, has strong resources and institutional frameworks (including private sector) that should be able to initiate and sustain effective nutrition actions at scale. To date, however, Egypt has not achieved a high or sustained level of impact from implementing a significant number of nutrition-relevant interventions over an extended period of time.

Recent global evidence points toward focusing on critical nutrition interventions during the 1,000-day period from a child's conception until second birthday. Because the majority of the linear growth deficits that make up the under-5 stunting burden accumulate during this time, reflecting nutrition deficiencies, interventions during this period have the greatest impact on nutrition outcomes and ensure that children have every opportunity to grow and thrive (Victora et al. 2010). The 2013 *Lancet* series on maternal and child nutrition identified 10 evidence-based, nutrition-specific interventions that would most effectively address undernutrition and micronutrient deficiencies within this period (Bhutta et al. 2013). However, Egypt is currently experiencing gaps in the coverage of many key interventions, resulting in suboptimal nutritional status among infants and young children.

Nutrition interventions provided at nominal fees (almost free of charge) by the public primary health care and maternal and child health system have mainly targeted pregnant and lactating women as well as children under 5. These interventions include growth monitoring and promotion (GMP), infant and young child feeding (IYCF), social and behavior change communication (SBCC), iron–folic acid (IFA) supplementation in pregnancy, iron supplementation in children 0–24 months of age, and vitamin A supplementation for postpartum mothers and infants and young children.

Other major investments in addressing hunger and malnutrition on a national scale have been primarily through food fortification and heavy food subsidies. Universal salt iodization (USI) can be considered a success story, currently reaching 91 percent of households. National programs to fortify oil with vitamin A and wheat flour with iron unfortunately were suspended in the aftermath of the 2011 revolution before they could be fully evaluated. Food subsidy interventions have existed for decades in Egypt. However, the mainly calorie-dense and nutrient-poor food items provided through the subsidy program may have encouraged greater consumption of these at the expense of other food groups, notably in urban Egypt. A recent study found that, when compared with nonbeneficiaries, the probability of mothers being overweight was higher among beneficiary families (Breisinger et al. 2013). However, recent changes to the subsidy program have added a wider range of subsidized foods, although beneficiaries are now required to submit a copayment for the subsidized commodities, which may limit access among poorer households.

As for other nutrition-sensitive interventions that involve the nonhealth sectors, emerging evidence points toward good opportunities in the area of water, sanitation, and hygiene (WASH) interventions (especially in underserved communities). The cash transfer scheme, Takaful, has added conditionalities that give households incentives to invest in health, nutrition, and education (regular school attendance and health care visits for pregnant women and young children). A 2018 evaluation by the International Food Policy Research Institute (IFPRI) revealed some encouraging results in terms of nutrition outcomes (Breisinger et al. 2018). The Ministry of Social Solidarity (MOSS) is also piloting an approach with the World Food Programme (WFP), MOHP, and the Ministry of Supply and Internal Trade (MOSIT) as part of the first 1,000 days program model in three governorates in Upper Egypt. The pilot is targeting Takaful beneficiaries, including pregnant women and children 0–24 months of age, for receipt of a food voucher for nutritious foods after they meet the conditionality that they receive regular nutrition services within the primary health care (PHC) units. However, the approach will have to be evaluated for impact in due course.

Although there are four recognized pathways through which agriculture can positively affect nutritional status (Ruel and Alderman 2013) and the GoE is investing heavily in national agriculture production and logistics, these investments do not have explicit objectives for affecting nutrition outcomes in Egypt. A countrywide early childhood development (ECD) initiative was recently launched to reorganize, revamp, and scale up a comprehensive ECD program linked to the health system, spanning from motherhood to early primary school. However, it is too early to determine whether it could have an impact on nutrition outcomes. In primary education, the focus is on school feeding. However, this aspect of the initiative is primarily aimed at encouraging enrollment and attendance at school and supporting learning by alleviating short-term hunger with, at best, modest effects on health and nutrition outcomes.

Overall, the analysis of nutrition status reveals still high levels of malnutrition in Egypt among children under 5, adolescents, and women of reproductive age, in particular. Moreover, there is little evidence that any of these interventions and programs are currently contributing as effectively as they could be to the control of the most urgent problems of malnutrition: stunting, wasting, overweight/obesity, and anemia and other forms of micronutrient deficiency. Meanwhile, there are some noticeable gaps in programming, particularly in interventions that could affect overweight and obesity.

Based on the identified gaps in programming, the global evidence base on the key effective nutrition-specific interventions, the available evidence around nutrition-sensitive programs, and the availability of delivery platforms in Egypt, interventions and programs with the most impact and scale-up potential were identified in order to address malnutrition more comprehensively in Egypt. The 16 interventions selected based on these criteria are listed in table ES.1.

TABLE ES.1 Sixteen interventions selected to address malnutrition in Egypt

INTERVENTION	DESCRIPTION	TARGET POPULATION
Infant and young child feeding (IYCF) and micronutrients		
1. Promotion and support of breastfeeding	Communication of optimal breastfeeding practices	Pregnant women and mothers of children 0-6 months
2. Promotion of complementary feeding	Communication of complementary feeding practices (excluding provision of food)	Mothers of children 6-23 months
3. Growth monitoring and promotion (GMP)	Systematic strengthening of GMP guidelines and operational procedures, training, and scale-up	Children 0-59 months
4. Iron supplementation	Weekly supplementation with iron drops for three months, followed by three months of no supplementation and repeated until child is 5 years old	Children 6-59 months
5. Vitamin A supplementation	Biannual supplementation of vitamin A capsules	Children 6-59 months
Curative interventions (MAM/SAM)		
6. Treatment of moderate acute malnutrition (MAM)	Treatment of MAM in supplementary feeding programs	Children 6-59 months
7. Management of severe acute malnutrition (SAM)	Severely malnourished children admitted in either inpatient or outpatient therapeutic feeding programs	Children 6-59 months
Disease prevention and management		
8. Treatment of diarrhea (ORS)	Management of mild and moderate diarrhea with oral rehydration solution (ORS)	Children 6-59 months
9. Therapeutic zinc supplementation	As part of diarrhea management with ORS	Children 6-59 months
10. Deworming	Annual or biannual single-dose albendazole (400 milligrams) or mebendazole (500 milligrams) to reduce the worm burden of soil-transmitted helminth infection	Children 12-59 months

continued

TABLE ES.1, *continued*

INTERVENTION	DESCRIPTION	TARGET POPULATION
Maternal nutrition		
11. Iron–folic acid supplementation	Three months supplementation of iron–folic acid during pregnancy	Pregnant women
Water, sanitation, and hygiene (WASH)		
12. Use of improved water source	Regulation and advocacy activities to ensure access to water supply services from an "improved" source within 1 kilometer of the user's dwelling. An "improved" source is one that is likely to provide "safe" water.	All households
13. Use of water connection in home	Regulation and advocacy activities to ensure access to safe water from a household connection	All households
14. Improved excreta disposal (latrine/toilet)	Promotional activities to ensure access to improved/hygienic excreta disposal (access to improved latrine or flush toilet)	All households
15. Hand washing with soap	Promotional activities for "appropriate" hand washing behavior	All households
16. Hygienic disposal of children's stools	Promotional activities for the proper disposal of children's stools	All households

Successful scaling up of these identified nutrition interventions in Egypt will require careful sequencing and selection of implementation approaches. It will be important to both demonstrate confidence-boosting early achievements and simultaneously build a foundation for sustained nutrition interventions reaching all vulnerable groups. Three potential scale-up scenarios were identified: (1) scale up all 16 interventions to full national coverage; (2) prioritize all 16 interventions only in the governorates with the highest burden of stunting; and (3) scale up to full national coverage the most cost-effective interventions for stunting reduction out of the 16.

Because the majority of the nutrition interventions proposed are delivered through the health system, strengthening this system is fundamental to the success of any nutrition scale-up plan. Key platforms for delivering nutrition-relevant interventions include antenatal care, well-baby clinic visits, community-based nutrition programs, and child health days. The GoE has already taken steps in this direction by initiating an operational trial to test the provision of an integrated "best practice" package of nutrition services under the primary health care (PHC) system in two districts in Lower Egypt in 2017. It includes a fully revised Standardized Protocol of Action for Nutrition Services (SPANS) within the first 1,000 days, aiming to address weaknesses in the demand side, supply side, and enabling environment for stunting prevention. The trial is intended to continue for a total cycle of five years, paying particular attention to cost and impact and a discussion of results as the trial proceeds. Egypt is also set to undergo broader health care system reform and health sector restructuring. Both are expected to improve public health care service dramatically in terms of quality and equity.

Furthermore, in the scaling-up process the GoE must assume effective leadership, while recognizing that effective internal coordination and linkages (among government sectors, administrative levels, and agencies) as well as external cooperation (with development partners, civil society organizations, and the private sector) will be critical for success.

Cost-effectiveness of potential scale-up scenarios

Although Egypt is a lower-middle-income country, the cost of scaling up even a limited number of high-impact nutrition interventions to improve nutrition outcomes may be prohibitive. However, the potential economic benefits from scaling up key interventions could far outweigh the costs of implementation. With that in mind, an economic analysis was carried out to help policy makers understand the potential benefits of scaling up key interventions and to identify and prioritize the most cost-effective package of interventions. This analysis was conducted by combining costs with estimates of impact to identify the most significant and cost-effective combinations of interventions in the Egyptian context based on the three scale-up scenarios just outlined.

Of the 16 interventions singled out as having the greatest potential to be scaled up and a positive effect on malnutrition (particularly stunting) in the Egyptian context, 13 could be modeled using the Lives Saved Tool (LiST). LiST estimates the global health impacts of scaling up key interventions by modeling outcomes around health and nutrition outcomes, among others. The modeled interventions included IYCF (promotion of breastfeeding and complementary feeding), micronutrients (IFA for pregnant women and vitamin A for children), MAM/SAM treatment, treatment of diarrhea (oral rehydration solution and zinc), and five WASH interventions.

Analysis of the three scale-up scenarios revealed that, to prevent stunting of the highest number children, Egypt should prioritize funding the most cost-effective interventions that achieve the same result as full coverage: IYCF (especially promotion of appropriate breastfeeding and complementary feeding), IFA supplementation, vitamin A supplementation for children, and promoting hygienic disposal of children's stools—all resulting in 421,360 cases of stunting prevented. When comparing the costs and benefits of delivering only the most cost-effective interventions in stunting reduction to the other two scenarios, this scenario provides better value for money: the cost per death prevented is $19,412; the cost per stunting case prevented is $196.

Prioritizing implementation of the most cost-effective interventions for stunting reduction is also estimated to translate into and return the highest economic benefits over the productive lives of children who receive the interventions (a return of $17.87 in economic benefits for each dollar invested). However, this approach comes at a cost: by not implementing the treatment of acute malnutrition (MAM/SAM), it will not have any impact on the current levels of wasting and will prevent only 4,249 additional deaths (30 percent of the full national coverage scenario). Maintaining the supplementation of oral rehydration solution (ORS) and zinc for the treatment of diarrhea at current coverage levels means that further potential gains in combating malnutrition will not be realized.

This scenario is also estimated to translate into and return the highest economic benefits over the productive lives of the children who receive the interventions. The estimated benefit-cost ratio for implementing this scenario in Egypt, 17.87, suggests that every dollar invested would result in about $18 in economic returns and $1,326 million in productivity gains, indicating that the benefits of investing in nutrition significantly outweigh the costs.

Fiscal space to scale up nutrition

Identification of funding options is critical to ensuring that one or more of the scale-up scenarios can be implemented to improve nutrition outcomes. Thus an analysis of the existing and projected fiscal space was carried out to understand whether it is conducive to absorbing the additional costs of implementing the scale-up scenarios.

The analysis found that improved macroeconomic conditions in the long run as well as medium-run efficiency gains are two areas with good prospects of generating significant additional resources for nutrition. Other potential sources offer more limited opportunities. These include (1) higher funding through the health budget but limited by competing priorities for finite resources and highly centralized decision making; (2) raising further funds in the health sector through, for example, earmarked taxes for health (or nutrition), and yet difficulties arise from the evolving and multisectoral nature of nutrition and the potential negative impacts of such taxes; and (3) foreign assistance, but Egypt is not reliant on external funding for nutrition.

In the long run, it is reasonable to expect significant economic growth from the increased productivity of Egypt's workforce arising from the reduction in stunting. Lower levels of stunting and the resulting improved health will also reduce reliance on social programs and cut stunting-related health costs. Aside from economic growth, the government's revenue could also increase if tax revenue grows through an expanded tax base, new taxes, or more efficient tax collection.

Allocative and operational efficiency gains can be obtained in the medium run by focusing on delivery of the most cost-effective interventions in stunting reduction: IYCF (especially complementary feeding), IFA supplementation for pregnant women, iron and vitamin A supplementation for children, and promotion of hygienic disposal of children's stools. These interventions are also those that can be scaled up quickly either with existing capacity or with relatively small investments. This strategy is expected to translate into substantial economic benefits and return the highest economic benefits over the productive lives of the children who receive the interventions.

REFERENCES

Bhutta, Z. A., J. K. Das, A. Rizvi, M. F. Gaffey, N. Walker, S. Horton, P. Webb, A. Lartey, and R. E. Black. 2013. "Evidence-Based Interventions for Improvement of Maternal and Child Nutrition: What Can Be Done and at What Cost?" *Lancet* 382 (9890): 452–77.

Black, R. E., C. G. Victora, S. P. Walker, Z. A. Bhutta, P. Christian, M. de Onis, M. Ezzati, S. Grantham-McGregor, J. Katz, R. Martorell, and R. Uauy. 2013. "Maternal and Child Undernutrition and Overweight in Low-Income and Middle-Income Countries." *Lancet* 382 (9890): 427–51. doi:10.1016/S0140-6736(13)60937-X.

Breisinger, C., P. Al-Riffai, O. Ecker, R. Abuismail, J. Waite, N. Abdelwahab, A. Zohery, H. El-Laithy, and D. Armanious. 2013. "Tackling Egypt's Rising Food Insecurity in a Time of Transition." Joint IFPRI-WFP Country Policy Note. IFPRI andWFP, Washington, DC, and Rome.

Breisinger, C., D. Gilligan, N. Karachiwalla, S. Kurdi, H. El-Enbaby, A. H. Jilani, and G. Thai. 2018. "Impact Evaluation Study for Egypt's *Takaful and Karama* Cash Transfer Program: Part 1: Quantitative Report." MENA RP Working Paper 14. International Food Policy Research Institute (IFPRI), Washington, DC, and Cairo, Egypt. http://ebrary.ifpri.org/cdm /ref/collection/p15738coll2/id/132719.

Horton, S., M. Shekar, C. McDonald, A. Mahal, and J. K. Brooks. 2010. *Scaling up Nutrition: What Will It Cost?* Washington, DC: World Bank. doi:10.1596/978-0-8213-8077-2.

IDSC (Egyptian Cabinet Information and Decision Support Center). 2014. *The Cost of Hunger in Egypt: Implications of Child Undernutrition on the Social and Economic Development of Egypt.* Cairo.

MOHP (Ministry of Health and Population). 2012. *Egypt Nutrition Landscape Analysis Report 2012.* Government of Egypt, Cairo.

MOHP (Ministry of Health and Population), NNI (National Nutrition Institute), and UNICEF (United Nations Children's Fund). 2017. *Nutrition Agenda for Action: A Policy Paper on Scaling Up Nutrition Interventions in Egypt.* Cairo: UNICEF. https://www.unicef.org/egypt /reports/nutrition-agenda-action-cairo-2017.

MOHP (Ministry of Health and Population) and UNICEF (United Nations Children's Fund). 2017. *Nutrition Stakeholder and Action Mapping Report.* Cairo: UNICEF. https://www .unnetworkforsun.org/sites/default/files/2018-08/Nutrition%20Stakeholder%20%26%20 Action%20Mapping%20Report-Egypt.pdf.

Ruel, M. T., and H. Alderman. 2013. "Nutrition-Sensitive Interventions and Programmes: How Can They Help to Accelerate Progress in Improving Maternal and Child Nutrition?" *Lancet* 382 (9891): 536–51. https://doi.org/10.1016/S0140-6736(13)60843-0.

Victora, C. G., M. de Onis, P. C. Hallal, M. Blössner, and R. Shrimpton. 2010. "Worldwide Timing of Growth Faltering: Revisiting Implications for Interventions." *Pediatrics* 125 (3): e473–e480. doi:10.1542/peds.2009-1519.

WFP (World Food Programme). 2013. *The Status of Poverty and Food Security in Egypt: Analysis and Policy Recommendations.* Preliminary Summary Report, Cairo.

WHO (World Health Organization). 2014. "Global Nutrition Targets 2025: Childhood Overweight Policy Brief." WHO/NMH/NHD/14.6. Geneva.

———. 2017. "Global Targets 2025 Tracking Tool: Country Progress Report 2017—Egypt." Geneva. https://extranet.who.int/sree/Reports?op=vs&path=%2FWHO_HQ_Reports/G16/PROD /EXT/Targets_Menu&VSPARAM_varLanguage=E&VSPARAM_varISOCODE=ALB.

Abbreviations

ANC	antenatal care
BFHI	Baby Friendly Hospital Initiative
BMI	body mass index
CAPMAS	Central Agency for Public Mobilization and Statistics
CCT	conditional cash transfer
CHW	community health worker
CRS	Creditor Reporting System
CSO	civil society organization
DAC	Development Assistance Committee
DALY	disability-adjusted life year
DHS	Demographic and Health Survey
ECD	early childhood development
EDHS	Egypt Demographic and Health Survey
EU	European Union
FAO	Food and Agriculture Organization of the United Nations
FDI	foreign direct investment
GAIN	Global Alliance for Improved Nutrition
GDP	gross domestic product
GMP	growth monitoring and promotion
GoE	Government of Egypt
HCWW	Holding Company for Water and Waste Water
IFA	iron–folic acid
IFPRI	International Food Policy Research Institute
IMAM	Integrated Management of Acute Malnutrition
IMCI	Integrated Management of Childhood Illness
IYCF	infant and young child feeding
LBW	low birthweight
LE	Egyptian pound
LiST	Lives Saved Tool
MAM	moderate acute malnutrition
MCH	maternal and child health
MOALR	Ministry of Agriculture and Land Reclamation
MOE	Ministry of Education

MOHP	Ministry of Health and Population
MOHUUC	Ministry of Housing, Utilities and Urban Communities
MOSIT	Ministry of Supply and Internal Trade
MOSS	Ministry of Social Solidarity
MOWRI	Ministry of Water Resources and Irrigation
NCD	noncommunicable disease
NFNPS	National Food and Nutrition Policy and Strategy
NGO	nongovernmental organization
NHA	National Health Accounts
NNI	National Nutrition Institute
NRSP	National Rural Sanitation Program
NSFP	National School Feeding Program
ODA	official development assistance
OECD	Organisation for Economic Co-operation and Development
ORS	oral rehydration solution
PER	public expenditure review
PHC	primary health care
SAM	severe acute malnutrition
SBCC	social and behavior change communication
SDG	Sustainable Development Goal
SHA	System of Health Accounts
SPANS	Standardized Protocol of Action for Nutrition Services
SUN	Scaling Up Nutrition (movement)
TGE	total government expenditure
TNE	total nutrition expenditure
UNICEF	United Nations Children's Fund
USAID	U.S. Agency for International Development
USI	universal salt iodization
WASH	water, sanitation, and hygiene
WFP	World Food Programme
WHA	World Health Assembly
WHO	World Health Organization

In this report, all dollar amounts are U.S. dollars, unless otherwise indicated.

Background

Since 1990, the Arab Republic of Egypt has achieved significant improvements in key health indicators, with maternal mortality falling from 106 to 33 deaths per 100,000 live births and infant mortality falling from 63 to 20 deaths per 1,000 births (World Bank 2015). Significant regional and urban/rural disparities persist, however, and more recent data suggest the rate of progress on these indicators is slowing. Life expectancy, though rising from 66 to 71 years over this period, remains below the Middle East and North Africa average of 73 years. However, during the same period Egypt has not made the same progress in reducing malnutrition, and it has been identified as one of 36 countries in which 90 percent of the global burden of malnutrition falls (Horton et al. 2010).

Egypt also faces the challenge of dealing with the double burden of malnutrition, with overweight and obesity rising, while stunting in children under 5 remains of high public health significance, and wasting has risen since 2005 from a low to a medium level of public health significance. Children who are overweight or obese are at a higher risk of developing serious health problems, including type 2 diabetes, high blood pressure, and liver disease (WHO 2014). At the same time, over one-third of child deaths in Egypt are caused by undernutrition, mostly from the greater severity of the disease. Globally, a large number of studies have confirmed the adverse impacts of malnutrition (undernutrition and overweight) on quality of life and life expectancy (Zheng et al. 2014). In 2014, Egypt ranked 59th out of 89 low- and middle-income countries in relation to the severity of nutrition indicators (Webb 2014), and it presently is not on track to meet the majority of the six nutrition targets established by the World Health Assembly in 2012 (WHO 2017).

Malnutrition is also a huge burden on Egypt's economy. According to the study *The Cost of Hunger in Egypt* (IDSC 2014), undernutrition, as is manifested by poor linear growth (stunting), wasting and micronutrient deficiencies in children, and anemia among adult women, is sapping an estimated 1.98 percent of Egypt's annual gross domestic product (GDP) through productivity foregone and costs to the health system, representing an economic hemorrhage of about $3.6 billion a year (reference year 2009). The study concludes that long-term sustainable development cannot happen without effectively combating undernutrition and eliminating childhood stunting, designating them key elements of the social development agenda.

The government of Egypt (GoE) has shown a strong political commitment to assessing and addressing malnutrition in Egypt. A nutrition landscape analysis, the first in Arab countries, was carried out by Egypt's Ministry of Health and Population (MOHP) and the United Nations Children's Fund (UNICEF) in 2011 to complement the country's 10-year National Food and Nutrition Policy and Strategy 2007–2017 (NFNPS). The landscape analysis described the extent of the malnutrition problem (including rising obesity rates) in Egypt, provided possible solutions to optimize outcomes with the available resources, and set out clear immediate, medium-term, and long-term recommendations to guide investments until 2017 (MOHP 2012). More recently, the MOHP, in close collaboration with UNICEF, developed a *Nutrition Agenda for Action* (MOHP, NNI, and UNICEF 2017) and *Nutrition Stakeholder and Action Mapping Report* (MOHP and UNICEF 2017). Both of these reports have helped to build momentum toward updating the National Food and Nutrition Policy and Strategy and developing an action plan (2018–25) as well as increasing Egypt's commitment to nutrition.

STUDY OBJECTIVE AND RATIONALE

This report was developed at the request of the government of Egypt and in close collaboration with UNICEF. It is intended to help inform the development of an updated national food and nutrition policy and strategy and to guide nutrition investments over the next five years. The report provides an updated overview of Egypt's nutrition situation, the programs currently in place, and opportunities to scale up the response to alleviate the burden of malnutrition. Beyond an assessment of the prevalence of overnutrition, the emphasis of the report is on undernutrition throughout. The specific aims are the following:

- Document the magnitude and severity of malnutrition in Egypt, including overweight and obesity, and country-specific key determinants. The last comprehensive assessment was the landscape analysis carried out in 2011.
- Provide an overview of the current nutrition-specific and nutrition-sensitive programs in Egypt; map the coverage of various donor and government programs; and document gaps in the scope, coverage, and financing of these programs.
- Identify for the government and the development partner community potential nutrition-specific and nutrition-sensitive policy options for scaling up programs and interventions and strengthening the overall response to address undernutrition in the country.
- Provide estimates and the costs and benefits of a select number of highly effective interventions and policy scenarios to address undernutrition.
- Analyze the fiscal space required to implement nutrition interventions at scale.

METHODS AND ANALYTICAL APPROACH

This report documents the current state of the nutrition landscape using recent data from a variety of sources, including:

- Demographic and nutrition epidemiology data from existing surveys
- Network assessment of key stakeholders in nutrition in Egypt

- Review of legal, strategy, policy, and guideline documents from the relevant ministries and agencies in the health and nonhealth sectors
- Review of gray and published literature, as well as program and evaluation reports in the health and nonhealth sectors from the GoE and nongovernment agencies.

Primary quantitative data were not collected as a part of the assessment, and the report does *not* serve as an evaluation of the impact and effectiveness of programs. It draws on extant data and sources to synthesize and analyze the nutrition situation, policies, and programs to identify promising areas for further consideration.

STRUCTURE OF THE REPORT

The remainder of this report is organized into five chapters. Chapters 1 and 2 analyze, respectively, the undernutrition and overnutrition status and determinants among children under 5 and women of reproductive age in Egypt. Chapter 3 is an overview of nutrition-specific and nutrition-sensitive programs, the existing gaps, and the opportunities to scale up such interventions. Chapter 4 calculates the cost-effectiveness of the scale-up of different policy scenarios, and chapter 5 assesses the fiscal space needed to scale up. Appendix A then presents the statistical methods used for the determinants of malnutrition among Egyptian children, and appendix B reports the distribution of the sample by key characteristics and regression analysis results.

Although chapter 2 highlights the growing overnutrition challenge in Egypt, the emphasis of all other chapters is on undernutrition. While not within the scope of this report, future research to help identify the high impact and cost effective solutions needed to address the growing overweight and obesity crisis in Egypt is critical.

REFERENCES

Horton, S., M. Shekar, C. McDonald, A. Mahal, and J. K. Brooks. 2010. *Scaling up Nutrition: What Will It Cost?* Washington, DC: World Bank. doi:10.1596/978-0-8213-8077-2.

IDSC (Egyptian Cabinet Information and Decision Support Center). 2014. *The Cost of Hunger in Egypt: Implications of Child Undernutrition on the Social and Economic Development of Egypt.* Cairo.

MOHP (Ministry of Health and Population). 2012. *Egypt Nutrition Landscape Analysis Report 2012.* Government of Egypt, Cairo.

MOHP (Ministry of Health and Population), NNI (National Nutrition Institute), and UNICEF (United Nations Children's Fund). 2017. *Nutrition Agenda for Action: A Policy Paper on Scaling Up Nutrition Interventions in Egypt.* Cairo: UNICEF. https://www.unicef.org/egypt/reports/nutrition-agenda-action-cairo-2017.

MOHP (Ministry of Health and Population) and UNICEF (United Nations Children's Fund). 2017. *Nutrition Stakeholder and Action Mapping Report.* Cairo: UNICEF. https://www.unicef.org/egypt/reports/nutrition-stakeholder-and-action-mapping-report-cairo-2017.

Webb, P. 2014. "Nutrition and the Post-2015 Sustainable Development Goals." A Policy Brief, Geneva, UNSCN Secretariat.

WHO (World Health Organization). 2014. "Global Nutrition Targets 2025: Childhood Overweight Policy Brief." WHO/NMH/NHD/14.6. Geneva.

———. 2017. "Global Targets 2025 Tracking Tool: Country Progress Report 2017—Egypt." Geneva. https://extranet.who.int/sree/Reports?op=vs&path=%2FWHO_HQ_Reports/G16/PROD /EXT/Targets_Menu&VSPARAM_varLanguage=E&VSPARAM_varISOCODE=ALB.

World Bank. 2015. World Bank Open Data (database): Egypt (2015). Washington, DC. https://data .worldbank.org/country/egypt-arab-rep.

Zheng, X. Y., Y. L. Han, C. Guo, L. Zhang, Y. Qin, and G. Chen. 2014. "Progress in Research of Nutrition and Life Expectancy." *Biomedical and Environmental Sciences* 27 (3): 155–61. https://pdfs.semanticscholar.org/26e8/ebd94de643a5e737ffccb21a3d3191f906be.pdf.

1 Undernutrition of Children Under 5 and Women of Reproductive Age in Egypt

JONATHAN KWEKU AKUOKU

KEY MESSAGES

- Stunting remains at a high level of public health significance in Egypt and the country continues to have higher prevalence of stunting than many of its regional counterparts.
  - Although there are fewer discernible differences in the levels across wealth quintiles, the diminished disparity has been due in part to a greater downward trend among children in the poorest wealth quintile and in part to a significant upward trend among children in the richest wealth quintiles.
  - A general downward trend across regions was evident in earlier years, but prevalence has sharply increased in urban Upper Egypt in more recent years.
  - The declining trend is significant for both boys and girls, as well as in rural but not urban areas.
  - Key determinants of stunting include being a boy, maternal education, size at birth, urban residence, and residence in urban Upper Egypt.
- Wasting has increased significantly since 2000, and the rising trend is considerably higher for the frontier governorates (versus the urban governorates) and among girls.
  - The upward trend in wasting prevalence is also significant across urban and rural areas.
  - Similarly, there is an upward trend across all wealth quintiles.
  - Key determinants of wasting include residence in the frontier governorates, younger age, birth order, and maternal body mass index (BMI)
- Although recent data on micronutrient status and deficiency are limited, the data available indicate high levels of anemia among children, adolescents, and women and falling consumption of iron- and vitamin A–rich foods among children under 5.

INTRODUCTION

This chapter describes undernutrition among children under 5 and women of reproductive age in Egypt. The chapter utilizes data from the 1992, 1995, 2000, 2005, 2008, and 2014 rounds of the Egypt Demographic and Health Survey (EDHS) (El-Zanaty et al. 1993, 1996; El-Zanaty and Way 2001, 2006, 2009;

MOHP, El-Zanaty and Associates, and ICF International 2015), as well as data from other literature and databases.

The chapter begins by presenting the methodology used to develop this overview of the nutrition situation among children under 5 and women of reproductive age in Egypt. It then examines the current prevalence and historical trends of and risk factors for stunting and wasting. The final section summarizes the findings.

METHODOLOGY

Understanding the determinants of malnutrition

The Conceptual Framework for the Determinants of Malnutrition, developed by the United Nations Children's Fund (UNICEF) and its partners is a multilevel, multisectoral framework for understanding the causes and consequences of maternal and child malnutrition (UNICEF 1990, 2013). In doing so, it identifies three levels of causes of malnutrition: immediate, underlying, and basic (figure 1.1).

FIGURE 1.1

UNICEF conceptual framework for the determinants of malnutrition

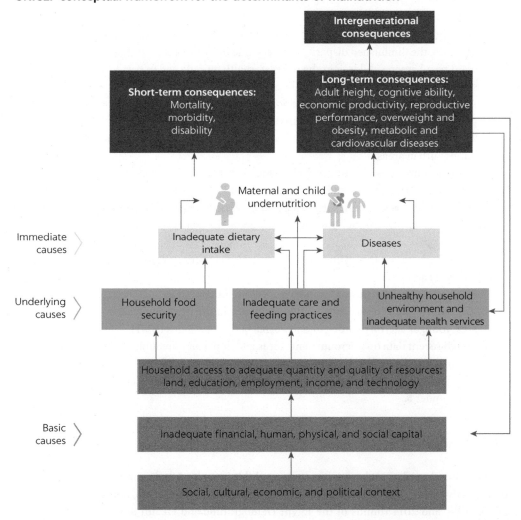

Source: UNICEF 2013 (CC by 3.0 Unported).

The *immediate causes* of malnutrition refer to adequacy of diet, including breastfeeding, frequency of feeding, and dietary diversity, along with disease, especially infections, which are direct causes of stunting (see box 1.1). Diet adequacy and disease act synergistically in their effect on childhood stunting. Infections can affect growth by reducing appetite, impairing the absorption of nutrients, and forcing the immune system to reallocate nutrients from growth to fighting the infection, while inadequacy in food intake increases the risk, severity, and prolonged morbidity of infections (Dewey and Mayers 2011). Diarrhea has a particularly strong dose–response relationship with increased likelihood of stunting (Checkley et al. 2008), and respiratory infections accompanied by fever are associated with increased risk of stunting (Dewey and Mayers 2011).

The *underlying causes* of malnutrition affect the immediate causes of stunting. Appropriate breastfeeding and complementary feeding to improve the adequacy of a child's diet are directly influenced by the availability of diverse foods in the household, caregivers' knowledge of the appropriate feeding and care practices, and the application of this knowledge to feeding a child appropriately. Likewise, disease incidence and severity are not only synergistic with feeding practices, but also affected by a hygienic household environment and access to and utilization of available health services (UNICEF 2015). Sociopolitical, economic, and cultural factors at the basic level affect the availability and utilization of resources at the underlying level. Household wealth and income may influence access to nutritious foods, utilization of health services, and availability of improved household infrastructure, while education of caregivers may influence access to information on improved child caring and feeding practices.

The *basic causes* of malnutrition include the extent of human and environmental resources, economic systems, and political and ideological factors at various levels of society that affect financial, human, physical, and social capital as well as a household's access to resources. Although determinants such as household wealth and maternal education are important and were included in the

---

Evidence of and recommendations on the increased nutritional needs of children

In their first two years of life, children have greater nutrient needs for proper physical and cognitive growth and development, and, more than adults, they must consume foods with higher nutrient density (Dewey 2016). For children under 6 months, lack of exclusive breastfeeding is associated with increased mortality and morbidity from infectious diseases such as diarrhea, pneumonia, and malaria. Diarrhea is especially important because of its impact on the absorption of nutrients from food (Black et al. 2008).

Although some studies find that exclusive breastfeeding may be a protective factor for children living in environments with high rates of infection (Dewey 2016), the evidence on the association between exclusive breastfeeding and stunting among children under 6 months is inconclusive. However, there is also an indirect pathway between breastfeeding and stunting through reductions in the incidence of diarrhea. It is recommended that children 6–24 months of age continue breastfeeding and be frequently fed with diverse nutrient-rich complementary foods (Dewey 2016; WHO 2008). Appropriate frequency and quantity of food provide a child with the caloric energy needed for this period of rapid growth, and a diet rich in nutrients such as zinc and vitamin A protects against the incidence and severity of diarrhea and respiratory infections (Black et al. 2013).

analytic model, they are not an explicit focus of this analysis. Rather, the main goal is to inform the design of effective interventions that can be implemented in the short to medium term—that is, interventions that focus on the immediate and underlying causes of malnutrition.

Data

Data for the foregoing analyses are from the 2014 round of the EDHS (MOHP, El-Zanaty and Associates, and ICF International 2015). The EDHS utilized a multistage cluster sampling design, allowing representative and precise estimates of population and health indicators at the national level and in six major subnational groupings: urban governorates, urban Lower Egypt, rural Lower Egypt, urban Upper Egypt, rural Upper Egypt, and frontier governorates. Two of the frontier governorates comprising less than 1 percent of the national population, North Sinai and South Sinai, were excluded from data collection in EDHS 2014 (MOHP, El-Zanaty and Associates, and ICFInternational 2015) because of security concerns.

The analysis described in this chapter is based on data from the women's questionnaire of the EDHS. This questionnaire contains information on women's demographic and health characteristics, as well as on children's health, nutrition, and care. The questionnaire is administered to all ever-married women 15–49 years of age resident in a household during the survey, and it includes height and weight measurements of resident children under 5 years. However, questions on feeding behavior are asked for children under 2 who reside with the mother. Therefore, the analytic sample is restricted to the youngest child of each woman 0–23 months of age.

Methods

The analysis uses the UNICEF conceptual framework of malnutrition and draws on data from the EDHS to undertake a regression analysis to identify the immediate, underlying, and basic determinants of malnutrition in Egypt. The key EDHS data analyzed at each level of the causes of malnutrition include the following:

- Immediate causes: disease incidence (infectious diseases)
- Underlying causes: feeding practices, care practices, household environment, health services, women's empowerment
- Basic causes: maternal education, household wealth.

A more detailed explanation of the methodology used to understand the key determinants of malnutrition in Egypt is provided in appendix A.

UNDERNUTRITION OF CHILDREN 0–59 MONTHS OF AGE

Stunting

Prevalence and trends

Stunting in Egypt is of high public health significance, according to the World Health Organization (WHO) classification[1]—more than one in five children under 5 are stunted. The WHO Child Growth Standards define stunting in young children as having height or length more than two standard deviations below the median height of a child of the same age and sex (de Onis and Onyango 2008).

Stunting is the result of multiple factors, from basic causes such as poverty and food insecurity to underlying and more immediate causes such as poor maternal health and nutrition during pregnancy, inadequate nutrition and health during the early years, and poor child care practices (de Onis, Blössner, and Borghi 2012). In the short term, stunting increases the risk of mortality and morbidity from diarrhea, pneumonia, and other childhood illnesses (Black et al. 2008, 2013). In the longer term, stunting may affect cognitive development, educational attendance and attainment, and economic productivity (de Onis, Blössner, and Borghi 2012).

Despite a small decline in prevalence since the early 1990s, the stunting prevalence in Egypt remains higher than the regional average of 15.8 percent among Middle East and North Africa countries (figure 1.2) and one of the highest among those with recent data. Between 1992 and 2014, stunting declined from 30.6 percent to 21.5 percent ($p < 0.001$ for trend),[2] but fluctuated and remained above the regional average during that period (figure 1.3).

Stunting prevalence is significantly higher in Upper Egypt, especially in rural ($p < 0.05$) and urban ($p < 0.001$) Upper Egypt when compared with the urban governorates (figure 1.4).

Since the early 1990s, stunting prevalence has steadily fallen in some regions. Across the regions, significant declining trends were experienced in the frontier governorates ($p < 0.001$), rural Upper Egypt ($p < 0.001$), and rural Lower Egypt ($p < 0.001$). The frontier governorates cover Sinai and the deserts that lie west and east of the Nile River and are home to less than 2 percent of the Egyptian population. The spike in stunting prevalence between 2005 and 2008 has been attributed to the reduced intake of animal protein in certain regions due to the outbreak of avian influenza. It affected the availability and cost of poultry and eggs and the incomes of certain households, and it created the perception that less nutritious substitutes were less likely to make children ill (Kavle, El-Zanaty, et al. 2015).

FIGURE 1.2

Prevalence of stunting among children under 5: Middle East and North Africa economies, various years

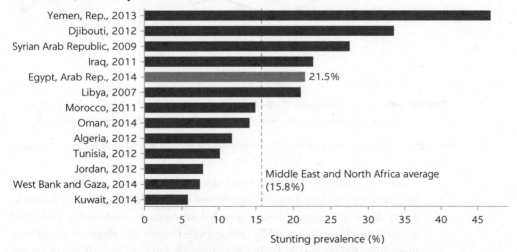

Sources: Egypt: EDHS microdata 2014 (dataset), Ministry of Health and Population and ICF International, Cairo, Egypt, and Rockville, MA, https://dhsprogram.com/data/; other countries: World Development Indicators (database), World Bank, Washington, DC, https://databank.worldbank.org/source/world-development-indicators.

FIGURE 1.3

Trends in stunting prevalence among children under 5: Middle East and North Africa economies, 1990–2016

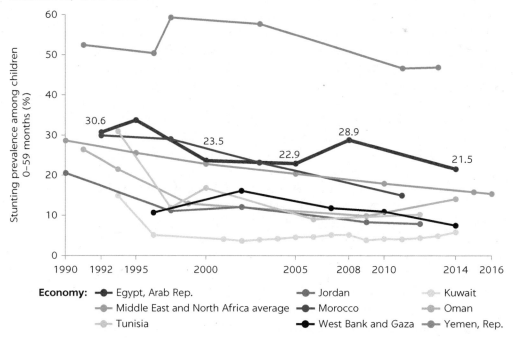

Sources: Egypt: EDHS microdata various years (dataset), ICF International, Rockville, MA, https://dhsprogram.com/data/; other countries: World Development Indicators (database), World Bank, Washington, DC, https://databank.worldbank.org/source/world-development-indicators.

FIGURE 1.4

Trends in stunting prevalence across regions: Egypt, 1992–2014

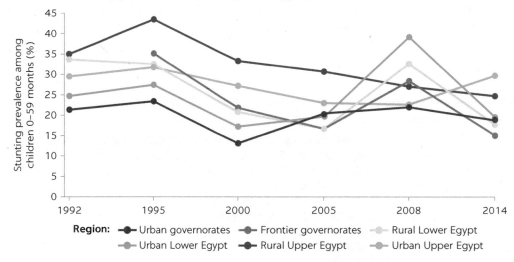

Source: EDHS microdata various years (dataset), ICF International, Rockville, MA, https://dhsprogram.com/data/.

Stunting affects children from both poor and rich households, and the prevalence among children from the wealthiest households has increased significantly. Although stunting is significantly lower among children from the third ($p < 0.001$) and fourth ($p < 0.01$) wealth quintile households when compared with those from the poorest households, stunting is not significantly lower among those in the wealthiest quintile ($p = 0.66$)—see figure 1.5. The gap in stunting prevalence between the poor and the rich has narrowed, driven in part by the

FIGURE 1.5
Trends in stunting prevalence across wealth quintiles: Egypt, 1995–2014

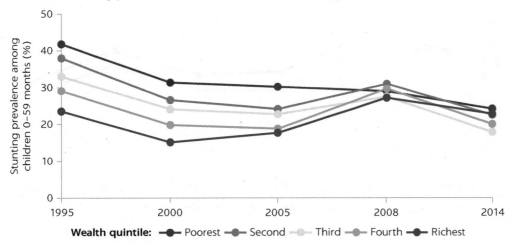

Source: EDHS microdata various years (dataset), ICF International, Rockville, MA, https://dhsprogram.com/data/.

FIGURE 1.6
Trends in stunting prevalence across urban and rural areas: Egypt, 1992–2014

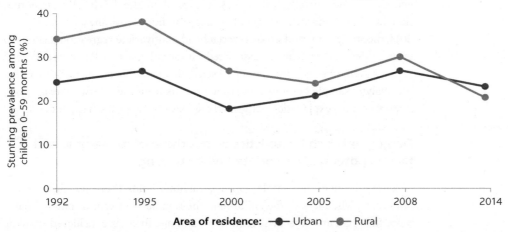

Source: EDHS microdata various years (dataset), ICF International, Rockville, MA, https://dhsprogram.com/data/.

increasing trend in prevalence among those from the wealthiest households ($p < 0.05$). Between 2008 and 2014, stunting declined across all wealth quintiles.

Stunting prevalence has been declining among children from rural areas (figure 1.6). Although stunting prevalence has historically been higher among children from rural households, these children have also experienced a more significant decline in stunting prevalence when compared with their urban counterparts ($p < 0.001$). Data from the most recent EDHS shows a higher prevalence of stunting among urban children, although this difference is not statistically significant ($p < 0.1$). In 2016 the rural population comprised 56.8 percent of Egypt's total population.[3]

Boys are more likely to be stunted than girls. Stunting prevalence has been consistently higher among boys than girls, and it was significantly higher in 2014 ($p < 0.001$)—see figure 1.7. However, the stunting prevalence among both groups have declined significantly ($p < 0.001$).

FIGURE 1.7

Trends in stunting prevalence by child's sex: Egypt, 1992–2014

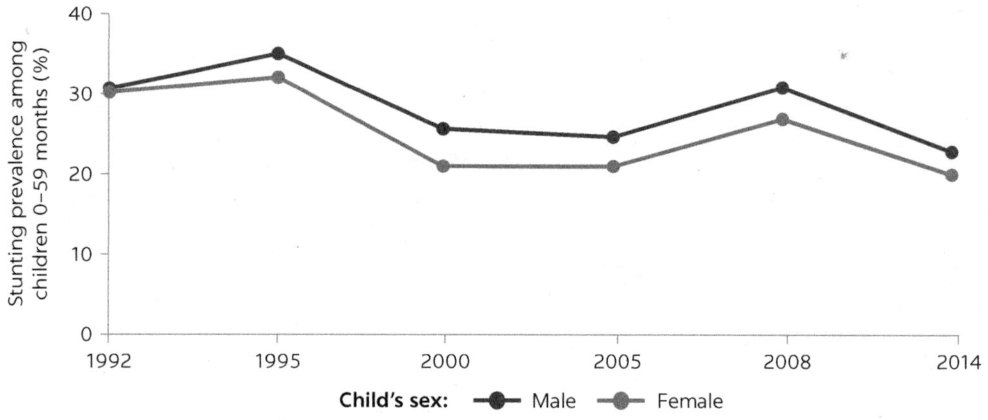

Source: EDHS microdata various years (dataset), ICF International, Rockville, MA, https://dhsprogram.com/data/.

Determinants of stunting among children 0–23 months of age

Stunting is the result of a complex interaction of household, environmental, socio-economic, and cultural influences, captured in the UNICEF conceptual framework on malnutrition (figure 1.1). Using this framework and data from EDHS 2014, the study team undertook bivariate and multivariate regression analysis to examine the significant factors associated with stunting among Egyptian children.[4] It first summarizes the distribution of select demographic characteristics across the analytic sample before summarizing results from the multivariate analysis. A more detailed explanation of the methodology used appears in appendix A.

Demographic characteristics across the analytic sample and factors potentially associated with stunting

Seventy percent of the sample is from rural households, there are slightly more boys than girls, and half the children in the sample are 1 year or older. Finally, more than half are first- or second-born, and one in six is considered small or very small at birth by his or her mother (see appendix B, table B.1).

An alarming 75 percent of mothers are overweight or obese. About two out of three (66.3 percent) have completed secondary school or higher education, whereas 16 percent have no education. Nearly 90 percent delivered at a health facility during their last pregnancy, almost all (97.7 percent) had a postnatal checkup after their last delivery, and more than 80 percent attended four or more antenatal care visits during their most recent pregnancy. Women reported they are involved in decision making about household purchases (64 percent), visits to their family (72 percent), and their own health care (80 percent).

A number of differences in characteristics are evident across urban and rural areas:

- Rural Upper Egypt and the rural frontier governorates have the highest proportions of women with no education (30 percent and 36 percent, respectively), and consequently the lowest proportions of women who have completed secondary school or higher education.
- Urban Upper Egypt has the highest proportion of women who are overweight or obese (80 percent).

- Relative to the national level and other regions, the rural frontier governorates have a lower proportion of women who attended four or more antenatal care visits during their most recent pregnancy (64 percent versus 83 percent nationally and 85 percent in urban frontier governorates).
- The rural frontier governorates also have the lowest proportion of women reporting being involved in decisions about their own health care (69 percent). In general, a lower proportion of women in the rural governorates reported being involved in decision making.
- None of the households from the rural governorates is in the highest wealth quintile, while nearly all of the households in the urban governorates are in the top two wealth quintiles.
- Although there is nearly universal coverage of piped water into dwellings, households in the frontier governorates are less likely to have access, with only 60 percent of households having access to piped water in the rural frontier governorates.

Overall, the prevalence of breastfeeding is relatively high. However, the prevalence of *early initiation and exclusive breastfeeding* is much lower, particularly in urban areas. Although the proportion of children 12–15 months of age who were still being breastfed ranges from 67 to 84 percent, low proportions of children were initially breastfed within one hour of birth (16 percent in urban governorates and 45 percent in rural frontier governorates) (figure 1.8).

FIGURE 1.8

Breastfeeding practices, complementary feeding practices, and incidence of disease among children 0–23 months of age: Egypt

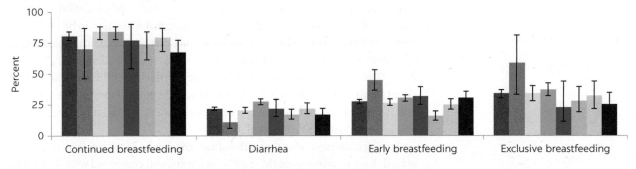

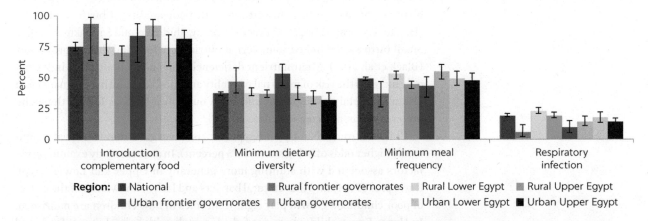

Source: Reanalysis of EDHS microdata 2014 (dataset), Ministry of Health and Population and ICF International, Cairo, Egypt, and Rockville, MA, https://dhsprogram.com/data/.
Note: I = 95% confidence interval.

The timely introduction of complementary foods is relatively high, but the proportion of children fed the minimum number of times and with a nutritionally diverse diet is generally very low (figure 1.8).

Disease incidence among children is particularly high in rural Upper Egypt. In the rural frontier governorates, one in 10 children had an episode of diarrhea in the two weeks preceding the survey compared with one in four children in rural Upper Egypt. The incidence of potential respiratory infection is also lowest in the frontier governorates (5.4 percent for rural and 9.5 percent for urban) and ranges from 15 to 24 percent in the other regions.

Results from the multivariate analysis examining significant factors associated with stunting

Boys are more likely than girls to be stunted, and this relationship remains statistically significant after adjusting for other covariates. Boys had 47 percent higher odds than girls of being stunted in a model with all children 0–23 months of age, and 100 percent higher odds among children 0–6 months of age. This finding is consistent with those across other countries[8] and previous findings in Egypt (Khatab 2010; Zottarelli, Sunil, and Rajaram 2007), as well as the trends from previous rounds of the EDHS (1992, 1995, 2000, 2005, 2008).

Children of mothers with an incomplete secondary education (versus completed secondary) have significantly higher odds of stunting (35 percent). In a recent review of the drivers of the decline in stunting across countries in Sub-Saharan Africa and South Asia, Headey, Hoddinott, and Park (2017) find strong positive associations between higher parental education and the height-for-age z-score. A multicountry study of the link between maternal education and child nutritional status also finds higher levels of maternal education to be protective against malnutrition, including stunting, noting that there is a threshold level of education at which this effect is significant (Makate and Makate 2017; Makoka 2013). Greater maternal education is thought to influence child health and nutritional status by empowering mothers to seek and appropriately utilize information, as well as to mobilize resources in the care of children (Caldwell 1979; Mosley and Chen 1984; Ruel et al. 1992).

Among children under 6 months of age, those who were small or very small at birth have nearly double the odds of being stunted compared with those who were average weight at birth. Although birth size is based on mothers' reports, previous studies have shown it to be a good predictor of outcomes related to birthweight, particularly in settings with poor quality of birthweight data (Haque, Tisha, and Huq 2015; Sreeramareddy, Shidhaye, and Sathiakumar 2011). Small birth size is linked to maternal nutrition before and during pregnancy (Black et al. 2013). Micronutrient deficiencies and a low body mass index not only increase the risk of maternal mortality and morbidity during pregnancy, but also affect fetal development and birth outcomes such as low birthweight, preterm births, and cognitive defects.

Children from urban Upper Egypt (versus urban governorates) are at significantly higher odds of being stunted (75 percent). In a recent study examining the factors associated with stunting more generally in Upper and Lower Egypt, Kavle et al. (2014) find that cultural barriers and lack of knowledge of the causes of poor childhood growth play significant roles in how children are nourished. In Upper Egypt, children are not fed adequately with animal source foods and are often given tea, juices, and energy-dense food of poor nutritional quality, a situation due in part to government subsidies on sugar and oil (Kavle, Mehanna, et al. 2015). This situation is contributing to the increasing double burden of undernutrition and overnutrition in Egyptian children.

Egyptian children from urban households are more likely to be stunted than children from rural households. This is contrary to findings from other countries and evidence from a large body of research indicating that children in rural areas are generally at greater risk for stunting than their urban counterparts (Menon, Ruel, and Morris 2000; Smith, Ruel, and Ndiaye 2005). The rationale is that urban areas have favorable endowments in the underlying determinants of stunting—that is, they are more likely to have access to improved water and sanitation, have residents in the higher wealth quintiles, and have access to better-quality health services. And yet the most recent national survey shows that children in urban areas are more likely to be stunted, and this analysis is stratified to examine the different factors associated with stunting across each area. The full regression results are presented in appendix B, tables B.2, B.3, and B.4.

Figure 1.9 shows that among Egyptian children 0–23 months of age from rural households, similar factors as found earlier are associated with the odds of stunting: being a boy, small size at birth, and lower maternal education are associated with a 40–50 percent higher odds of stunting, similar to the associations found for the whole sample. Early initiation of breastfeeding is even more protective for rural children than the national average (36 percent reduced odds versus 25 percent). For the rural sample of children 6–23 months of age, being large at birth and early initiation of breastfeeding significantly reduce the odds of stunting (65 percent and 35 percent reductions, respectively). Beyond the increased odds of stunting in male infants, there are no other significant determinants of stunting among rural children under 6 months of age.

FIGURE 1.9

Adjusted odds ratio for significant determinants of stunting among rural Egyptian children 0–23 months of age

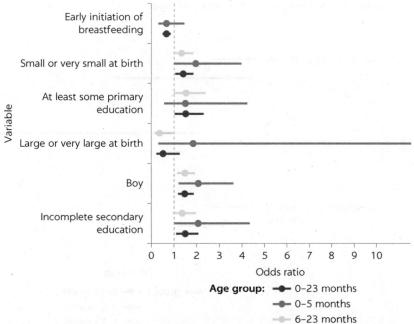

Source: EDHS microdata 2014 (dataset), Ministry of Health and Population and ICF International, Cairo, Egypt, and Rockville, MA, https://dhsprogram.com/data/.

In urban children, large size at birth and child postnatal checkup appear to significantly reduce the odds of stunting among children under 6 months of age (95 percent and 79 percent odds reduction, respectively)—see figure 1.10. However, only 15 percent of urban children under 6 months of age had a postnatal checkup, and mothers reported that less than 3 percent of urban children were large or very large at birth.

Among children 0–6 months of age, increasing socioeconomic status is associated with higher odds of being stunted. However, this finding is in line with the fact that urban children are more likely to be stunted in Egypt and are more likely to reside in households in the higher wealth quintiles. This finding is statistically significant among children from households in the fourth wealth quintile, with their odds of stunting more than double that of those in the poorest wealth quintile.

A comparison of the prevalence of some key determinants of stunting by household wealth quintile reveals that children in the higher wealth quintiles are more likely than those in lower quintiles to have been delivered in a health facility (96 percent versus 78 percent). In addition, they are more likely to have had a postnatal check after birth (17 percent versus 13 percent), are just as likely to have been exclusively breastfed and for their mother to have had a postnatal checkup, and are less likely to have had an incidence of diarrhea or symptoms of respiratory infection in the past two weeks (17 percent versus 25 percent and 13 percent versus 17 percent, respectively). Children in the higher wealth quintiles, however, are less likely to have been initiated on breastfeeding within one hour of birth, although a chi-squared test found no significant difference in early breastfeeding initiation (p = 0.101). This analysis shows, then, that other factors are likely at play among higher wealth quintiles in determining the increased odds of being stunted.

FIGURE 1.10

Adjusted odds ratio for significant determinants of stunting among urban Egyptian children 0–23 months of age

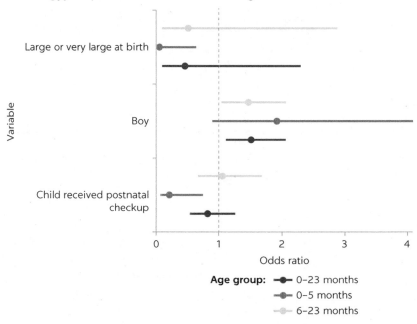

Source: EDHS microdata 2014 (dataset), Ministry of Health and Population and ICF International, Cairo, Egypt, and Rockville, MA, https://dhsprogram.com/data/.

Wasting

Prevalence and trends

Almost one in 10 children under 5 in Egypt is wasted, which is substantially higher than the regional average (figure 1.11) and of medium public health significance, according to the WHO classification.[5] Childhood wasting[6] is symptomatic of acute malnutrition caused by insufficient consumption of foods or frequent episodes of infectious diseases such as diarrhea. These causes can act synergistically, with inadequate food consumption increasing the severity of diseases, while severe and multiple episodes of infectious diseases may decrease the absorption of nutrients from food.

Wasting among children under 5 has increased steadily since 2000. As shown in figure 1.12, each round of the EDHS since 2000 has shown a consistent increase in wasting among Egyptian children ($p < 0.001$ for trend), and this upward trend is present across several demographic categories. It increased from 3.8 percent in 1992 to 8.5 percent in 2014, and if the trend continues it could soon become of high public health significance, according to the WHO classification.

The prevalence of wasting has increased across all regions in Egypt since 2000, with the frontier governorates having a significantly higher increasing trend when compared with the urban governorates ($p < 0.05$ for interaction between year and region). However, there was no statistically significant difference in wasting prevalence across the regions in 2014 (figure 1.13).

Wasting prevalence has increased for children from both rich and poor households. Across wealth quintiles, wasting prevalence increased significantly as of 2000 ($p < 0.001$ for trend in each wealth quintile), although there is no significant difference in the increasing trend across the quintiles and no significant difference in prevalence in 2014 (figure 1.14).

The prevalence of wasting has increased for children in both urban and rural areas. Over the study period, wasting increased among both urban ($p < 0.001$)

FIGURE 1.11

Prevalence of wasting among children under 5: Middle East and North Africa economies, various years

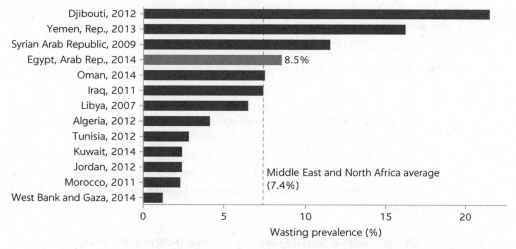

Sources: Egypt: EDHS microdata 2014 (dataset), Ministry of Health and Population and ICF International, Cairo, Egypt, and Rockville, MA, https://dhsprogram.com/data/; other countries: World Development Indicators (database), World Bank, Washington, DC, https://databank.worldbank.org/source/world-development-indicators.

FIGURE 1.12

Trends in wasting prevalence: Middle East and North Africa economies, 1990–2014

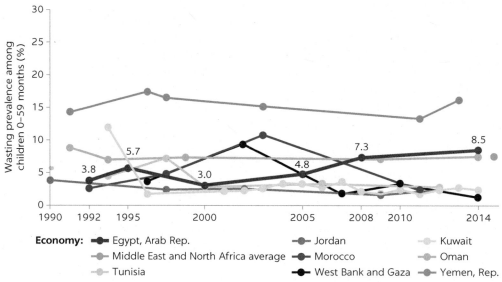

Source: Egypt: EDHS microdata various years (dataset), ICF International, Rockville, MA, https://dhsprogram.com/data/; other countries: World Development Indicators (database), World Bank, Washington, DC, https://databank.worldbank.org/source/world-development-indicators.

FIGURE 1.13

Trends in wasting prevalence across regions: Egypt, 1992–2014

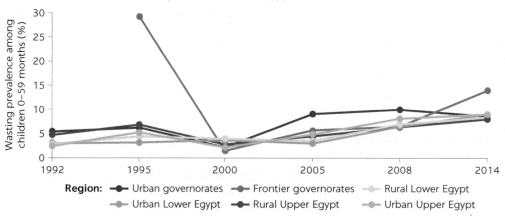

Source: EDHS microdata various years (dataset), ICF International, Rockville, MA, https://dhsprogram.com/data/.

and rural ($p < 0.001$) children, with no significant difference in trend and no significant difference in prevalence in 2014 (figure 1.15).

Since 2000, there have been significant increasing trends in wasting for both boys and girls, with a significant difference between them in trends ($p < 0.05$ for interaction between year and child's sex) but no difference in prevalence in 2014 (figure 1.16).

Determinants of wasting among children 0–59 months of age

Using the UNICEF framework and a set of covariates with significant bivariate associations with wasting, the study team found several factors significantly associated with the odds of wasting in a multivariate model.

FIGURE 1.14

Trends in wasting prevalence across wealth quintiles: Egypt, 1995-2014

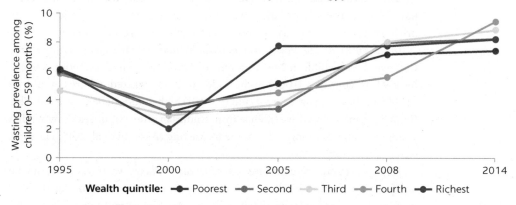

Source: EDHS microdata various years (dataset), ICF International, Rockville, MA, https://dhsprogram.com/data/.

FIGURE 1.15

Trends in wasting prevalence across urban and rural areas: Egypt, 1992-2014

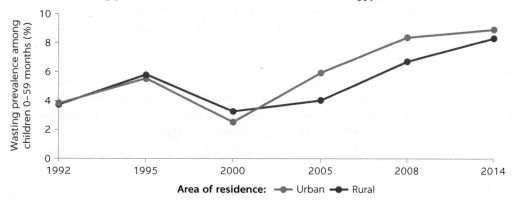

Source: EDHS microdata various years (dataset), ICF International, Rockville, MA, https://dhsprogram.com/data/.

FIGURE 1.16

Trends in wasting prevalence by child's sex: Egypt, 1992-2014

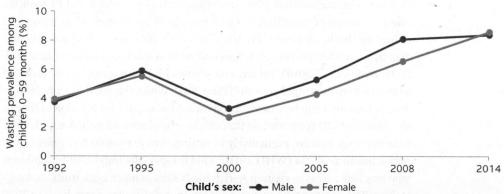

Source: EDHS microdata various years (dataset), ICF International, Rockville, MA, https://dhsprogram.com/data/.

Children in the frontier governorates have increased odds of wasting. After adjustments are made for multiple factors, children from frontier governorates have 72 percent higher odds of wasting when compared with children from urban governorates. The association is not significant in other regions.

In the multivariate model, younger children have increased odds of wasting. Compared with children 24–59 months of age, children under 6 months of age have 94 percent ($p < 0.001$) higher odds of being wasted, whereas children 12–23 months of age have 26 percent ($p < 0.01$) higher odds of being wasted. This finding is consistent with evidence from studies in other countries showing that younger infants are more vulnerable to wasting (Akombi et al. 2017; Harding, Aguayo, and Webb 2018).

Higher birth order is associated with increased odds of wasting. Children who are fourth or higher birth order have 31 percent ($p < 0.01$) higher odds of wasting. This finding is consistent with prior evidence that lower birth order children have better nutritional status (Horton 1988). Furthermore, because higher birth order children would be of younger age, this finding is also consistent with the negative association between age and the odds of wasting reported earlier.

Mother's BMI status and health decision-making power are significantly associated with the odds of child wasting. In the multivariate-adjusted model, children whose mothers are overweight or obese have 20 percent lower odds of wasting ($p < 0.05$), and those whose mothers participate in decisions about their own health care have 25 percent lower odds of wasting ($p < 0.01$). The association between maternal BMI and child wasting has been documented in previous studies (such as Rahman, Chowdhury, and Hossain 2009), and it may stem from the fact that these children likely live in households with greater food security. Measures of women's empowerment have been associated with improved child nutritional status, although this is dependent on how this concept is operationalized (Carlson, Kordas, and Murray-Kolb 2015; Cunningham et al. 2015).

Micronutrient status among children 6–59 months of age

Vitamin A

In EDHS 2014, 16.7 percent of children 6–59 months of age were reported to have had a vitamin A supplement in the six months preceding the survey, compared with 12.4 percent in 2008.[7] As further explained and discussed in chapter 3, this low figure may be a result of only providing vitamin A capsule (VAC) supplementation in conjunction with the immunization visits at 9 and 18 months. Adequate levels of vitamin A in children help to boost immune function and reduce morbidity and mortality from infectious diseases such as measles and diarrhea, as well as prevent blindness and other vision impairments (Black et al. 2008; Imdad et al. 2010). Infants and young children require higher levels of vitamin A to sustain rapid growth (WHO 2011). With evidence that a single large dose of vitamin A can be absorbed and utilized as needed for a period of four to six months, WHO recommends that children be given a vitamin A supplement once every six months, particularly in settings where vitamin A deficiency is a public health problem (WHO 2011).[8] This is especially important for children who may lack access to vitamin A–rich foods such as meat, eggs, fruits, and vegetables. The most recent survey on vitamin A deficiency dates back to 1999 (Stevens et al. 2015; Wirth et al. 2017).

Whereas there is generally no difference in boys and girls, more children from richer households receive vitamin A supplements than children from poorer households. Boys and girls are just as likely to receive vitamin A supplements (16.7 percent and 16.8 percent, respectively), whereas more children in the richest wealth quintile receive the supplements, compared with those in the poorest (19.6 percent versus 14.5 percent). A greater proportion of children in urban Lower Egypt receive supplementation (20.2 percent), whereas the lowest proportion of children in the frontier governorates receive supplementation.

Consumption of vitamin A–rich foods by children is fairly low, particularly in Upper Egypt. Diet is one key pathway for children to maintain adequate levels of micronutrients, including vitamin A. In EDHS 2014, 61 percent of children 6–23 months of age were reported to have consumed foods rich in vitamin A the day preceding the survey, compared with 71 percent in 2008. Consumption of vitamin A–rich foods in 2014 was highest among children from the frontier governorates (73 percent) and rural Lower Egypt (64.4 percent), and lowest among those from rural and urban Upper Egypt (57.5 percent).

Iron and iron-deficiency anemia

In 2014 almost one-third of children in Egypt were anemic, an improvement since 2008 but still detrimentally high. As shown in figure 1.17, among children 6–59 months of age the prevalence of any anemia significantly increased between 2000 and 2005, from 30 to nearly 50 percent, before declining to 27 percent in 2014 ($p < 0.001$ for declining trend), which, according to the WHO classification, is a moderate public health problem.[9] The prevalence of moderate anemia was 9.6 percent and mild anemia was 17 percent.

Iron deficiency has been identified as a major cause of anemia in young children. It can be caused by inadequate dietary intake of iron-rich foods and

FIGURE 1.17

Trends in anemia among children 6–59 months of age: Egypt, 2000, 2005, 2014

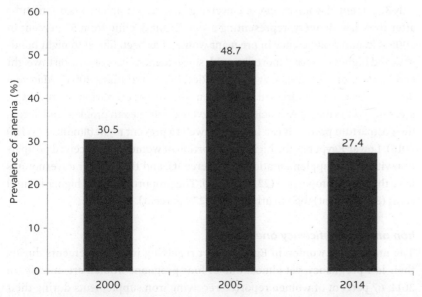

Source: EDHS microdata various years (dataset), ICF International, Rockville, MA, https://dhsprogram.com/data/.

helminthic infections (FAO and WHO 2004). Although term infants are born with an adequate supply of iron stores (provided that the mother is not anemic), iron requirements after six months are supplied largely by the appropriate complementary foods. Iron deficiency can result in reduced immune function and increased susceptibility to infectious disease, as well as impaired physical development and cognitive function among children (Black et al. 2013; FAO and WHO 2004). Fortification of staple foods, daily iron supplementation, as well as consumption of iron-rich foods such as meat, fish, poultry, and eggs, have been recommended as preventive measures against iron deficiency (FAO and WHO 2004; WHO 2016). According to EDHS 2014, less than 8 percent of children 6–59 months of age received an iron supplement in the seven days prior to the survey.

Anemia prevalence among children is particularly high in the frontier governorates, in rural areas, and in poorer households. Compared with the urban governorates, anemia prevalence is significantly higher in the frontier governorates (44.5 percent, $p < 0.001$) and rural areas of both Upper Egypt (30.3 percent, $p < 0.01$) and Lower Egypt (28.5 percent, $p < 0.05$). Prevalence is significantly higher in rural areas than urban areas (29.4 percent versus 23.2 percent, $p < 0.001$) and highest among children from the poorest households (34.6 percent versus 21.2 percent in richest, $p < 0.001$), and it decreases with increasing wealth quintile ($p < 0.001$).

Only about half of children under 2 consume iron-rich foods, a situation that has worsened since 2008. Consumption of iron-rich foods by children 6–23 months of age declined from 65.6 percent in 2008 to 53 percent in 2014.[10] The highest proportion of children consuming iron-rich foods are from the frontier governorates (66.3 percent), and the lowest proportion are from rural Upper Egypt (47.1 percent). The proportions are similar by sex, area of residence, and wealth quintile.

Micronutrient status among women of reproductive age

Vitamin A

About one in three women of reproductive age in Egypt report receiving vitamin A supplements after their delivery of a child. In the EDHS 2014 survey, only 31 percent of women reported receiving vitamin A supplements two months after their last delivery, representing a significant decline from 57 percent in 2008. Vitamin A deficiency in pregnant women has been linked to night blindness and higher maternal mortality, with subsequent effects on low birthweight and infant mortality (Black et al. 2013; Rice, West, and Black 2004). Maternal deficiencies can be addressed through supplementation during pregnancy in areas in which vitamin A deficiency is a severe public health problem and during the postpartum period. It can be used as well to prevent night blindness (WHO 2016). Lower Egypt has the highest proportion of women who received postpartum vitamin A supplementation (32.3 percent), and the frontier governorates have the lowest proportion (22.2 percent). The proportion is also higher in rural areas (32.8 percent) than in urban areas (27.9 percent).

Iron and iron-deficiency anemia

The majority of women in Egypt report receiving iron supplements during their last pregnancy, yet almost one in four pregnant women are anemic. In 2014, 67 percent of women reported receiving iron supplements during their last pregnancy, a significant increase over 2008 (42.5 percent). The prevalence of anemia among nonpregnant Egyptian women of reproductive age in 2012 was 29.6 percent and among pregnant women, 24.7 percent,[11] both of which are of moderate public health significance, according to the WHO classification (WHO 2001). These percentages are lower than in some Middle East and North Africa countries (such as Tunisia, 27.9 percent and 34.4 percent; Morocco, 34 percent and 38.6 percent, respectively; Jordan, 20.6 percent and 34 percent) but higher than others (such as Kuwait, 20.7 percent and 28.8 percent). Anemia in pregnancy is associated with higher maternal mortality, low birthweight, and higher perinatal mortality (Black et al. 2013; Stoltzfus, Mullany, and Black 2004). Deficiency can result from inadequate consumption of iron-rich foods and, among women of reproductive age, the depletion of iron stores during menstruation. Proper fetal development requires higher levels of iron, and thus pregnant women are at greater risk of deficiency (Black et al. 2008). Increased consumption of iron-rich foods, as well as routine supplementation during pregnancy and deworming, are recommended solutions to improving the iron levels of pregnant women (WHO 2012).

CONCLUSIONS

Malnutrition, both chronic (stunting) and acute (wasting) remain at elevated levels of public health significance in Egypt, and they are at levels higher than those found in most of Egypt's regional counterparts and the Middle East and North Africa regional average.

This analysis found that one in five children 0–23 months of age in Egypt is stunted. Stunting prevalence varies across Egypt's regions, from a low of 15.3 percent in the rural frontier governorates, to a high of 28.9 percent in urban Upper Egypt. Disparities in stunting prevalence between the richest and poorest wealth quintiles have significantly narrowed due in part to a more consistent decline in the poorest quintile since 2000 and in part as a result of slower declines or increases in the top wealth quintiles.

In the multivariate regressions, several determinants are consistently associated with stunting across the models. A child's sex, reported size at birth, early initiation of breastfeeding, maternal education, and household wealth remain consistent determinants of childhood stunting in this analysis. Boys have from 50 to 100 percent higher odds of being stunted, and small birth size is associated with a 90 percent increase in the odds of stunting among children under 6 months of age. Early initiation of breastfeeding appears to protect against stunting, reducing the odds by 35 percent among children in rural households in the analysis, although the current global evidence base on the relationship between stunting and breastfeeding is inconclusive. Maternal education below completion of secondary schooling increases the odds of childhood stunting by 50 percent. Studies have shown that boys, particularly in Sub-Saharan Africa and some Asian countries, face greater odds of stunting, although the mechanism for this differential remains unclear (Keino et al. 2014; Rakotomanana et al. 2017; Wamani et al. 2007). Some studies have theorized that males are more vulnerable to morbidity in early life (Green 1992), and thus increased morbidity will affect early nutrition.

The prevalence of wasting has consistently increased since the 2000 round of the EDHS, and this upward trend is evident and significant across several demographic factors. Wasting has sharply increased in the frontier governorates since 2000, and the upward trend is higher than in the urban governorates. There is an increasing trend among children from both rural and urban households, and although prevalence is nearly identical in both boys and girls, the upward trend is more pronounced among girls than boys.

For the wasting outcome, a child's age, birth order, mother's BMI, and residence in the frontier governorates are significant factors in the multivariate regression. Younger children, children of later births, and children living in frontier governorates have significantly greater odds of wasting, whereas children whose mothers are overweight or obese have significantly reduced odds of wasting. Frontier governorates, comprising largely desert areas, may be more susceptible to climate change and greater food insecurity and thus have a greater likelihood of acute malnutrition among children.

The prevalence of key underlying determinants was high: 90 percent of women delivered in a health facility; 98 percent received a postnatal checkup after delivery; 80 percent attended four or more antenatal care visits during their most recent pregnancy; and 80 percent were involved in decisions about their own health care. Women in the frontier governorates generally have lower participation in health care decision making, which is in line with women in rural frontier governorates having the lowest attendance at four or more antenatal care visits during their most recent pregnancy. Although access to improved sanitation is nearly universal, there are significant disparities in access to piped water, with only 60 percent of households in the rural frontier governorates having such access.

Overall, the prevalence of key feeding and care practices is low nationally and varies considerably across regions. Only one in three children under 6 months of age is exclusively breastfed, which drops to one in eight at 4–5 months of age. Although almost four in five children are introduced to complementary foods in a timely manner, only one in four children 6–23 months of age are fed both an adequate number of times and with a nutritionally diverse diet.

This analysis indicates that five key areas for interventions should be explored:

1. Priority should be given to interventions that improve maternal nutrition before and during pregnancy as well as in the postpartum period to ensure optimal birth and early childhood outcomes. Such interventions should include ensuring adequate micronutrient status by providing antenatal micronutrient supplements, screening and treating micronutrient deficiencies (mainly anemia), improving access to and consumption of nutritionally diverse foods among pregnant women, and monitoring weight gain during pregnancy as part of antenatal care.

2. Meeting nutritional requirements is a key factor in ensuring that infants and young children are able to survive and thrive. Suboptimal breastfeeding and complementary feeding practices along with micronutrient deficiencies hinder their potential. Therefore, a focus on implementation of an infant and young child feeding (IYCF) social and behavioral change strategy and ensuring infants and young children are receiving sufficient micronutrients through either complementary feeding or supplementation are important areas to explore.

3. Infections have a negative effect on malnutrition, including in Egypt. Ensuring that key interventions are systematically implemented at scale can help to

break this vicious cycle, including therapeutic zinc supplementation in cases of diarrhea, deworming, and ensuring proper sanitation and hygiene practices to control intestinal infections during infancy and childhood. Scaling up water, sanitation, and hygiene (WASH) interventions, particularly in rural areas with lower coverage, can also help to reduce the cycle of infection and malnutrition.

4. Other nutrition-sensitive interventions should be investigated to understand the potential to decrease food insecurity and poverty, improve health and nutrition knowledge, and broadly contribute to meeting nutrition goals.

5. Because of the current high level of wasting (8 percent), development and implementation of an integrated management of acute malnutrition (IMAM) strategy would help to ensure the short-term effective treatment of children with severe or moderate acute malnutrition, thereby reducing rates of mortality among this age group.

NOTES

1. WHO classifies the country-level prevalence of stunting into levels of public health significance. The latest revised threshold levels for stunting are as follows: prevalence of <2.5 percent (very low public health significance), 2.5–9 percent (low), 10–19 percent (medium), 20–29 percent (high), ≥30 percent (very high)—see de Onis et al. (2018).
2. Test for trend was based on a logistic regression model fitting the outcome, stunting, on a continuous year variable. The model accounted for weighting and clustering inherent in the complex design of the EDHS survey.
3. World Development Indicators (database), World Bank, Washington, DC, https://databank .worldbank.org/source/world-development-indicators..
4. Because stunting stems from a multitude of factors, other significant factors may not be captured in the EDHS (and so are not examined here), and yet they also affect the levels and severity of stunting.
5. WHO classifies the country-level prevalence of wasting into levels of public health significance. The latest revised threshold levels for wasting are as follows: prevalence of less than 2.5 percent (very low public health significance), 2.5–9 percent (low), 10–19 percent (medium), 20–29 percent (high), equal to or greater than 30 percent (very high)—see de Onis et al. (2018).
6. Children are classified as wasted if their weight-for-height (WHZ) z-score is more than two standard deviations below the median weight of a child of the same height and sex, according to the WHO Child Growth Standards median.
7. Based on EDHS data compiled by ICF International on the STATcompiler.com website.
8. WHO recommends that in settings where vitamin A deficiency is a public health problem (that is, where the prevalence of night blindness is 1 percent or higher in children 24–59 months of age or where the prevalence of vitamin A deficiency—serum retinol of 0.70 micromoles per liter or lower—is 20 percent or higher in infants and children 6–59 months of age), high-dose vitamin A supplementation be given to infants and children 6–59 months of age.
9. WHO classifies the country-level prevalence of anemia into levels of public health significance (2001). The threshold levels for anemia are as follows: prevalence of <4.9 percent, no public health problem; 5–19.9 percent, low; 20–39.9 percent, moderate, and ≥40 percent, severe.
10. Based on EDHS data compiled by ICF International on the STATcompiler.com website.
11. Data retrieved from WHO's Global Targets Tracking Tool, http://www.who.int/nutrition /global-target-2025/en/.

REFERENCES

Akombi, B. J., K. E. Agho, D. Merom, J. J. Hall, and A. M. Renzaho. 2017. "Multilevel Analysis of Factors Associated with Wasting and Underweight among Children Under-Five Years in Nigeria." *Nutrients* 9 (1): 44. doi:10.3390/nu9010044.

Black, R. E., L. H. Allen, Z. A. Bhutta, L. E. Caufield, M. de Onis, M. Ezzati, C. Mathers, and J. Rivera. 2008. "Maternal and Child Undernutrition: Global and Regional Exposures and Health Consequences." *Lancet* 371: 243–60.

Black, R. E., C. G. Victora, S. P. Walker, Z. A. Bhutta, P. Christian, M. de Onis, M. Ezzati, S. Grantham-McGregor, J. Katz, R. Martorell, and R. Uauy. 2013. "Maternal and Child Undernutrition and Overweight in Low-Income and Middle-Income Countries." *Lancet* 382 (9890): 427–51. doi:10.1016/S0140-6736(13)60937-X.

Caldwell, J. C. 1979. "Education as a Factor in Mortality Decline: An Examination of Nigerian Data." *Population Studies* (NY) 33 (3): 395–413.

Carlson, G. J., K. Kordas, and L. E. Murray-Kolb. 2015. "Associations between Women's Autonomy and Child Nutritional Status: A Review of the Literature." *Maternal and Child Nutrition* 11 (4): 452–82. doi:10.1111/mcn.12113.

Checkley, W., G. Buckley, R. H. Gilman, A. M. Assis, R. L. Guerrant, S. S. Morris, K. Mølbak, P. Valentiner-Branth, C. F. Lanata, and R. E. Black. 2008. "Multi-country Analysis of the Effects of Diarrhoea on Childhood Stunting." *International Journal of Epidemiology* 37 (4): 816–30.

Cunningham, K., M. Ruel, E. Ferguson, and R. Uauy. 2015. "Women's Empowerment and Child Nutritional Status in South Asia: A Synthesis of the Literature." *Maternal and Child Nutrition* 11 (1): 1–19. doi:10.1111/mcn.12125.

de Onis, M., M. Blössner, and E. Borghi. 2012. "Prevalence and Trends of Stunting among Pre-school Children, 1990–2020." *Public Health Nutrition* 15 (01): 142–48. doi:10.1017/S1368980011001315.

de Onis, M., E. Borghi, M. Arimond, P. Webb, T. Croft, K. Saha, L. M. De-Regil, F. Thuita, R. Heidkamp, J. Krasevec, C. Hayashi, and R. Flores-Ayala. 2018. "Prevalence Thresholds for Wasting, Overweight and Stunting in Children under 5 Years." *Public Health Nutrition* 22 (1): 175–79. doi: 10.1017/S1368980018002434.

de Onis, M., and A. Onyango. 2008. "WHO Child Growth Standards." *Paediatric Croatian Supplement* 52 (suppl. 1): 13–17. doi:10.4067/S0370-41062009000400012.

Dewey, K. G. 2016. "Reducing Stunting by Improving Maternal, Infant and Young Child Nutrition in Regions such as South Asia: Evidence, Challenges and Opportunities." *Maternal and Child Nutrition* 12: 27–38.

Dewey K. G., and D. R. Mayers. 2011. "Early Child Growth: How Do Nutrition and Infection Interact?" *Maternal and Child Nutrition* 7 (suppl. 3): 129–42.

El-Zanaty, F. H., E. M. Hussein, G. A. Shawky, A. A. Way, and S. Kishor. 1996. *Egypt Demographic and Health Survey 1995.* Calverton, MA: National Population Council Egypt and Macro International. https://dhsprogram.com/pubs/pdf/FR71/FR71.pdf.

El-Zanaty, F. H., H. A. A. Sayed, H. H. M. Zaky, and A. A. Way. 1993. *Egypt Demographic and Health Survey 1992.* Cairo, Egypt and Calverton, MA: National Population Council Egypt and Macro International. https://dhsprogram.com/pubs/pdf/FR48/FR48.pdf.

El-Zanaty, F., and A. A. Way. 2001. *Egypt Demographic and Health Survey 2000.* Calverton, MA: Ministry of Health and Population Egypt, National Population Council Egypt, and ORC Macro. https://dhsprogram.com/pubs/pdf/FR117/FR117.pdf.

———. 2006. *Egypt Demographic and Health Survey 2005.* Cairo, Egypt: Ministry of Health and Population Egypt, National Population Council, El-Zanaty and Associates, and ORC Macro. https://dhsprogram.com/pubs/pdf/FR176/FR176.pdf.

———. 2009. *Egypt Demographic and Health Survey 2008.* Cairo, Egypt: Ministry of Health Egypt, El-Zanaty and Associates, and Macro International. https://dhsprogram.com/pubs/pdf/FR220/FR220.pdf.

FAO (Food and Agriculture Organization) and WHO (World Health Organization). 2004. *Vitamin and Mineral Requirements in Human Nutrition,* Second Edition. Geneva. ISBN: 9241546123.

Green M. S. 1992. "The Male Predominance in the Incidence of Infectious Diseases in Children: A Postulated Explanation for Disparities in the Literature." *International Journal of Epidemiology* 21 (2): 381–86.

Haque, S. M. R., S. Tisha, and N. Huq. 2015. "Poor Birth Size a Badge of Low Birth Weight Accompanying Less Antenatal Care in Bangladesh with Substantial Divisional Variation: Evidence from BDHS-2011." *Public Health Research* 5 (6): 184–91. doi:10.5923/j.phr.20150506.03.

Harding, K. L., V. M. Aguayo, and P. Webb. 2018. "Factors Associated with Wasting among Children under Five Years Old in South Asia: Implications for Action." *PLOS One* (July 3): 1–7. doi:10.1371/journal.pone.0198749.

Headey, D., J. Hoddinott, and S. Park. 2017. "Accounting for Nutritional Changes in Six Success Stories: A Regression-Decomposition Approach." *Global Food Security* 13: 12–20. doi:10.1016/j.gfs.2017.02.003.

Horton, S. 1988. "Birth Order and Child Nutritional Status: Evidence from the Philippines." *Economic Development and Cultural Change* 36 (2): 341–54. doi:10.1086/451655.

Imdad, A., K. Herzer, E. Mayo-Wilson, M. Y. Yakoob, and Z. A. Bhutta. 2010. "Vitamin A Supplementation for Preventing Morbidity and Mortality in Children from 6 Months to 5 Years of Age." *Cochrane Database of Systematic Reviews* (12): CD008524. doi:10.1002/14651858.CD008524.pub2.

Kavle, J. A., F. El-Zanaty, M. Landry, and R. Galloway. 2015. "The Rise in Stunting in Relation to Avian Influenza and Food Consumption Patterns in Lower Egypt in Comparison to Upper Egypt: Results from 2005 and 2008 Demographic and Health Surveys." *BMC Public Health* 15 (1): 1–18. doi:10.1186/s12889-015-1627-3.

Kavle, J. A., S. Mehanna, G. Saleh, M. A. Fouad, M. Ramzy, D. Hamed, M. Hassan, G. Khan, and R. Galloway. 2014. *Examining Factors Associated with Stunting in Lower Egypt in Comparison to Upper Egypt: Bridging the Gap between Cultural Beliefs and Feasible Feeding Practices through Trials for Improved Practices.* Washington, DC: Maternal and Child Health Integrated Program (MCHIP), U.S. Agency for International Development.

——. 2015. "Exploring Why Junk Foods Are 'Essential' Foods and How Culturally Tailored Recommendations Improved Feeding in Egyptian Children." *Maternal and Child Nutrition* 11 (3): 346–70.

Keino, S., G. Plasqui, G. Ettyang, and B. van den Borne. 2014. "Determinants of Stunting and Overweight among Young Children and Adolescents in Sub-Saharan Africa." *Food and Nutrition Bulletin* 35 (2): 167–78.

Khatab, K. 2010. "Childhood Malnutrition in Egypt Using Geoadditive Gaussian and Latent Variable Models." *American Journal of Tropical Medicine and Hygiene* 82 (4): 653–63. doi:10.4269/ajtmh.2010.09-0501.

Makate, M., and C. Makate. 2017. "Educated Mothers, Well-Fed and Healthy Children? Assessing the Impact of the 1980 School Reform on Dietary Diversity and Nutrition Outcomes of Zimbabwean Children." *Journal of Development Studies* 2017: 1–21.

Makoka, D. 2013. "The Impact of Maternal Education on Child Nutrition: Evidence from Malawi, Tanzania and Zimbabwe." DHS Working Paper 84, ICF International, Calverton. http://www.dhsprogram.com/pubs/pdf/WP84/WP84.pdf.

Menon, P., M. T. Ruel, and S. S. Morris. 2000. "Socio-economic Differentials in Child Stunting Are Considerably Larger in Urban than Rural Areas: Analysis of 10 DHS Data Sets." *Food and Nutrition Bulletin* 21 (3): 282–89. doi:10.1177/156482650002100305.

MOHP (Ministry of Health and Population), El-Zanaty and Associates, and ICF International. 2015. *Egypt Demographic and Health Survey 2014.* Cairo, Egypt and Rockville, MD: Ministry of Health and Population and ICF International. https://dhsprogram.com/pubs/pdf/FR302/FR302.pdf.

Mosley, W. H., and L. C. Chen. 1984. "An Analytical Framework for the Study of Child Survival in Developing Countries." *Bulletin of the World Health Organization* 10: 25–45. doi:10.2307/2807954.

Rahman, A., S. Chowdhury, and D. Hossain. 2009. "Acute Malnutrition in Bangladeshi Children: Levels and Determinants." *Asia-Pacific Journal of Public Health* 31 (3): 294–302. doi:10.1177/1010539509335399.

Rakotomanana, H., G. E. Gates, D. Hildebrand, and B. J. Stoecker. 2017. "Determinants of Stunting in Children under 5 Years in Madagascar." *Maternal and Child Nutrition* 13 (4). doi:10.1111/mcn.12409.

Rice, A. L., K. P. West, and R. E. Black. 2004. "Vitamin A Deficiency." In *Comparative Quantification of Health Risks,* edited by M. Ezzati, A. D. Lopez, A. Rodgers, and C. J. L. Murray, Vol. 1, 211–57. https://apps.who.int/iris/handle/10665/42770.

Ruel, M. T., J. P. Habicht, P. Pinstrup-Andersen, and Y. Gröhn. 1992. "The Mediating Effect of Maternal Nutrition Knowledge on the Association between Maternal Schooling and Child Nutritional Status in Lesotho." *American Journal of Epidemiology* 135 (8): 904–14. http://www.ncbi.nlm.nih.gov/pubmed/1585903.

Smith, L., M. Ruel, and A. Ndiaye. 2005. "Why Is Child Malnutrition Lower in Urban than in Rural Areas? Evidence from 36 Developing Countries." *World Development* 33 (8): 1285–1305.

Sreeramareddy, C. T., R. R. Shidhaye, and N. Sathiakumar. 2011. "Association between Biomass Fuel Use and Maternal Report of Child Size at Birth—An Analysis of 2005–06 India Demographic Health Survey Data." *BMC Public Health* 11 (1): 403. doi:10.1186/1471-2458-11-403.

Stevens, G. A., J. E. Bennett, Q. Hennocq, Y. Lu, L. M. De-Regil, L. Rogers, G. Danaei, G. Li, R. A. White, S. R. Flaxman, S. P. Oehrle, M. M. Finucane, R. Guerrero, Y. A. Bhutta, A. Then-Paulino, W. Fawzi, R. E. Black, and M. Ezzati. 2015. "Trends and Mortality Effects of Vitamin A Deficiency in Children in 138 Low-Income and Middle-Income Countries between 1991 and 2013: A Pooled Analysis of Population-Based Surveys." *Lancet Global Health* 3 (9): 528–36. doi:10.1016/S2214-109X(15)00039-X.

Stoltzfus, R. J., L. Mullany, and R. E. Black. 2004. "Iron Deficiency Anaemia." In *Comparative Quantification of Health Risks,* edited by M. Ezzati, A. D. Lopez, A. Rodgers, and C. J. L. Murray, Vol. 1, 163–209. https://apps.who.int/iris/handle/10665/42770.

UNICEF (United Nations Children's Fund). 1990. *Strategy for Improved Nutrition of Children and Women in Developing Countries.* New York: UNICEF.

——. 2013. *Improving Child Nutrition: The Achievable Imperative for Global Progress.* New York: UNICEF. doi:978-92-806-4686-3.

——. 2015. "UNICEF's Approach to Scaling up Nutrition for Mothers and Their Children." Discussion Paper, Programme Division, UNICEF, New York. https://www.unicef.org/nutrition/files/Unicef_Nutrition_Strategy.pdf.

Wamani, H., A. N. Åstrøm, S. Peterson, J. K. Tumwine, and T. Tylleskär. 2007. "Boys Are More Stunted than Girls in Sub-Saharan Africa: A Meta-analysis of 16 Demographic and Health Surveys." *BMC Pediatrics* 7: 1–10. doi:10.1186/1471-2431-7-17.

WHO (World Health Organization). 2001. "Iron Deficiency Anaemia: Assessment, Prevention, and Control. A Guide for Programme Managers." WHO/NHD/01.3. Geneva.

——.2008. "Indicators for Assessing Infant and Young Child Feeding Practices: Part 1—Definitions: Conclusions of a Consensus Meeting Held 6-8 November 2007 in Washington D.C., USA." World Health Organization, Geneva. http://apps.who.int/iris/bitstream/handle/10665/43895/9789241596664_eng.pdf?sequence=1.

——. 2011. "Guideline: Vitamin A Supplementation in Infants and Children 6–59 Months of Age." Geneva.

——. 2012. "Guideline: Daily Iron and Folic Acid Supplementation in Pregnant Women." Geneva.

——. 2016. "Daily Iron Supplementation in Infants and Children." Geneva.

Wirth, J. P., N. Petry, S. A. Tanumihardjo, L. M. Rogers, E. McLean, A. Greig, G. S. Garrett, R. D. W. Klemm, and F. Rohner. 2017. "Vitamin A Supplementation Programs and Country-Level Evidence of Vitamin A Deficiency." *Nutrients* 9 (3):1–18. doi:10.3390/nu9030190.

Zottarelli, L. K., T. S. Sunil, and S. Rajaram. 2007. "Influence of Parental and Socioeconomic Factors on Stunting in Children under 5 Years in Egypt." *Eastern Mediterranean Health Journal* 13 (6): 1330–42.

2 Overnutrition of Children Under 5 and Women of Reproductive Age in Egypt

FRANK HU AND YANPING LI

KEY MESSAGES

- There is a rising trend in childhood overweight (and obesity) in Egypt, and the prevalence is higher than in most countries in the Middle East and North Africa region.
  - The proportion of overweight children with stunting has also increased in the last few decades.
  - Key determinants of overweight and obesity in children include urban living, maternal obesity, and a calorie-dense diet.
- High levels of overnutrition among women of reproductive age predominate in Egypt, with more than 80 percent of such women overweight or obese.

  - More than 10 percent of women in Egypt show signs of both obesity and anemia.
  - Based on data from the Egypt Demographic and Health Survey and the literature, maternal obesity is a critical factor in the development of childhood obesity.
  - Key determinants of overweight and obesity among women of reproductive age include sedentary lifestyles and consumption of energy-dense foods, with women from richer households and urban areas slightly more likely to be overweight.

INTRODUCTION

This chapter describes the situation on overnutrition among children under 5 and women of reproductive age in Egypt. The chapter utilizes data from the 1992, 1995, 2000, 2005, 2008, and 2014 rounds of the Egypt Demographic and Health Survey (EDHS) (El-Zanaty et al. 1993, 1996; El-Zanaty and Way 2001, 2006, 2009; MOHP, El-Zanaty and Associates, and ICF International 2015), as well as data from other literature and databases. This chapter also examines the trends in overweight and obesity and the prevalence of anemia among women of reproductive age.

CHILDHOOD OVERWEIGHT AND OBESITY

Prevalence and trends

In Egypt, almost 15 percent of children under 5 are overweight, and of those almost 5 percent are obese. Overweight among children, defined as having a weight-for-height z-score greater than two standard deviations above the WHO Child Growth Standards median (WHO 2008), has both immediate and long-term consequences (Black et al. 2013), and it increases the risk of obesity in adulthood. According to the World Health Organization (WHO) classification (WHO 2008), the prevalence of overweight individuals in Egypt is currently a significant public health problem with growing concern over the increasing pervasiveness and long-lasting impact.

The prevalence of overweight in children under 5 was 14.9 percent in Egypt in 2014, the third-highest in Middle East and North Africa countries (figure 2.1). In Egypt, 10.1 percent of overweight children had a weight-for-height z-score (WHZ) of greater than 2, but less than or equal to 3, and 4.8 percent of these children were obese, with a weight-for-height z-score above 3, according to the WHO criteria (WHO 2008).

Despite fluctuations, Egypt has seen a steady increase in child overweight prevalence since the early 1990s, with a small reduction recorded after 2008. The prevalence of overweight among children in Egypt was 13.8 percent in 1992, 13.4 percent in 1995, 17.6 percent in 2000, 13.2 percent in 2005, 19.1 percent in 2008, and 14.9 percent in 2014, with a significant upward trend over time (p = 0.001 for trend). In all of the survey years, the estimates in Egypt were much higher than the average level of overweight in Middle East and North Africa countries for which data are available (figure 2.2).

In 2014 in Egypt, the prevalence of overweight (including obesity) is 15.3 percent among boys and 14.3 percent among girls, while the prevalence of obesity is 4.9 percent among boys and 4.7 percent among girls (figure 2.3).

FIGURE 2.1

Prevalence of overweight among children under 5: Middle East and North Africa economies, various years

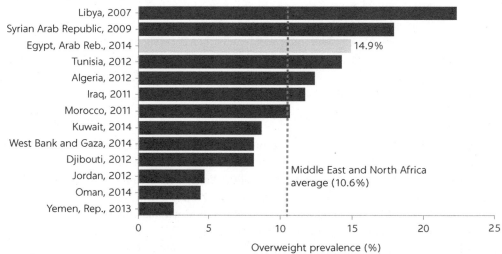

Sources: Egypt: EDHS microdata 2014 (dataset), Ministry of Health and Population and ICF International, Cairo, Egypt, and Rockville, MA, https://dhsprogram.com/data/; other countries: World Development Indicators (database), World Bank, Washington, DC, https://databank.worldbank.org/source/world-development-indicators.

FIGURE 2.2

Trends in prevalence of childhood overweight: Middle East and North Africa economies, various years

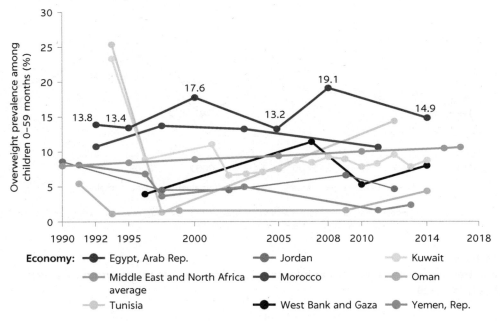

Sources: EDHS microdata various years (dataset), ICF International, Rockville, MA, https://dhsprogram.com /data/; other countries: World Development Indicators (database), World Bank, Washington, DC, https:// databank.worldbank.org/source/world-development-indicators.

FIGURE 2.3

Prevalence of overweight and obesity among children: Egypt, 2014

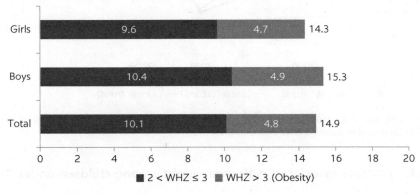

Source: EDHS 2014 (MOHP, El-Zanaty and Associates, and ICF International 2015).
Note: WHZ = weight-for-height z-score.

The steady increase in overweight is consistent for both girls and boys. As shown in figure 2.4, the upward trend in overweight is consistent in boys (p =0.08 for trend) and girls (p = 0.004 for trend) without significant gender differences (p = 0.4 for interaction).

The upward trend in overweight prevalence is greater in urban than in rural areas. When stratified by living area (figure 2.5), a significant upward trend in overweight prevalence is observed among children living in urban areas (p < 0.0001 for trend) but not rural areas (p = 0.33 for trend; p = 0.005 for interaction).

FIGURE 2.4

Time trend of overweight among infants and children by sex: Egypt, 1992–2014

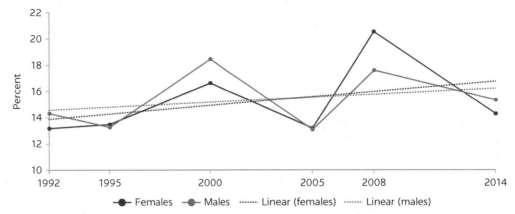

Sources: EDHS 1992, 1995, 2000, 2005, 2008, 2014 (El-Zanaty et al. 1993, 1996; El-Zanaty and Way 2001, 2006, 2009; MOHP, El-Zanaty and Associates, and ICF International 2015).

FIGURE 2.5

Time trend of overweight among infants and children across urban and rural areas: Egypt, 1992–2014

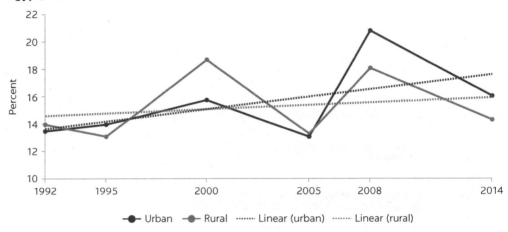

Sources: EDHS 1992, 1995, 2000, 2005, 2008, 2014(El-Zanaty et al. 1993, 1996; El-Zanaty and Way 2001, 2006, 2009; MOHP, El-Zanaty and Associates, and ICF International 2015).

Risk factors associated with overweight among children under 5

Childhood overweight and obesity are caused by increased energy storage from overconsumption of calories beyond growth needs and energy expenditure (Anderson and Butcher 2006; Goran and Treuth 2001). The increasing prevalence of overweight in Egyptian children could be attributed largely to rapid urbanization and the accompanying nutritional transition characterized by dietary shifts from traditional foods and local fruits and vegetables to Westernized diets that are higher in fat, sugar, and calories (Aboul-Enein, Bernstein, and Neary 2016; Farrag, Cheskin, and Farag 2017). According to Hassanyn (2000), as early as between 1981 and 2000 the consumption of meat and dairy increased substantially (also see Aly et al. 1981; Hassan, Moussa, and Ismail 2006).

In Egypt, children from both the poorest and richest households have a significantly higher likelihood of being overweight. And yet socioeconomic status and obesity tend to be inversely related in high-income countries and positively related in developing countries (Kim and von dem Knesebeck 2018; Newton, Braithwaite, and Akinyemiju 2017; Wu et al. 2015). In Egypt, however, the prevalence of overweight is 17.7 percent among children under 5 from the richest households, 15.8 percent among children from the poorest households, and 13.9 percent among households within the middle wealth index (figure 2.6, panel a). The government of Egypt (GoE) subsidizes certain foods such as sugar and flour despite their low nutritional value, and thus the poorest households have access to affordable, energy-dense foods. The high prevalence of overweight among the richest households may be explained by urbanization and its associated transition to more Western diets and sedentary lifestyles (Angkurawaranon et al. 2014). The negative coping strategies employed by poor families, including reverting to calorie-dense foods to cope with higher food prices and food inaccessibility rather than consuming nutrient-rich foods, may explain their greater likelihood of being overweight (WFP 2013).

Children in urban governorates tend to be more overweight in Egypt, indicating a link with urbanization. The prevalence of overweight is 8.4 percent among children living in frontier governorates and 14.5 percent among children living in the urban governorates, suggesting a link between urbanization and obesity rates (figure 2.6, panel b).

FIGURE 2.6

Prevalence of overweight children by wealth index and region: Egypt, 2014

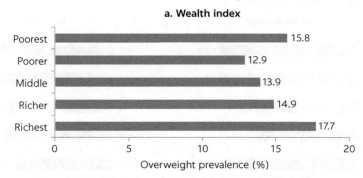

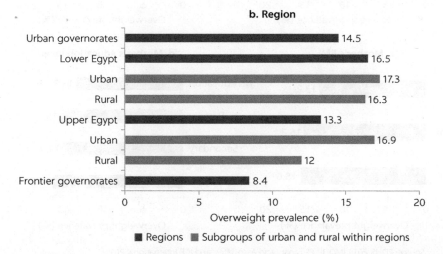

■ Regions ■ Subgroups of urban and rural within regions

Source: EDHS 2014 (MOHP, El-Zanaty and Associates, and ICF International 2015).

In Egypt, children with large birth size as well as very small birth size have a higher prevalence of overweight than those with normal birth size, although birth size does not reach a significant level in the multivariate-adjusted model (figure 2.7, panel a). This finding partially supports the finding in a recent meta-analysis that high birthweight is associated with increased risk of obesity from childhood to early adulthood (Yu et al. 2011).

Several other characteristics are relevant to childhood overweight, including family size and birth order. In particular, a smaller family size is associated with childhood obesity. For children under 5, the childhood overweight prevalence is 15.3 percent in families with one child; 14.9 percent, two children; 13.9 percent, three children; 12.7 percent, four children; and 8.1 percent, five or more children. Birth order also seems to be relevant to childhood overweight. Children who are born first have a 15.7 percent prevalence of overweight, whereas children born second have a 15.5 percent prevalence; third, 14.6 percent; and fourth or later, 13.7 percent. However, when simultaneously adjusting for birth order, the number of children under 5, and family size, only family size is significantly associated with the likelihood of being overweight: children from households with fewer members are more likely to be overweight (figure 2.7, panel b; figure 2.8).

FIGURE 2.7

Prevalence of overweight children by birthweight, family size, mother's obesity level, and mother's education level: Egypt, 2014

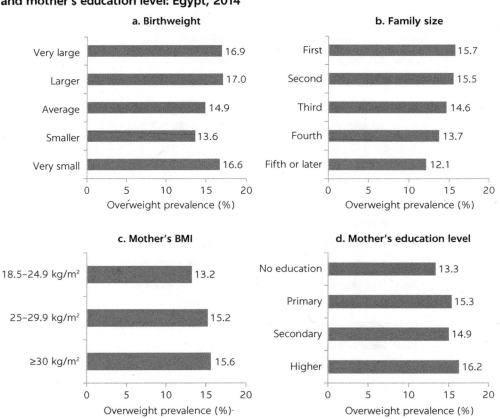

Source: EDHS 2014 (MOHP, El-Zanaty and Associates, and ICF International 2015).
Note: BMI = body mass index; kg/m² = kilograms per square meter.

FIGURE 2.8

Multivariate-adjusted odds ratio for overweight among children under 5: Egypt, 2014

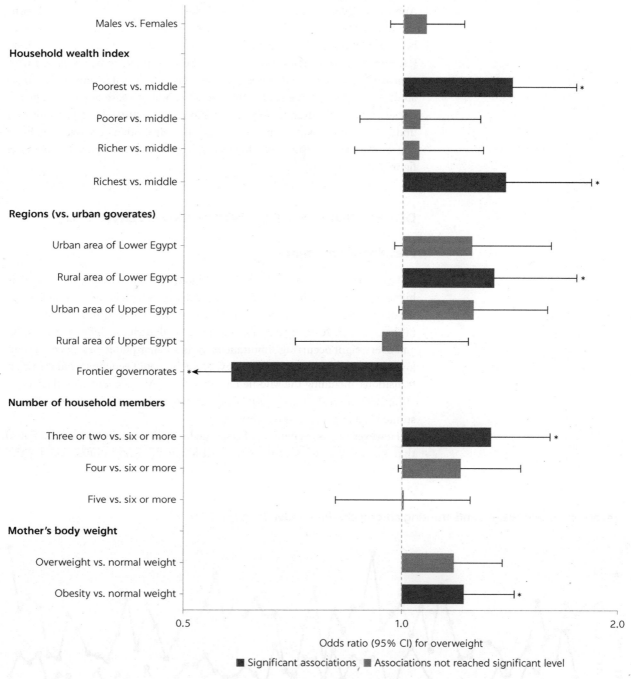

Source: EDHS 2014 (MOHP, El-Zanaty and Associates, and ICF International 2015).
Note: CI = confidence interval.
p < 0.05.

Finally, children from mothers who have higher levels of education, as well as from mothers who are obese, are more likely to be overweight. A recent study in Egypt finds that children whose mothers had higher education levels were less likely to be stunted than children whose mothers had lower education levels (Sharaf, Mansour, and Rashad 2018). Data from EDHS 2014 suggests that children from mothers with higher education levels are more likely to be overweight than children from mothers with lower education levels, but the association is not statistically significant after multivariate adjustment (figure 2.7, panel d). Another study of Egyptian mothers and children indicates that maternal consumption of beverages with added sugar is a significant predictor of children's body mass index, likely because of the access to these beverages in the household (Hassan et al. 2016). Elsewhere, parental obesity is found to be associated with approximately a threefold increase in the odds of overweight among Lebanese adolescents (Nasreddine et al. 2014) and a twofold increase in the presence of obesity among children in Jordan (Al-Kloub et al. 2010). In Egypt, children under 5 are more likely to be overweight if their mothers are overweight or obese, even after adjustment for multiple risk factors (figure 2.7, panel c; figure 2.8).

DOUBLE BURDEN OF STUNTING AND OVERWEIGHT

Prevalence and trends

In Egypt, for all age groups from 3 to 59 months, the prevalence of stunting is higher than overweight (figure 2.9). Although overweight is generally an indicator of overnutrition, stunting reflects the cumulative effects of undernutrition (Tzioumis et al. 2016). The double burden of malnutrition, defined as stunting and overweight occurring simultaneously, is a major public health concern in low- and middle-income countries experiencing rapid economic and nutrition transitions, including the Middle East and North Africa countries (Black et al. 2013; Tzioumis et al. 2016). In 2014, 22 percent of Egyptian children under 5 were stunted and 15 percent were overweight.

However, almost 51 percent of overweight children are also stunted, a figure that has increased by more than half since the early 1990s. Among the

FIGURE 2.9

Prevalence of overweight and stunting among children under 5: Egypt, 2014

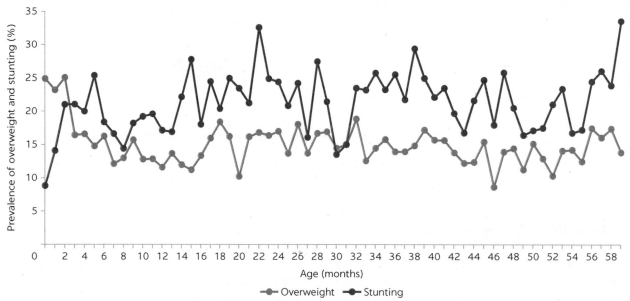

Source: EDHS 2014 (MOHP, El-Zanaty and Associates, and ICF International 2015).

14.9 percent of overweight children in Egypt in 2014, 7.6 percent were overweight with stunting (accounting for 50.9 percent of all of the overweight children). In 1992, out of 13.8 percent of children overweight, only 36.6 percent were stunted (figure 2.10). However, only a few studies—in China (Li et al. 2011), Mexico (Fernald and Neufeld 2007), and South Africa (Mamabolo et al. 2005)— have examined the presence and determinants of undernutrition (stunting) and overnutrition (overweight) within the same individuals. The following section examines risk factors of the double burden of stunting and overweight among children 0–59 months of age in Egypt.

Risk factors associated with double burden of stunting and overweight among children 0–59 months of age

Compared with single-birth children, twins were more likely to be overweight with stunting but less likely to be overweight without stunting in Egypt in 2014 (figure 2.11). Being a twin has also been found to be inversely related to children's height-for-age z-score (Sharaf, Mansour, and Rashad 2018). In addition, according to the EDHS data, boys are more likely to be overweight with stunting than girls. A meta-analysis of 16 Demographic and Health Survey (DHS) data sets also found that boys were more stunted than girls in Sub-Saharan countries (Wamani et al. 2007).

Children from the poorest households have a higher likelihood of being overweight with or without stunting, compared with children from households within the middle wealth index. Children from the richest households have a significantly higher likelihood of being overweight without stunting (figure 2.11).

Compared with those living in urban governorates, children living in frontier governorates have a lower likelihood of being overweight with and without stunting. Children living in urban areas of Upper Egypt have a significantly higher likelihood of being overweight with stunting (figure 2.11). Upper Egypt is the poorest region in Egypt, and therefore undernutrition and stunting

FIGURE 2.10

Prevalence of overweight with and without stunting: Egypt, 1992–2014

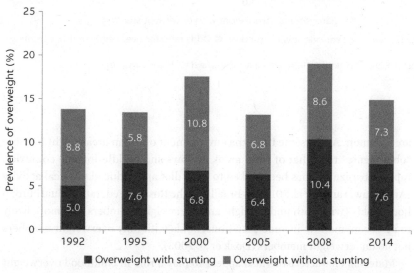

Sources: EDHS 1992, 1995, 2000, 2005, 2008, 2014 (El-Zanaty et al. 1993, 1996; El-Zanaty and Way 2001, 2006, 2009; MOHP, El-Zanaty and Associates, and ICF International 2015).

FIGURE 2.11

Odds ratio for overweight (including obesity) with or without stunting: Egypt, 2014

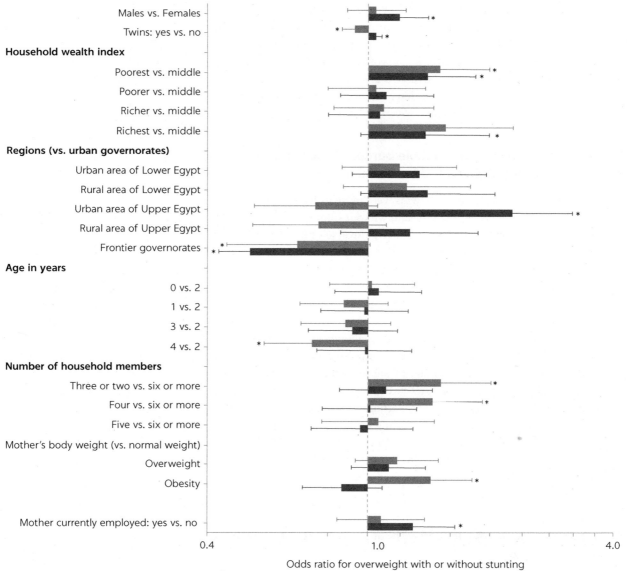

Source: EDHS 2014 (MOHP, El-Zanaty and Associates, and ICF International 2015).
*p < 0.05.

are common. At the same time, the environment of urban areas might be more "obesogenic" than that of rural areas. In low- and middle-income countries, rapid urbanization has been linked to poor diet and reduced physical activity (Angkurawaranon et al. 2014). In Brazil and the Russian Federation, dual burden households (with both underweight and overweight members) are more likely to be urban and low-income than households with only overweight members but no underweight members (Doak et al. 2005).

Maternal characteristics also appear to play a role in childhood overweight and stunting. Obese mothers in Egypt are more likely to have an overweight child without stunting, compared with normal weight mothers (figure 2.11).

Another study in Egypt finds that maternal employment has a significant negative impact on child nutritional status as measured by the height-for-age z- score; children of unemployed mothers are taller than those of employed mothers (Rashad and Sharaf 2017). Employed mothers were also more likely to have stunted overweight children (figure 2.11). Maternal employment may reduce the time mothers can devote to childcare, feeding, and preparation of nutritious food. Additional data from Egypt suggest that older siblings play an important role in feeding young children when mothers are away from home, and often feed them junk foods such as processed snack foods containing added sugar (Kavle et al. 2015). A prospective study in rural South Africa found that having a working or student mother increased the risk of concurrent stunting and overweight among children 3 years of age (Mamabolo et al. 2005).

Perceptions and the availability of certain complementary foods may also affect childhood obesity rates in Egypt. Complementary foods given to children weaning from breastfeeding are important for balancing weight and height growth. In the Middle East and North Africa region, including Egypt, complementary foods are often sugary drinks and snacks that are low in nutritional value and high in calories (Aitsi-Selmi et al. 2014; Nasreddine et al. 2012; Popkin, Adair, and Ng 2012; Zottarelli, Sunil, and Rajaram 2007). Government subsidies of sugar and oil have played an important role in the Egyptian diet by increasing the accessibility and affordability of these types of energy-dense foods (Asfaw 2007; Austin, Hill, and Fawzi 2013; Kavle et al. 2014, 2015). Among the Egyptian population, sponge cakes and sugary biscuits are not perceived as unhealthy and are considered "ideal" common complementary foods. Unhealthy foods such as sugary biscuits, candy, chips, and cakes make up one-third of the foods consumed daily by Egyptian infants (Kavle et al. 2015). Child consumption of sugary snack foods is associated with a 51 percent higher likelihood of being part of a "stunted child and obese mother" household (Aitsi-Selmi 2015).

Poor dietary diversity can also obstruct healthy child growth. One study finds that of 300 Egyptian infants, only half meet the WHO cutoff for adequate diversity at 12 months (Kavle et al. 2016). The same study finds a significant association between a minimum dietary diversity (infants consuming at least four food groups from 6 months of age) and the weight-for-length z-score in Lower Egypt (Kavle et al. 2016). An earlier study in China (Li et al. 2010) indicated that the overall dietary diversity score was significantly lower in stunted overweight children than in normal weight and overweight children. Specifically, stunted overweight children consume a lower diversity of vegetables and fruits and animal food groups than normal weight and overweight children. On the other hand, stunted overweight children consume a larger diversity of cereal and tubers than stunted children without overweight.

As recommended by WHO for measuring dietary diversity in infants and young children 6–23 months of age (WHO 2008), EDHS 2014 collected food intake data on children under 2. The following food groups were used to calculate dietary diversity scores: (1) infant formula, milk other than breast milk, cheese, or yogurt or other milk products; (2) foods made from grains, roots, and tubers; (3) vitamin A–rich fruits and vegetables; (4) other fruits and vegetables; (5) eggs; (6) meat, poultry, fish, shellfish, and organ meats; (7) legumes and nuts.

Children who did not consume any foods within the seven identified food groups had the highest prevalence of overweight with stunting. The prevalence of overweight was highest among children who consumed foods in all seven food groups in the last 24 hours, especially overweight without stunting (figure 2.12).

FIGURE 2.12

Prevalence of overweight with and without stunting according to the number of food groups children 6–23 months of age living with their mother were fed in last 24 hours: Egypt, 2014

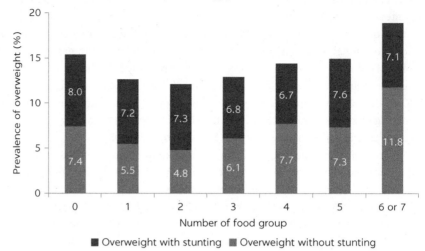

Source: EDHS 2014 (MOHP, El-Zanaty and Associates, and ICF International 2015).
Note: Food groups: (0) = children did not eat any food from the following seven food groups; (1) infant formula, milk other than breast milk, cheese, or yogurt or other milk products; (2) foods made from grains, roots, and tubers; (3) vitamin A–rich fruits and vegetables; (4) other fruits and vegetables; (5) eggs; (6) meat, poultry, fish, shellfish, and organ meats; (7) legumes and nuts.

Because research has indicated that Egyptian children under 2 frequently consume energy-dense junk foods, children not consuming foods in the seven groups may have been consuming more junk food (Kavle et al. 2015). In the study by Kavle et al. (2015), Egyptian mothers stated that their primary reasons for withholding the introduction of nutritious food and delaying family/table foods until 1 year of age were fears of illness, inability to digest these foods, or allergies. After analyzing each of the seven food groups, this study found that infant formula, milk other than breast milk, cheese, or yogurt or other milk products was the only food group significantly associated with a lower likelihood of being overweight with stunting.

Although the consumption of soft drinks in Egypt was not assessed in EDHS 2014, there is evidence that it has increased substantially over the past few decades. A 2011 survey of the health behavior of Egyptian teenagers indicated that 60 percent of boys and 51 percent of girls consumed one or more carbonated, sugar-sweetened drink daily, and 87 percent did not participate in regular physical activity (WHO and UNICEF 2003). Future EDHS surveys should include an assessment of sugar-sweetened beverage consumption.

OVERWEIGHT AND OBESITY IN WOMEN OF REPRODUCTIVE AGE

Prevalence and trends

In Egypt, more than a third of women are overweight and close to half of all women are obese—a situation that has worsened since 2000. Overweight and obesity, defined as having a body mass index of 25–29.9 for overweight and 30 or

FIGURE 2.13

Trends in overweight and obesity among women of reproductive age: Egypt, 2000–2014

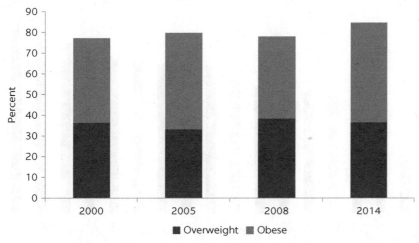

Sources: EDHS 2000, 2005, 2008, 2014 (El-Zanaty and Way 2001, 2006, 2009; MOHP, El-Zanaty and Associates, and ICF International 2015).

greater for obesity, increase the risk of adverse pregnancy outcomes such as hemorrhaging and maternal death, as well as increased infant mortality and preterm birth (Black et al. 2013).

According to EDHS 2014, the prevalence of overweight and obesity among Egyptian women of reproductive age is 36.5 percent and 48.1 percent, respectively (figure 2.13). Moreover, more than five out of every six Egyptian women 15–49 years of age are overweight or obese (85 percent). Only 15.1 percent of women are at a normal weight, and the prevalence of underweight is very low (0.3 percent).

In a WHO report on obesity in adults over age 18 (WHO 2014), Egypt had a prevalence of obesity among women of 37.5 percent, ranking it in the middle of the Middle East and North Africa countries (figure 2.14, panel a). However, the average BMI among Egyptian women was higher than that in all the other Middle East and North Africa countries, except for Kuwait at 31 percent (figure 2.14, panel b). Another analysis of obesity among urban women found that Egyptian women had the highest prevalence of overweight and obesity among the 24 African countries in 2014 (Amugsi et al. 2017).

Whereas the prevalence of obesity among women tends to increase rapidly with age, the prevalence of overweight tends to decrease slightly with age. In 2014, 16.4 percent of women age 16 were obese, compared with 67.2 percent of women age 49. By contrast, 29 percent of women age 16 were overweight, compared with 27.3 percent of women age 49. Considering overweight and obesity together, 45.4 percent of 16-year-old and 90 percent of 36-year-old Egyptian women were overweight or obese. Nearly all 49-year-old Egyptian women (94.5 percent) were overweight or obese (figure 2.15). For women in Egypt, the likelihood of obesity increases by approximately 8 percent a year as they age (figure 2.18).

The prevalence of overweight and obesity is higher among women from urban households than among their rural counterparts (figure 2.16). This finding has emerged over several rounds of the EDHS.

FIGURE 2.14

Prevalence of obesity among women in Middle East and North Africa countries, 2014

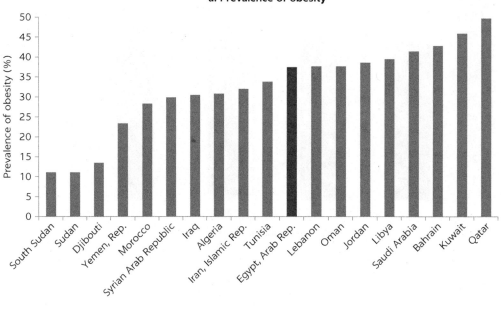

Source: WHO 2014.

Risk factors associated with overweight and obesity in women of reproductive age in 2014

Women from poorer households in rural areas tend to be slightly less obese than women from richer households in urban areas. The prevalence of obesity is 44.6 percent among the poorest women, 51.3 percent among women living in richer households, and 47.7 percent among the richest women (figure 2.17, panel a). After multivariate adjustment, the poorest women have

FIGURE 2.15

Prevalence of overweight and obesity across women 15–49 years of age: Egypt, 2014

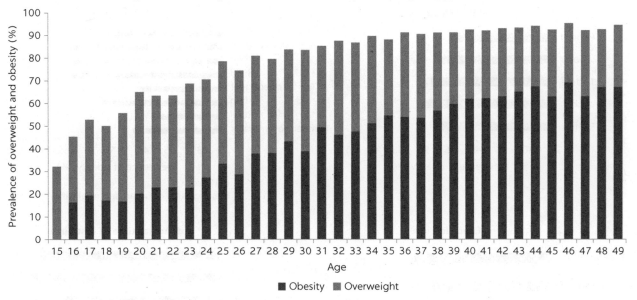

Source: EDHS 2014 (MOHP, El-Zanaty and Associates, and ICF International 2015).

FIGURE 2.16

Overweight and obesity prevalence among women in rural and urban areas: Egypt, 2014

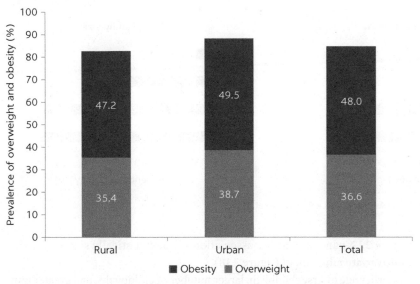

Source: EDHS 2014 (MOHP, El-Zanaty and Associates, and ICF International 2015).

a significantly lower likelihood of obesity, compared with those in the middle wealth index. A positive association between wealth index and obesity is observed for all women except for the richest (figure 2.18). Obesity prevalence varies across regions of Egypt, ranging from 37.4 percent in rural areas of Upper Egypt to 54.6 percent in urban areas of Lower Egypt (figure 2.17, panel b) and the difference persists after adjustment for wealth index, education level, and age (figure 2.18). There is a dose-response relationship between lower education levels and increased prevalence of obesity

FIGURE 2.17

Prevalence of obesity across sociodemographic factors: Egypt, 2014

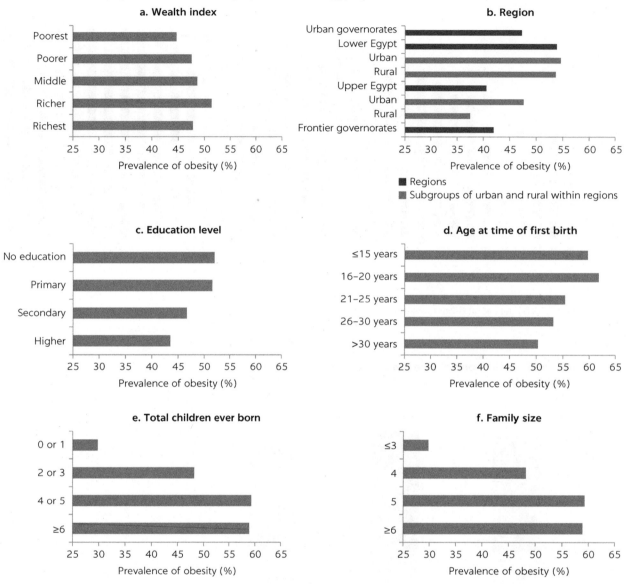

Source: EDHS 2014 (MOHP, El-Zanaty and Associates, and ICF International 2015).

(figure 2.17, panel c), but the association is not statistically significant after multivariate adjustment (figure 2.18).

Earlier age of first childbirth, larger number of childbirths, and greater number of household members are all significantly associated with a higher likelihood of obesity. Childbirth is commonly associated with weight gain and obesity (Davis et al. 2009; Onubi et al. 2016; Smith et al. 1994). Among Egyptian women, the age of first childbirth appears to influence obesity risk; the prevalence of obesity is 59.6 percent among those who had their first child before age 16 and 50.3 percent for women who had their first child after age 30 (figure 2.17, panel d). The prevalence of obesity among women also increases with number of children (figure 2.17, panel e), consistent with a meta-analysis by Onubi et al. (2016) that observed an increased risk of obesity in multiparous women compared with nulliparous women in African countries. Larger family size is associated with a

FIGURE 2.18

Multivariate-adjusted odds ratio for obesity among women 15–49 years of age: Egypt, 2014

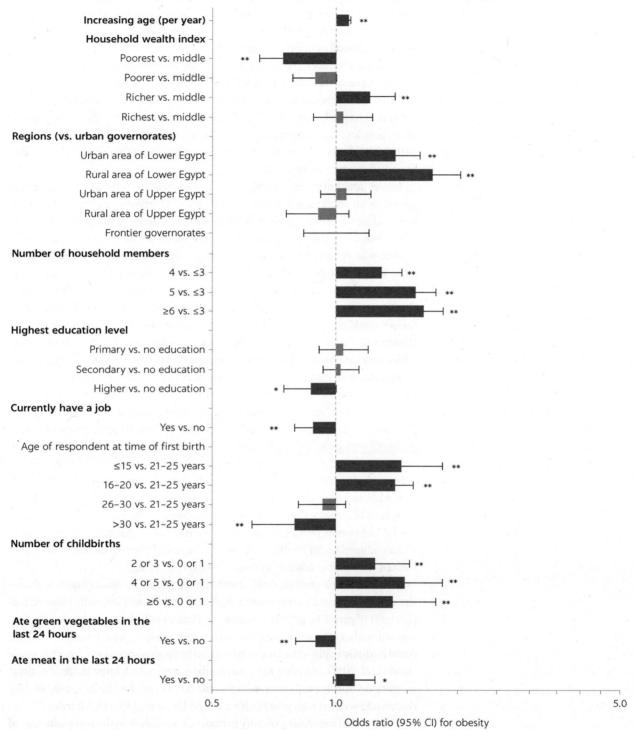

Source: EDHS 2014 (MOHP, El-Zanaty and Associates, and ICF International 2015).

Note: Figure reflects survey logistic models with listed factors simultaneously adjusted. Analyses of sociodemographic factors are based on women 15–49 years of age from EDHS 2014. Analyses of age of first birth and total number of children born are limited to women 30–49 years of age. Analysis of dietary factors is based on EDHS 2005 and EDHS 2008 when dietary surveys are included. Orange bar represents nonsignificant associations at p > 0.1. CI = confidence interval.

*p < 0.1   **p < 0.05.

higher likelihood of obesity (figure 2.17, panel f), which is also consistent with previous findings in Egyptian women (Hassan et al. 2016). After multivariate adjustment, earlier age of first childbirth, larger number of childbirths, and greater number of household members are all significantly associated with a higher likelihood of obesity (figure 2.18).

Previous studies have also observed that overweight and obese Egyptian women have a statistically significant higher incidence of unemployment (Hassan et al. 2016), in agreement with studies from Gulf countries (ALNohair 2014) that have shown that high obesity prevalence is strongly related to low education level and unemployment. Consistent with previous findings, the EDHS 2014 data indicate that employed women have a significantly lower likelihood of obesity (figure 2.18).

Lower intake of green vegetables and higher meat consumption by women are linked to an increased likelihood of obesity. Thirty-one percent of women reported intake of green leafy vegetables within 24 hours of the EDHS interview. Those women had a significantly lower likelihood of obesity as compared with women who reported not eating green leafy vegetables, even after multivariate adjustment (p = 0.04). A study of overweight and obese Egyptian women found that vegetable consumption was the only significant dietary factor related to obesity; 71.4 percent of the nonobese women consumed vegetables four to seven times a week, compared with only 30.5 percent of overweight and obese women (Hassan, El Shebini, and Ahmed 2016). The subsidization of energy-dense foods, which may have resulted in the overconsumption of calories among Egyptians, is likely a factor in this trend (Aboulenein et al. 2010). As shown in figure 2.18, in the EDHS analysis there is also an association between higher meat consumption and an increased likelihood of obesity at a marginally significant level (p = 0.06).

There is a strong association between household wealth and the obesity prevalence of women with no education. Using EDHS 2005 and EDHS 2008 data, Aitsi-Selmi et al. (2014) find a significant interaction effect between wealth index and education level on odds of obesity among Egyptian women. The interaction is also present in the EDHS 2014 data (p < 0.01 for interaction). As shown in figure 2.19, panel a, there was a strong positive association between household wealth and obesity prevalence among women with no education, primary or secondary education (all p's < 0.001 for trend), but a slightly decreasing trend among women with higher education levels (p = 0.06 for trend).

When the number of total childbirths increases, the increase in maternal obesity is slower among women with a high education level than with a low education level (figure 2.19, panel b). A study by Onubi et al. (2016) indicates that only women with a tertiary education know their pre-pregnancy weights, which could partially explain the role of education in these associations. Another study (Kavle et al. 2018) finds that Egyptian mothers tend to lack knowledge of optimal weight gain during pregnancy, which could be a reason for the increased obesity risk among women who give birth earlier and have multiple childbirths.

The trend of decreasing obesity prevalence according to the increasing age of first childbirth is less pronounced among women with higher levels of education. Specifically, this trend is less pronounced among women with a tertiary education than women with less education (figure 2.19, panel c). Among women with a tertiary education in EDHS 2014, no one gave birth at or before age 15. However, the interactions between education levels and age at first birth or total number of childbirths are not statistically significant (p > 0.05 for both interactions), which may be due to the small sample size.

FIGURE 2.19

Interactions between education levels and household wealth, total number of childbirths, and age at first birth and their effects on obesity prevalence in women: Egypt, 2014

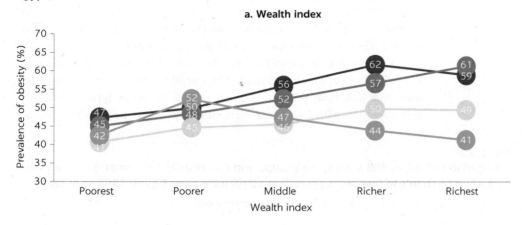

a. Wealth index

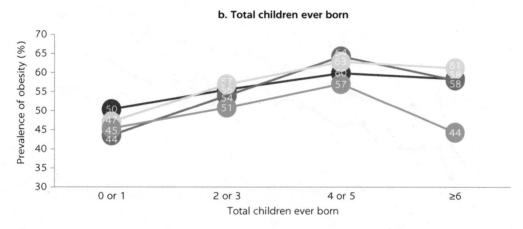

b. Total children ever born

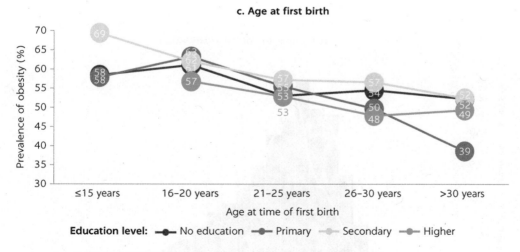

c. Age at first birth

Education level: ● No education ● Primary ● Secondary ● Higher

Source: EDHS 2014 (MOHP, El-Zanaty and Associates, and ICF International 2015).

Time trends of BMI and obesity

The obesity prevalence and BMI of women who have had a child have increased steadily since the early 1990s. In reproductive-age Egyptian women who had a living birth within five years but not within two months preceding the EDHS interview, the prevalence of obesity was 24.1 percent in 1992 and 35.8 percent in 2012. This prevalence increased an average of 1 percent every two years across all age groups (figure 2.20, panel a). Over the last 22 years, the overall BMI distribution has shifted toward higher BMIs; the mean BMI increased from 26.8 kilograms per square meter in 1992 to 29.1 kilograms per square meter in 2014, with an average increasing rate of one BMI unit per decade

FIGURE 2.20

Comparison of mean BMI across age groups and BMI distribution among women who had a live birth in the five years preceding EDHS interview: Egypt, 1992 and 2014

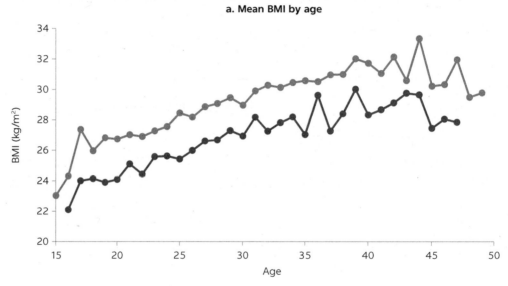

a. Mean BMI by age

b. Comparison of BMI distribution

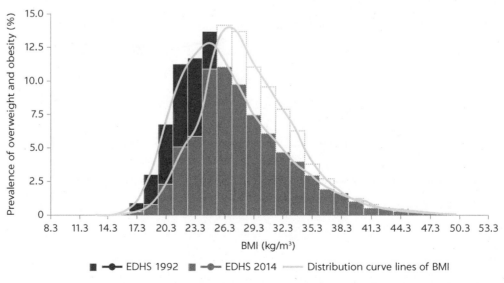

Sources: EDHS 1992, 2014 (El-Zanaty et al. 1993; MOHP, El-Zanaty and Associates, and ICF International 2015).
Note: BMI = body mass index; EDHS = Egypt Demographic and Health Survey; kg/m² = kilograms per square meter.

(figure 2.20, panel b). Time trend analysis is based on data on women who had a live birth in the five years before the EDHS interview—those were comparable across different surveys.

After 1992, the prevalence of both overweight and obesity in women had significantly increased in urban and rural areas ($p < 0.0001$ for all), although the increasing trend was more pronounced in rural areas (p for interaction < 0.0001—see figure 2.21. A previous study among Egyptian women observed a similar trend and suggested that government subsidies of high-energy, low-nutrient density foods that form a large part of the diet in poor rural populations may have contributed to the trend (Austin, Hill, and Fawzi 2013).

In the early 1990s, women with higher education levels were obese, but by 2014 women with lower education levels were obese as well. Indeed, this remarkable change in the obesity pattern among Egyptian women shows that women with higher education levels were more likely to be obese in 1992, but that this trend was reversed in 2014 (figure 2.22).

Whereas in the early 1990s obesity was more problematic for richer than for poorer households, by 2014 obesity was largely a problem of both the rich and the poor. As shown in figure 2.23, women from rich households were more likely to be obese in 1995; the prevalence of obesity was only 6.4 percent among the poorest but 38.2 percent among the richest. The large difference in obesity prevalence between the poorest and richest disappeared in 2014 when obesity became an epidemic across all wealth levels.

Coexisting undernutrition and overnutrition in Egyptian women

A significant proportion of women in Egypt are both obese and anemic. EDHS 2014 reveals an overall obesity prevalence of 48.0 percent and an increasing

FIGURE 2.21

Overweight and obesity prevalence among women who had a live birth in the five years preceding EDHS interview: Egypt, 1992–2014

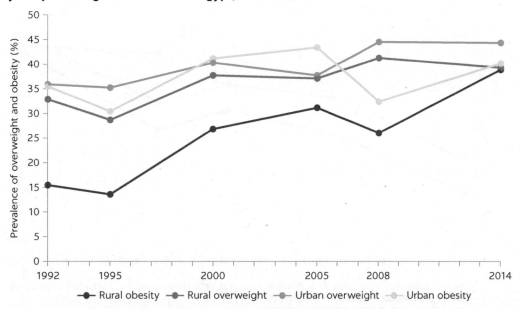

Sources: EDHS 1992, 1995, 2000, 2005, 2008, 2014 El-Zanaty et al. 1993, 1996; El-Zanaty and Way 2001, 2006, 2009; MOHP, El-Zanaty and Associates, and ICF International 2015).
Note: EDHS = Egypt Demographic and Health Survey.

FIGURE 2.22

Trends of obesity prevalence across education levels among women who had a live birth in the five years preceding EDHS interview: Egypt, 1992–2014

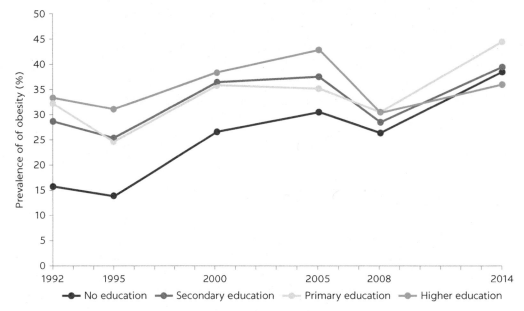

Sources: EDHS 1992, 1995, 2000, 2005, 2008, 2014 (El-Zanaty et al. 1993, 1996; El-Zanaty and Way 2001, 2006, 2009; MOHP, El-Zanaty and Associates, and ICF International 2015).
Note: EDHS = Egypt Demographic and Health Survey.

FIGURE 2.23

Obesity prevalence and household wealth among women who had a live birth in the five years preceding the EDHS interview: Egypt, 1995–2014

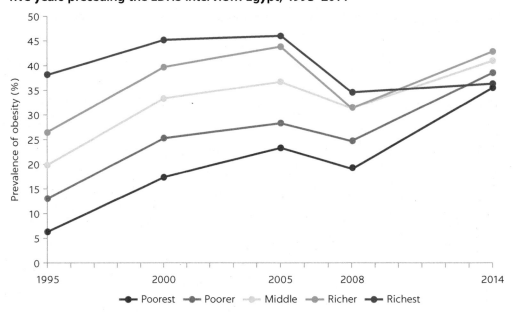

Sources: EDHS 1995, 2000, 2005, 2008, 2014 (El-Zanaty et al. 1996; El-Zanaty and Way 2001, 2006, 2009; MOHP, El-Zanaty and Associates, and ICF International 2015).
Note: EDHS = Egypt Demographic and Health Survey.

trend with age. The overall prevalence of anemia is 25.6 percent, with no clear difference across age groups (figure 2.24).

Anemia is a common sign of malnutrition, whereas obesity is generally indicative of overnutrition. The coexistence of anemia and obesity is observed not only at population level, as shown in figure 2.24, but also within the same individual (figure 2.25). In 2000 more than 10 percent of women Egypt showed signs of both obesity and anemia, which is 16.5 percent in 2005 and 11.3 percent in 2014 (figure 2.25). Several studies from Ghana and Mexico have also reported the coexistence of anemia and obesity (Anderson 2017; Samper-Ternent, Michaels-Obregon, and Wong 2011).

In 2014 women living in urban areas of Upper Egypt had a significantly higher likelihood of being obese and anemic at the same time compared with women living in other urban governorates. This finding is consistent with the EDHS data for children, indicating a double burden of malnutrition and overnutrition in urban Upper Egypt. These associations are likely due to a combination of the "obesogenic" environment in urban areas that is conducive to obesity and an overall low diet quality contributing to malnutrition because Upper Egypt is the poorest region in the country. In low- and middle-income countries, rapid urbanization has been linked to poor diet and reduced physical activity (Angkurawaranon et al. 2014). In Mexico, living in urban areas has been associated with a higher probability of obesity and anemia within the same individuals (Samper-Ternent, Michaels-Obregon, and Wong 2011). In addition, in EDHS 2014 women who had their first birth before age 20 had a significantly higher likelihood of obesity with or without anemia, compared with women who had their first birth between 21 and 25 years of age.

FIGURE 2.24

Coexistence of anemia and obesity by age among women: Egypt, 2014

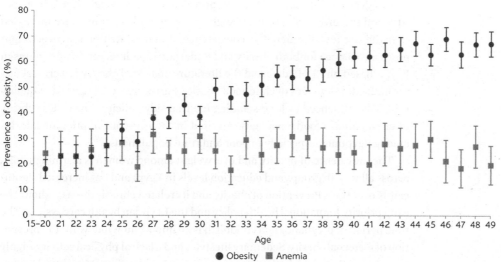

Source: EDHS 2014 (MOHP, El-Zanaty and Associates, and ICF International 2015).

FIGURE 2.25

Coexistence of anemia and obesity among women: Egypt, 2000, 2005, 2014

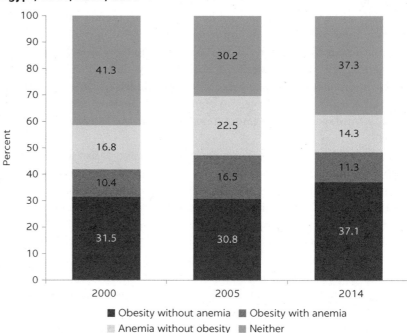

Sources: EDHS 2000, 2005, 2008 (El-Zanaty and Way 2001, 2006, 2009).

CONCLUSIONS

In addition to malnutrition, both chronic (stunting) and acute (wasting), overweight remain at elevated levels of public health significance in Egypt, and, likewise, is at levels higher than those found for most of Egypt's regional counterparts and the Middle East and North Africa regional average.

In Egyptian children under 5, the prevalence of overweight (including obesity) and the proportion of overweight children with stunting have increased over the last few decades. The coexistence of undernutrition and overweight poses a challenge for both obesity and undernutrition intervention programs in Egypt. Based on EDHS data and the literature, maternal obesity is a critical factor in the development of childhood obesity. Furthermore, in Egypt diet quality is heavily influenced by long-standing food subsidy policies. The GoE's subsidy of energy-dense foods may have resulted in the overconsumption of calories among Egyptians, especially in poor and rural populations.

The prevalence of obesity and overweight among women is alarmingly high across all wealth groups and education levels in Egypt and has increased significantly over time. Prevention of obesity and its related chronic diseases should be a top priority for national health policy and the Egyptian health care system. The time period of pregnancy and childbirth is an important window for the prevention of maternal obesity. Sedentary lifestyles and a lack of physical activity, highly prevalent in Egypt and other countries in the Middle East (Musaiger, Hassan, and Obeid 2011), are problematic, as is the consumption of energy-dense foods, particularly by poorer and rural populations.

Although the remainder of this book focuses on the interventions and options needed to address the undernutrition situation in Egypt—identified by the government as an immediate priority—future efforts will need to take into account the growing obesity epidemic among women, adolescents, and children. The double burden of malnutrition requires careful consideration of the common causes of over- and undernutrition, and programmatic and policy interventions must ultimately be harmonized to minimize the possibility that solutions to address one area of malnutrition do not exacerbate problems in the other (Ecker et al. 2016).

REFERENCES

Aboulenein, S., H. El-Laithy, O. Helmy, H. Kheir-El-Din, and D. Mandour. 2010. "Impact of the Global Food Price Shock on the Poor in Egypt." Working Paper 157, Egyptian Center for Economic Studies. http://www.eces.org.eg/Publication.aspx?Id=313.

Aboul-Enein, B. H., J. Bernstein, and A. C. Neary. 2016. "Dietary Transition and Obesity in Selected Arabic-Speaking Countries: A Review of the Current Evidence." *Eastern Mediterranean Health Journal* 22 (10): 763–70.

Aitsi-Selmi, A. 2015. "Households with a Stunted Child and Obese Mother: Trends and Child Feeding Practices in a Middle-Income Country, 1992–2008." *Maternal and Child Health Journal* 19 (6): 1284–91.

Aitsi-Selmi, A., R. Bell, J. Shipley, and M. G. Marmot. 2014. "Education Modifies the Association of Wealth with Obesity in Women in Middle-Income but Not Low-Income Countries: An Interaction Study Using Seven National Datasets, 2005–2010." *PloS One* 9 (3): e90403.

Al-Kloub, M. I., M. A. Al-Hassan, E. S. Froelicher, and A. M. Ibrahim. 2010. "Predictors of Obesity in School-Aged Jordanian Adolescents." *International Journal of Nursing Practice* 16 (4): 397–405.

ALNohair, S. 2014. "Obesity in Gulf Countries." *International Journal of Health Science* (Qassim) 8 (1): 79–83.

Aly, H., A. Dakroury, A. Said, W. Moussa, F. Shaheen, F. Ghoneme, M. Hassein, M. Hathout, M. Shehata, and H. Gomaa. 1981. "National Food Consumption Study, Final Report." National Nutrition Institute, Ministry of Health and Population, Cairo.

Amugsi, D. A., Z. T. Dimbuene, B. Mberu, S. Muthhri, and A. C. Ezeh. 2017. "Prevalence and Time Trends in Overweight and Obesity among Urban Women: An Analysis of Demographic and Health Surveys Data from 24 African Countries, 1991–2014." *BMJ Open* 7 (10): e017344.

Anderson, A. K. 2017. "Prevalence of Anemia, Overweight/Obesity, and Undiagnosed Hypertension and Diabetes among Residents of Selected Communities in Ghana." *International Journal of Chronic Diseases* 2017: 7836019.

Anderson, P. M., and K. F. Butcher. 2006. "Childhood Obesity: Trends and Potential Causes." *The Future of Children:* 16 (1): 19–46.

Angkurawaranon, C., W. Jiraporncharoen, B. Chenthanakij, P. Doyle, and D. Nitsch. 2014. "Urban Environments and Obesity in Southeast Asia: A Systematic Review, Meta-Analysis and Meta-Regression." *PloS One* 9 (11): e113547.

Asfaw, A. 2007. "Do Government Good Price Policies Affect the Prevalence of Obesity? Empirical Evidence from Egypt." *World Development* 35 (4): 687–701.

Austin, A. M., A. G. Hill, and W. W. Fawzi. 2013. "Maternal Obesity Trends in Egypt 1995–2005." *Maternal Child Nutrition* 9 (2): 167–79.

Black, R. E., C. G. Victora, S. P. Walker, Z. A. Bhutta, P. Christian, M. de Onis, M. Ezzati, S. Grantham-McGregor, J. Katz, R. Martorell, and R. Uauy. 2013. "Maternal and Child Undernutrition and Overweight in Low-Income and Middle-Income Countries." *Lancet* 382 (9890): 427–51. doi:10.1016/S0140-6736(13)60937-X.

Davis, E. M., S. J. Zyzanski, C. M. Olson, K. C. Stange, and R. I. Horowitz. 2009. "Racial, Ethnic, and Socioeconomic Differences in the Incidence of Obesity Related to Childbirth." *American Journal of Public Health* 99 (2): 294–99.

Doak, C. M., L. S. Adair, M. Bentley, C. Monteiro, and B. M. Popkin. 2005. "The Dual Burden Household and the Nutrition Transition Paradox." *International Journal of Obesity* (London) 29 (1): 129–36.

Ecker, O., P. Al-Riffai, C. Breisinger, and R. El-Batrawy. 2016. *Nutrition and Economic Development: Exploring Egypt's Exceptionalism and the Role of Food Subsidies.* Washington, DC: International Food Policy Research Institute. doi:10.2499/9780896292383.

EI-Zanaty, F. H., E. M. Hussein, G. A. Shawky, A. A. Way, and S. Kishor. 1996. *Egypt Demographic and Health Survey 1995.* Calverton, MA: National Population Council Egypt and Macro International. https://dhsprogram.com/pubs/pdf/FR71/FR71.pdf.

El-Zanaty, F. H., H. A. A. Sayed, H. H. M. Zaky, and A. A. Way. 1993. *Egypt Demographic and Health Survey 1992.* Cairo, Egypt and Calverton, MA: National Population Council Egypt and Macro International. https://dhsprogram.com/pubs/pdf/FR48/FR48.pdf.

El-Zanaty, F., and A. A. Way. 2001. *Egypt Demographic and Health Survey 2000.* Calverton, MA: Ministry of Health and Population Egypt, National Population Council Egypt, and ORC Macro. https://dhsprogram.com/pubs/pdf/FR117/FR117.pdf.

———. 2006. *Egypt Demographic and Health Survey 2005.* Cairo, Egypt: Ministry of Health and Population Egypt, National Population Council, El-Zanaty and Associates, and ORC Macro. https://dhsprogram.com/pubs/pdf/FR176/FR176.pdf.

———. 2009. *Egypt Demographic and Health Survey 2008.* Cairo, Egypt: Ministry of Health Egypt, El-Zanaty and Associates, and Macro International. https://dhsprogram.com/pubs/pdf/FR220/FR220.pdf.

Farrag, N. S., L. J. Cheskin, and M. K. Farag. 2017. "A Systematic Review of Childhood Obesity in the Middle East and North Africa (MENA) Region: Prevalence and Risk Factors Meta-analysis." *Advances in Pediatric Research* 4 (8).

Fernald, L. C., and L. M. Neufeld. 2007. "Overweight with Concurrent Stunting in Very Young Children from Rural Mexico: Prevalence and Associated Factors." *European Journal of Clinical Nutrition* 61 (5): 623–32.

Goran, M. I., and M. S. Treuth. 2001. "Energy Expenditure, Physical Activity, and Obesity in Children." *Pediatric Clinics of North America* 48 (4): 931–53.

Hassan, H., W. Moussa, and I. Ismail. 2006. "Assessment of Dietary Changes and Their Health Implications in Countries Facing the Double Burden of Malnutrition: Egypt, 1980 to 2005." In *The Double Burden of Malnutrition: Case Studies from Six Developing Countries.* FAO Food and Nutrition Paper 84, 43–97. Rome: Food and Agriculture Organization. doi: http://www.fao.org/tempref/docrep/fao/009/a0442e/a0442e00.pdf.

Hassan, N. E., S. M. El Shebini, and N. H. Ahmed. 2016. "Association between Dietary Patterns, Breakfast Skipping and Familial Obesity among a Sample of Egyptian Families." *Open Access Macedonian Journal of Medical Sciences* 4 (2): 213–18.

Hassan, N. E., S. Wahba, I. R. El-Ala Meey, S. A. El-Masry, M. M. Abushady, E. R. Abdel Hamed, T. S. Ibrahim, and S. Boseila. 2016. "Dietary Behaviour Pattern and Physical Activity in Overweight and Obese Egyptian Mothers: Relationships with Their Children's Body Mass Index." *Open Access Macedonian Journal of Medical Sciences* 4 (3): 353–58.

Hassanyn, S. A. 2000. "Food Consumption Pattern and Nutrients Intake among Different Population Groups in Egypt. Final Report (Part 1)." National Nutrition Institute, WHO/EMRO, Cairo.

Kavle, J. A., V. L. Flax, A. Abdelmegeid, F. Salah, S. Hafez, M. Ramzy, D. Hamed, G. Saleh, and R. Galloway. 2016. "Factors Associated with Early Growth in Egyptian Infants: Implications for Addressing the Dual Burden of Malnutrition." *Maternal and Child Nutrition* 12 (1): 139–51.

Kavle, J. A., S. Mehanna, G. Khan, M. Hassan, G. Saleh, and C. Engmann. 2018. "Program Considerations for Integration of Nutrition and Family Planning: Beliefs around Maternal Diet and Breastfeeding within the Context of the Nutrition Transition in Egypt." *Maternal and Child Nutrition* 14 (1).

Kavle, J., S. Mehanna, G. Saleh, M. A. Fouad, M. Ramzy, D. Hamed, M. Hassan, G. Khan, and R. Galloway. 2014. *Examining Factors Associated with Stunting in Lower Egypt in Comparison to Upper Egypt: Bridging the Gap between Cultural Beliefs and Feasible Feeding Practices through Trials for Improved Practices.* Washington, DC: Maternal and Child Health Integrated Program (MCHIP). U.S. Agency for International Development.

———. 2015. "Exploring Why Junk Foods Are 'Essential' Foods and How Culturally Tailored Recommendations Improved Feeding in Egyptian Children." *Maternal and Child Nutrition* 11 (3): 346–70.

Kim, T. J., and O. von dem Knesebeck. 2018. "Income and Obesity: What Is the Direction of the Relationship? A Systematic Review and Meta-analysis." *BMJ Open* 8 (1): e019862.

Li, Y., J. M. Gibson, P. Jat, G. Puggioni, M. Hasan, J. H. West, et al. 2010. "Burden of Disease Attributed to Anthropogenic Air Pollution in the United Arab Emirates: Estimates Based on Observed Air Quality Data." *Science of the Total Environment* 408 (23): 5784–93.

Li, Y., N. M. Wedick, J. Lai, Y. He, X. Hu, A. Liu, S. Du, J. Zhang, X. Yang, C. Chen, F. B. Hu, and G. Ma. 2011. "Lack of Dietary Diversity and Dyslipidaemia among Stunted Overweight Children: The 2002 China National Nutrition and Health Survey." *Public Health Nutrition* 14 (5): 896–903.

Mamabolo, R. L., M. Alberts, N. P. Steyn, H. A. Delemarre-van de Waal, and N. S. Levitt. 2005. "Prevalence and Determinants of Stunting and Overweight in 3-Year-Old Black South African Children Residing in the Central Region of Limpopo Province, South Africa." *Public Health Nutrition* 8 (5): 501–8.

MOHP (Ministry of Health and Population), El-Zanaty and Associates, and ICF International. 2015. *Egypt Demographic and Health Survey 2014*. Cairo, Egypt and Rockville, MD: Ministry of Health and Population and ICF International. https://dhsprogram.com/pubs/pdf/FR302/FR302.pdf.

Musaiger, A. O., A. S. Hassan, and O. Obeid. 2011. "The Paradox of Nutrition-Related Diseases in the Arab Countries: The Need for Action." *International Journal of Environmental Research and Public Health* 8 (9): 3637–71.

Nasreddine, L., F. Naja, C. Aki, M. C. Chamieh, S. Karam, A. M. Sibai, and N. Hwalla. 2014. "Dietary, Lifestyle and Socio-economic Correlates of Overweight, Obesity and Central Adiposity in Lebanese Children and Adolescents." *Nutrients* 6 (3): 1038–62.

Nasreddine, L., M. N. Zeidan, F. Naja, and N. Hwalla. 2012. "Complementary Feeding in the MENA Region: Practices and Challenges." *Nutrition, Metabolism, and Cardiovascular Diseases* 22 (10): 793–98.

Newton, S., D. Braithwaite, and T. F. Akinyemiju. 2017. "Socio-economic Status over the Life Course and Obesity: Systematic Review and Meta-analysis." *PloS One* 12 (5): e0177151.

Onubi, O. J., D. Marais, L. Aucott, F. Okonofua, and A. S. Poobalan. 2016. "Maternal Obesity in Africa: A Systematic Review and Meta-analysis." *Journal of Public Health* (Oxford) 38 (3): e218-e231.

Popkin, B. M., L. S. Adair, and S. W. Ng. 2012. "Global Nutrition Transition and the Pandemic of Obesity in Developing Countries." *Nutrition Review* 70 (1): 3–21.

Rashad, A.S., and M. F. Sharaf. 2017. "Does Maternal Employment Affect Child Nutrition Status? New Evidence from Egypt." Working Paper 7, University of Alberta, Calgary.

Samper-Ternent, R., A. Michaels-Obregon, and R. Wong. 2011. "Coexistence of Obesity and Anemia in Older Mexican Adults." *Ageing International* 37 (1): 104–17.

Sharaf, M. F., E. I. Mansour, and A. S. Rashad. 2018. "Child Nutritional Status in Egypt: A Comprehensive Analysis of Socioeconomic Determinants Using a Quantile Regression Approach." *Journal of Biosocial Science* 51 (1): 1–17.

Smith, D. E., C. E. Lewis, J. L. Caveny, L. L. Perkins, G. L. Burke, and D. E. Bild. 1994. "Longitudinal Changes in Adiposity Associated with Pregnancy. The CARDIA Study. Coronary Artery Risk Development in Young Adults Study." *Journal of the American Medical Association* 271 (22): 1747–51.

Tzioumis, E., M. C. Kay, M. E. Bentley, and L. S. Adair. 2016. "Prevalence and Trends in the Childhood Dual Burden of Malnutrition in Low- and Middle-Income Countries, 1990–2012." *Public Health Nutrition* 19 (8): 1375–88.

Wamani, H., A. N. Astrøm, S. Peterson, J. K. Tumwine, and T. Tylleskär. 2007. "Boys Are More Stunted than Girls in Sub-Saharan Africa: A Meta-analysis of 16 Demographic and Health Surveys." *BMC Pediatrics* 7: 17.

WFP (World Food Programme). 2013. *The Status of Poverty and Food Security in Egypt: Analysis and Policy Recommendations*. Preliminary Summary Report, Cairo. https://documents.wfp.org/stellent/groups/public/documents/ena/wfp257467.pdf.

WHO (World Health Organization). 2008. "World Health Organization (WHO) Child Growth Standards: Training Course on Child Growth Assessment." Geneva.

——. 2014. *Global Status Report on Noncommunicable Diseases 2014*. Geneva: WHO.

WHO (World Health Organization) and UNICEF (United Nations Children's Fund). 2003. *Global Strategy for Infant and Young Child Feeding*. Geneva: WHO.

Wu, S., Y. Ding, F. Wu, R. Li, J. Han, and P. Mao. 2015. "Socio-economic Position as an Intervention against Overweight and Obesity in Children: A Systematic Review and Meta-analysis." *Scientific Reports* 5: 11354.

Yu, Z. B., S. P. Han, G. Z. Zhu, C. Zhu, X. J. Wang, X. G. Cao, and X. R. Guo. 2011. "Birth Weight and Subsequent Risk of Obesity: A Systematic Review and Meta-analysis." *Obesity Review* 12 (7): 525–42.

Zottarelli, L. K., T. S. Sunil, and S. Rajaram. 2007. "Influence of Parental and Socioeconomic Factors on Stunting in Children under 5 Years in Egypt." *Eastern Mediterranean Health Journal* 13 (6): 1330–42.

3 Undernutrition Interventions in Egypt: Status, Gaps, and Opportunities

FAYROUZ SAKR-ASHOUR, BJORN LJUNGQVIST, AND MATTHEW ROBINSON

KEY MESSAGES

- Focusing on interventions during the 1,000-day period from a child's conception to second birthday is critical to ensuring that all children have every opportunity to grow and thrive.
- The 2013 *Lancet* series on maternal and child nutrition identified 10 evidence-based, nutrition-specific interventions that are the most effective for addressing undernutrition and micronutrient deficiencies during the 1,000-day period. However, currently in Egypt there are gaps in coverage of many key interventions, resulting in suboptimal nutritional status among infants and young children (Bhutta et al. 2013).
- The only nutrition-specific intervention that can be considered at scale is universal salt iodization.
- There are also a wide range of interventions across sectors—agriculture, social protection, early childhood development, child education, and water, sanitation, and hygiene (WASH)—which either are or have the potential to be nutrition-sensitive. However, many do not focus on nutrition outcomes, and only WASH interventions have demonstrated nutrition impacts. The recent revisions of the Takaful conditional cash transfer show promise, but further evaluation is required.
- Based on the review of the status of key nutrition interventions in Egypt, it is recommended that 16 interventions in the areas of infant and young child feeding (IYCF), micronutrient, disease prevention and management, and WASH are scaled up (see table 3.10).
- A number of approaches are identified to scale up the identified interventions, including (1) scaling up to full national coverage, (2) scaling up by region, and (3) scaling up by prioritizing interventions. Considerations of the approach taken should include potential nutritional impact, cost, and capacity to implement, among others.
- Key elements identified for successful scaling up of the identified interventions include strengthening the health system (because most of the interventions identified are implemented primarily through the health system) and the multisectoral involvement of ministries and partners to support implementation.

INTRODUCTION

This chapter focuses on the status, challenges, and the responses needed in Egypt to implement or scale up interventions considered most critical to positively affecting the 1,000 days from a child's conception to second birthday. This includes 10 high-impact interventions that have already proven to be effective in similar settings, along with key WASH interventions. The chapter also reviews any programs in other sectors (agriculture, social protection, early child development, and education) that are currently supporting or have the potential to support nutrition goals and assesses the challenges and next steps.

The chapter begins with an overview of the current nutrition-*specific* and nutrition-*sensitive* interventions being implemented in Egypt with the aim of identifying critical gaps and opportunities for further investment. Based on these findings, it then discusses the key policy and program options (multisectoral) that could be considered for scale-up to address the prevailing and emerging problems of malnutrition in the Egyptian context, as well as the potential approaches to scaling up the identified interventions. The government of Egypt (GoE) is committed to improving the health and nutrition status of the people of Egypt, paying special attention to this critical 1,000-day window. Thus this analysis of scale-up options will support the GoE's commitment to action.

Stunting is one of the pressing challenges faced by Egyptians, and the implication of this problem on individuals, families, and the development of the entire nation is well established. However, no "standardized" package of large-scale nutrition interventions has been proven to combat stunting because the causes of stunting are likely to differ from one situation to the next and are also likely to change over time.

The 2013 *Lancet* series on maternal and child nutrition (Lancet 2013) developed a new model intended to point the way to optimum fetal and child growth and development. Within this framework, it introduced two concepts. *Nutrition-specific interventions and programs* would address the immediate determinants of fetal and child nutrition and development—adequate food and nutrient intake, feeding, caregiving and parenting practices (such as hygiene and psychosocial and emotional support), and low burden of infectious diseases. *Nutrition-sensitive interventions and programs* would address the underlying determinants of fetal and child nutrition and development—food security; adequate caregiving resources at the maternal, household, and community levels; and access to health services and a safe and hygienic environment—as well as incorporate specific nutrition goals and interventions. Nutrition-sensitive programs can also serve as delivery platforms for nutrition-specific interventions, potentially increasing their scale, coverage, and effectiveness.

The same *Lancet* series identified 10 evidence-based, nutrition-specific interventions that would be the most effective for addressing undernutrition and micronutrient deficiencies in women of reproductive age, pregnant women, neonates, infants, and children (Bhutta et al. 2013). Although less evidence is available on the impact of nutrition-sensitive interventions and programs than on nutrition-specific ones, a number of sectors have the potential to contribute to reaching nutrition goals. The *Lancet* series concludes that nutrition-sensitive programs hold great promise for supporting nutrition improvements and boosting the scale, coverage, and benefits of nutrition-specific interventions, including in agriculture, social protection, early child

BOX 3.1

Why 1,000 days?

- Both the 2008 and 2013 *Lancet* nutrition series (Lancet 2008, 2013) called for focusing on pregnancy and the first two years of life—the crucial 1,000 days—recognizing that this period is the most critical for the physical and cognitive development of children. The majority of the linear growth deficits that make up the under-5 stunting burden are accumulated during this time, reflecting nutritional deficiencies (Victora et al. 2010).

- This 1,000-day period offers a unique window of opportunity to ensure that a child has the best possible start in life by providing the mother and the child with the right nutrition, thereby helping the child to grow, secure development of critical mental and physiological faculties, learn, and thrive. A growing body of scientific evidence shows that the foundations of a person's lifelong health are largely set during this 1,000-day window.

- When mothers and children receive the right nutrition during this period, the foundation is laid for a child's stronger physical growth, higher learning capacity, improved performance in school, lower susceptibility to disease, and higher lifetime earning potential. Thus this period has a positive impact not only on the lives of individual children, but also on the health and prosperity of a nation.

- Key interventions include integrated maternal and newborn care, implementation of a comprehensive infant and young child feeding strategy, prevention and treatment of micronutrient deficiencies (iron supplementation, vitamin A supplementation, and salt iodization), prevention and treatment of severe acute malnutrition, improving water, sanitation, and hygiene, and expanding access to and use of health services.

development, and education (Ruel and Alderman 2013). For example, there is a growing body of evidence on how improving water, sanitation, and hygiene (WASH) can promote healthy environments, reduce the work burden of women, and reduce the prevalence of infectious diseases, thereby having an impact on nutrition status (USAID 2015).

The 2008 *Lancet* maternal and child undernutrition series (Lancet 2008) called for focusing on the 1,000 days from a child's conception to second birthday, and the 2013 series on maternal and child nutrition reinforced this approach (box 3.1). This approach is directed at the key nutrition interventions that can ensure the nutritional status of a woman at conception, during pregnancy, and through the first two years of a child's life so that a child has every opportunity to grow and thrive. However, interventions implemented during other time frames are likely to carry over to this 1,000-day period. Indeed, the positive impact of proper nutrition on other age groups, such as adolescent girls, will likely positively affect their children during these critical 1,000 days.

NUTRITION-SPECIFIC INTERVENTIONS

Nutrition-specific interventions include treatment of acute forms of malnutrition and also target the immediate causes of undernutrition: inadequate dietary intake and ill health. The next section discusses the existing nutrition-specific interventions and gaps in Egypt in three categories that reflect the key focus areas and target groups for nutrition-specific interventions: (1) newborn, infant, and young child nutrition interventions; (2) maternal nutrition and adolescent interventions; and (3) cross-cutting interventions: national food fortification.

Newborn, infant, and young child nutrition interventions

The newborn, infant, and young child nutrition interventions discussed in this section target the immediate factors affecting suboptimal growth and development, with a focus on the 1,000 days from conception to second birthday (Black et al. 2013). Interventions are framed within a life cycle approach, recognizing that nutrition interventions at each life stage can affect the 1,000 days and beyond. Specifically, this section describes (1) infant and young child feeding interventions, (2) growth monitoring and promotion (GMP), (3) micronutrient supplementation in young children, (4) integrated management of acute malnutrition (IMAM), and (5) deworming.

Infant and young child feeding (IYCF)

Optimal infant and young child feeding (IYCF) interventions have the greatest potential to singlehandedly influence child survival (UNICEF 2011). The *Lancet* maternal and child undernutrition series estimated that optimal IYCF practices, especially exclusive breastfeeding, could prevent up to 1.4 million deaths a year among children under 5 out of the approximately 10 million deaths a year (Black et al. 2008). Furthermore, optimal IYCF ensures that a child is protected from both under- and overnutrition and their consequences later in life, and breastfed infants have a lower risk of several chronic conditions later in life such as diabetes and heart disease (Horta, Loret de Mola, and Victora 2015; Peters et al. 2016). The IYCF practices recommended by the World Health Organization and UNICEF call for early initiation and exclusive breastfeeding for six months and for continued breastfeeding, together with nutritionally adequate, safe, age-appropriate, complementary feeding, from six months to two years (WHO and UNICEF 2003). Adherence to these guidelines can result in optimal nutrition in the first two years of life, and they are crucial to prevent stunting in infancy and early childhood and breaking the intergenerational cycle of undernutrition. Breastfeeding is also an important factor in preventing childhood obesity. A longer duration of breastfeeding is associated with a lower risk of childhood obesity in a dose-response manner (Yan et al. 2014).

In Egypt, IYCF interventions primarily center on social and behavioral change communication (SBCC) in the primary health care (PHC) system, and the government is committed to strengthening these interventions. Although breastfeeding is common in Egypt, exclusive breastfeeding is not very common; almost a third of infants are bottle-fed or consume complementary foods and liquids before reaching 6 months of age. Timely introduction of complementary foods is relatively high, but the proportion of children fed the minimum number of times and with a nutritionally diverse diet is generally very low (see chapter 1). Thus the GoE and its partners have shown a commitment to updating the messages, tools, and overall communications approaches to strengthen the counseling skills of PHC workers related to breastfeeding and complementary feeding practices.

In 2014 the Ministry of Health and Population (MOHP) began implementing the National Breastfeeding Program and the Baby Friendly Hospital Initiative (BFHI), based on the 2009 WHO and UNICEF BFHI guidelines (WHO and UNICEF 2009), in both the public and private sector. The MOHP is working with all partners to advocate and scale up the national BFHI program, integrating the BFHI guidelines into national policies and strategies. The goal of the National Breastfeeding Program and the BFHI is to strengthen the implementation of practices that protect, promote, and support breastfeeding (WHO and UNICEF 2009) and improve complementary feeding within the context of the IYCF strategy. In the model introduced by the MOHP, five PHC units and a hospital within the same catchment area provide pregnant women and lactating mothers with counseling services, while ensuring that they are referred to a baby-friendly hospital within their reach.

Under the umbrella of the BFHI program, the MOHP has developed updated national IYCF counseling guidelines targeting frontline health care workers, including community health workers, as well as nongovernmental organizations (NGOs). This counseling package provides standardized guidelines for nutrition during preconception, pregnancy, lactation, and complementary feeding. The aim is to strengthen the capacity of medical doctors, nurses, and community health workers within PHC facilities to deliver nutrition counseling to pregnant women and mothers of children 0–24 months of age visiting PHC units. A co-branded IYCF and early childhood development (ECD) audiovisual package was produced by UNICEF, the World Food Programme (WFP), and the MOHP for this purpose. The BFHI faces many challenges, as reported nationally, and through other Eastern Mediterranean country experiences. The successful implementation of the BFHI is contingent on addressing the existing national challenges and evaluating the experiences of these countries (Al-Jawaldeh and Abul-Fadl 2018; WHO 2017a).

The National Breastfeeding Program and the BFHI can be strengthened in several ways moving forward. This includes expanding the BFHI within the ongoing social health insurance program where quality services are provided to mothers attending PHC units, as well as continually strengthening the counseling skills of PHC workers. Strengthening the policy framework supporting implementation of the code of marketing of breast milk substitutes is key to the sustainability of breastfeeding support at the national level.

Target groups should extend beyond mothers and caregivers to include fathers, grandmothers, mothers-in-law, and the community at large. The presence of numerous harmonized delivery channels would be an advantage by reinforcing messages during immunization, treatment of diarrhea, and family planning services, and not solely through pre- and postnatal care visits. In addition, breastfeeding should be promoted through every possible communication and education channel in order to encourage mothers to adopt proper breastfeeding practices and reverse the present negative trends. Enforcement of the code of marketing of breast milk substitutes is another critical part of this approach. In addition, for complementary feeding SBCC it is important to include WASH messages, mainly relating to the hygienic preparation of complementary foods and hand washing by mothers and caregivers.

To address the double burden of undernutrition and overweight in children at the community and individual levels, promotion of dietary diversity through reducing the consumption of energy-dense, micronutrient-poor foods and increasing the consumption of fruits, vegetables, and other healthy foods should be encouraged. According to Egypt's Central Agency for Public Mobilization and Statistics (CAPMAS), households living in poverty represent more than one-quarter of the population (27.8 percent), mostly concentrated in Upper Egypt (and almost 60 percent in the governorates of Asyut and Sohag). In these settings, advice on adequate and proper complementary feeding practices and diverse diets may not be practical or sufficient. These families may need additional assistance to prevent chronic undernutrition as well as overnutrition in their offspring. Providing nutrient-dense complementary foods for such families to enhance complementary feeding could help ensure that these children receive adequate nutrition. Moreover, because diet quality is heavily influenced by long-standing food subsidy policies, particularly among poorer households, it will be important for nutritionally diverse commodities to be included in the scheme. Ready-to-use foods could be provided as part of the food ration cards for families with children under 5 who are at a high risk of malnutrition. Such approaches, however, could be considered in the design of future social protection programs as they do not seem warranted as a nationwide intervention.

Finally, development of a national IYCF social and behavioral change communication strategy would allow more efficient coordination and evaluation of the efficacy of efforts, whether among private, public, and NGO sectors or different donor agencies. And it would bring together the different stakeholders working particularly on IYCF promotion. Table 3.1 summarizes the proposed breastfeeding and complementary feeding practice interventions.

Growth monitoring and promotion

Growth monitoring and promotion (GMP) is an important intervention for detecting cases of growth faltering as early as possible and is particularly important to help combat Egypt's alarming stunting and obesity trends.[1] GMP sessions also give parents an opportunity to understand their child's development and

TABLE 3.1 Proposed breastfeeding support and complementary feeding practice interventions

INTERVENTION	TARGET BENEFICIARY	DELIVERY CHANNELS	KEY PLAYERS[a]	PARTNERS[b]
Promotion and support of breastfeeding	Mothers of children 0–23 months	Health units, health centers, public hospitals, community nutrition programs, midwives (*dayaas*), mass media[c]	Ministry of Health and Population: primary health care and family planning departments, National Population Council, Motherhood and Childhood Council	UN agencies, national and international NGOs
Promotion of appropriate complementary feeding practices	Mothers of children 0–23 months	Health units, health centers, public hospitals, community nutrition programs, mass media[c]	Ministry of Health and Population: primary health care department, Motherhood and Childhood Council	UN agencies, national and international NGOs

a. The key players listed are key state players.
b. Partners are UN agencies, nongovernmental organizations (NGOs), civil society organizations (CSOs), and the private sector. Such organizations should be involved in each of the interventions, giving appropriate consideration to interventions relevant to their mandate/vision.
c. Mass media are included as a delivery channel for interventions that involve behavior change communication. However, all other interventions should have some media outlet to promote awareness.

can act as an entry point for discussions about changes in behavior to improve child growth, as well as for other nutrition-relevant interventions such as deworming or vitamin A and iron supplementation.

In Egypt, GMP is a component of the regular maternal and child health (MCH) well-baby clinic checkup of children during their first years of life. Within health facilities, GMP refers to anthropometric measurement of children to screen malnourished cases, including stunting, wasting, underweight, over-weight, and obesity. Data are then plotted against standardized WHO growth curves, and malnourished cases are identified if there is a significant deviation from the median of the population. Once such cases are identified, a nutrition counselor provides counseling support to mothers, and follow-up visits are scheduled. The routine immunization clinic visits provide a good opportunity to combine health checkups and treatments with nutrition assessments (GMP and hemoglobin screening). It also is an opportunity for the mother to receive nutrition counseling suggesting that children receive specific interventions such as vitamin A and iron (prophylactic and treatment) supplementation.

The current system is facing a number of challenges. First, GMP is just one of the components of the regular well-baby clinic visits, which means it may not be a priority during such visits. Second, the large number of children at a clinic for other routine purposes and pressing health challenges (often acute medical conditions) require attention, which means less time is available for careful measurements, discussions, and counseling (UNICEF, MOHP, and USAID 2017). Third, there are currently no standardized protocols for refer-ral of severe cases of malnutrition, often referrals are informal and nonsys-tematic, and children are monitored within the PHC units in parallel. This situation arises in part from lack of capacity at the peripheral level to manage severe cases of malnutrition. As a result, many cases of severe acute malnu-trition may either be missed or, if picked up, not be referred for proper treatment.

The MOHP is committed, as part of implementing the first 1,000-day model within PHC facilities, to systematically strengthening GMP guidelines and related approaches. These include (1) regular assessments during routine child visits (accurate measurement of birthweight as well as the weight and length/height of children after birth up to 5 years of age); (2) responding to early signs of under- or overnutrition through education, counseling of individual mothers and fathers, and referrals and other actions in case child growth continues to falter; (3) training health care workers in monitoring the growth and develop-ment of children; and (4) systematic monitoring, feedback, and evaluation of the GMP system at the PHC unit, district, governorate, and central level, including on the quality of anthropometric measurements. The initial focus of these and other selected efforts is within the specially dedicated MOHP "1,000-day trial" to establish the operational procedures and costs for a nationwide scaling up of the improved Standardized Protocol of Action for Nutrition Services (SPANS) to be provided by all government and private PHC/MCH units (see the case study later in this chapter on strengthening the integrated nutrition package at the primary health care level).

Recently, the MOHP increased the number of routine well-baby clinic vis-its in the second year of life, thereby providing more opportunities to identify and address cases of malnutrition before the age of 2. Until recently, regular MCH well-baby clinic visits in Egypt normally take place at the scheduled immunization visits at 2, 4, 6, 9, 12, 15, and 18 months of age. However, two more visits have been added at 21 and 24 months, which altogether provide an excellent opportunity to detect, monitor, and address any malnutrition problems (including overweight) throughout early childhood and to link up the MCH health and nutrition monitoring and interventions with early childhood development such as including psychomotor, psychosocial, and cognitive assessments in these periodic clinic visits (see the section on child protection later in this chapter). The MOHP has updated the GMP and early childhood development capacity building package for health care workers, including the ECD component of child monitoring health cards, to strengthen the capacity of PHC workers to detect any deviation of child growth and development within a child's first two years. Table 3.2 summarizes the GMP intervention just described.

Micronutrient supplementation in young children

Micronutrient deficiencies often result in "hidden hunger," which may occur despite a diet with adequate calories. Micronutrient deficiencies are especially worrisome in infants and children because of the critical role micronutrients play in early growth and development. Vitamin A, iron, iodine, and zinc are the most prominent of these micronutrients and the target of many interventions based on evidence of prevailing deficiencies and the important role they play in health and disease.

Vitamin A supplementation. Vitamin A is essential for the functioning of the immune system and the healthy growth and development of children. Vitamin A deficiency could lead to visual impairment, illness, and also death. WHO (2011b) recommends that vitamin A supplements be given every four to six months to children 6–59 months of age in areas where vitamin A deficiency is seen as a public health problem. It is an inexpensive, quick, and effective way to improve vitamin A status and reduce child morbidity and mortality in the long term.

Egypt's vitamin A supplementation program is integrated into the Expanded Program on Immunization in PHC facilities. However, the existing implementation is ineffective and inconsistent. WHO guidelines (WHO 2011b) recommend that children 6–59 months of age be given a first dose of vitamin A of 100,000 international units (IU) between six and 11 months, followed by a dose of 200,000 IU every four to six months between the age of 12 and 59 months. In Egypt, the first dose (100,000 IU) of vitamin A supplementation is received with the measles vaccine at 9 months of age, and the second is given with the activated polio booster at 18 months of age (200,000 IU). Coupling supplementation with the immunization program increases the likelihood of reaching a greater number of children at these times regardless of location, education, wealth quintiles, and other sociodemographic variables that normally determine whether one seeks

TABLE 3.2 **Proposed growth monitoring and promotion interventions**

INTERVENTION	TARGET BENEFICIARY	DELIVERY CHANNELS	KEY PLAYERS	PARTNERS
Growth monitoring and promotion	Infants and children 0–59 months	Health units, health centers, public hospital outpatient clinics, community nutrition programs, preschools	Ministry of Health and Population: Noncommunicable disease and primary health care departments, National Nutrition Institute	UN agencies, national and international nongovernmental organizations

public versus private health care (because a majority complete the child vaccination schedule in the free state-run health services).

The nine-month gap between doses is not in line with the WHO guidelines, and further opportunities for distribution of vitamin A to children up to the age of 5 are limited at best. These shortcomings are reflected in the 2014 Egypt Demographic and Health Survey (EDHS) data (MOHP, El-Zanaty and Associates, and ICF International 2015), which shows that vitamin A supplementation is only at 16.7 percent for children 6–59 months of age. EDHS 2014 data for the age group 18–23 months, who would have received the second dose of vitamin A at 18 months of age, reveals the coverage to be 81.6 percent. Furthermore, the *Nutrition Stakeholder and Action Mapping Report* issued in 2017 found coverage to be >75 percent for vitamin A supplementation among children under 2 (MOHP and UNICEF 2017a).

The recent addition of well-baby clinic visits at 21 and 24 months of age, coupled with the regular MCH clinic visits at 36, 48 and 60 months, creates further opportunities to provide additional doses of 200,000 IU at 24, 36, 48 and 60 months. Even with this new schedule, however, the provision of vitamin A would be too far apart after age 2 according to the current international recommendations (WHO 2011b), but it would be a step in the right direction. As a first step, a needs assessment and review of the current recommendations by the Micronutrient Committee of the MOHP, which is coordinated by the National Nutrition Institute (NNI), would be needed to evaluate the best way forward. It would also be beneficial to carry out a full review of procurement, supply, and training needs, as well as costs, in order to assess whether this would be the best use of the resources required. Such a review should include a bottleneck analysis to understand what is currently limiting coverage for the age groups that currently receive vitamin A supplementation. Together, these assessments could inform the planning process moving forward. Table 3.3 summarizes the proposed vitamin A intervention for children.

Iron supplementation. Iron is an essential nutrient for growth and development. Lack of iron, caused by a low intake of iron-rich foods or an infection with intestinal helminths, can lead to anemia. The economic costs of iron-deficiency anemia from annual physical productivity losses have been calculated to be about $2.32 per capita, or 0.57 percent of the gross domestic product (GDP) in low- and middle-income countries (Horton and Ross 2003). The 2011 WHO Guidelines for Intermittent Iron Supplementation for Preschool and School-Age Children recommend that in settings where the prevalence of anemia in preschool or school-age children is 20 percent or higher, intermittent use of iron supplements be adopted as a public health intervention to improve iron status and reduce the risk of anemia among children (WHO 2011a).

TABLE 3.3 Proposed vitamin A intervention for children

INTERVENTION	TARGET BENEFICIARY	DELIVERY CHANNELS	KEY PLAYERS	PARTNERS
Vitamin A supplementation	Children 6–59 months	Health units, health centers during immunization days and regular MCH clinic visits, public hospitals, community nutrition programs	Ministry of Health and Population: primary health care department, Motherhood and Childhood Council	UN agencies

Note: MCH = maternal and child health.

The PHC system of the MOHP currently has in place an iron supplementation program for children 6–23 months of age, and it follows the WHO 2011 guidelines. These guidelines recommend 25 milligrams of elemental iron syrup or drops every week for three months, followed by a three-month gap, and then repeated until the child is 5 years old (WHO 2011a). WHO released new guidelines in 2016 that focus on daily iron supplementation in infants and children. These guidelines recommend daily iron supplementation in infants and young children 6–23 months of age and preschool-age children 24–59 months living in settings where anemia prevalence is greater than 40 percent. Because the current prevalence rate in Egypt is 27 percent among children 6–59 months of age (EDHS 2014), the current protocols can continue, although these protocols may need to be updated if the prevalence rate rises again above 40 percent.

Currently, efforts to provide this age group with iron supplementation are insufficient because only 10 percent of infants 6–8 months and 6 percent of children 48–59 months were given iron supplementation in the week prior to the EDHS 2014 survey. The situation is exacerbated by the suboptimal consumption of iron-rich foods, especially by infants 6–8 months of age (EDHS 2014). A contributing factor may also be the increasing cost of animal source foods, recognizing that heme-bound iron has much higher bioavailability than other sources of iron (López and Martos 2004).

Increasing the coverage of iron supplementation through the MCH clinic visits will be critical to the success of this intervention. However, another mechanism would be required to continue supplementation of children 24–59 months of age because the MCH clinic visits are only yearly from 2 years of age and up. Continuation will, however, require investments in retraining, supplies, and monitoring and reporting. In addition, services provided for vulnerable populations through the social safety net programs by the Ministry of Social Solidarity (MOSS) could present an opportunity to reach vulnerable populations such as through food ration cards and conditional cash transfers.

It will also be critical to ensure that iron supplementation is continued as part of an integrated program. This program would include management and prevention of anemia during pregnancy, promotion of adequate weight gain, hand washing, SBCC to increase diet diversity and knowledge of food combinations that increase iron absorption, control of parasitic infections, and appropriate fortification of complementary foods with iron and other micronutrient powders (see box 3.2). The barrier to optimal coverage has sometimes been lack of understanding of potential benefits, and so education should be emphasized through nationwide campaigns (De-Regil et al. 2011). In addition, a clear referral system for the management of clinically diagnosed anemic children should be put in place. A cheap, fast, "field-friendly" method for measuring hemoglobin in remote and rural health settings could further facilitate diagnosis of anemic children for treatment. Table 3.4 summarizes the proposed iron intervention for children.

TABLE 3.4 Proposed iron intervention for children

INTERVENTION	TARGET BENEFICIARY	DELIVERY CHANNELS	KEY PLAYERS	PARTNERS
Iron supplementation (weekly)	Children 6–59 months	Health units, health centers, public hospitals, cash transfer programs	Ministry of Health and Population, Ministry of Social Solidarity	UN agencies

---

BOX 3.2

Common challenges in micronutrient supplementation programs in Egypt

Significant challenges face each of the supplementation programs in Egypt. A well-defined and updated strategy for micronutrient supplementation does not exist in part because of the lack of efforts to review, update, and monitor all relevant micronutrient control strategies (including coordinating actions with food fortification, public nutrition education, and food subsidies and regulations). This lack partly stems in turn from a lack of overall awareness of the importance of prioritizing a range of micronutrient interventions.

Attention should be paid as well to the current challenges in implementing key micronutrient interventions such as vitamin A and iron in order to improve coverage and efficiency. The lack of a needs assessment and monitoring capacity, along with a weak supply chain and the questionable quality of data captured in the health information system, hinder accurate planning, implementation, and monitoring of micronutrient deficiency control in Egypt. That said, there is also a need to ensure that the available information is used as effectively as possible in decision making.

Although investments are needed in infrastructure and materials for screening of micronutrient deficiencies, particularly for iron deficiency (hemoglobin screening) and in training of key personnel to ensure improved implementation of key micronutrient interventions at scale, there is generally a lack of funding available. The MOHP and UNICEF, as part of the first 1,000 days model, have developed tools to improve the efficiency of the existing micronutrient supply chain system, including assessment and monitoring tools, capacity-building packages for health care workers, and data monitoring. However, sufficient funding will be required to fully implement this approach successfully.

Integrated management of acute malnutrition

Severe acute malnutrition (SAM) is a major cause of death in children under 5, either directly because their nutritional needs are not being met or indirectly because of the elevated risk of death from common childhood illnesses such as diarrhea, pneumonia, and malaria (WHO, UNICEF, and WFP 2014). The many potential causes could include poverty, lack of food, repeated illnesses, inappropriate feeding practices, lack of care, and poor hygiene. Children with SAM need urgent life-saving treatment in order to survive. Children with moderate acute malnutrition (MAM) have an increased risk of mortality, and if not treated, they run the risk of progressing toward SAM. Until relatively recently, children diagnosed with SAM were only treated in hospitals where they received therapeutic feeding along with medical care. Many more were never reached or lacked access to health facilities. However, with the recent availability of ready-to-use therapeutic food (RUTF) much of the treatment can be provided outside of the hospital system.

IMAM is an integrated approach to tackling malnutrition that targets children 6–59 months of age. The approach creates maximum coverage and access by not only relying on inpatient care for treatment (SAM with complications), but also introducing outpatient care (SAM without complications) and decentralization of services down to the community level. As a result, a far higher number of children with SAM or MAM can potentially be identified through community outreach, referred, and then treated, with the defaulter rate and number of relapse cases declining because of the continued monitoring in the community.

In Egypt, the MOHP, using the WHO guidelines (WHO 2005) for integrated management of childhood illnesses (IMCI), developed its own integrated IMCI package. However, it currently lacks specific protocols for the effective management of malnutrition. The IMCI strategy is a simple, effective approach geared toward outpatient clinical settings with limited resources. In these settings, health care providers can deliver appropriate treatments for the major illnesses, counsel caretakers, and refer severer cases that warrant care at a more fully equipped health care facility. Severe acute malnutrition and anemia are an integral part of identifying dangerous conditions requiring urgent care and hospitalization, follow-up, and nutrition counseling (WHO 2013b).

Despite this, the effective treatment of malnutrition—especially in its severer and more complex forms (that is, linked to other forms of infections and medical conditions)—remains inadequate. The treatment of malnourished children at home, and from health staff and community health workers (CHWs) at the PHC unit level, as well as at referral hospitals at the district and governorate level, is currently not taking place at scale. Despite the fact that Egypt has a comparatively well-established system of hospitals with pediatric departments down to district level, very few referred cases of SAM or severe pediatric anemia have been recorded. The recent *Nutrition Stakeholder and Action Mapping Report* concluded that treatment of SAM (and MAM) is simply "not done" (MOHP and UNICEF 2017a).

The capacity constraints of facilities and staff and weaknesses in referral systems may help explain the prevailing problems. As was observed for neonatal risk cases in the integrated perinatal health and nutrition (IPHN) review, the links between the health sector hospital and preventive services are not working well, and referrals are thus often left to the individual parents to pursue and with costs they may not be able to meet (UNICEF, MOHP, and USAID 2017). The capacity of pediatric referral departments to provide the SAM/MAM and severe anemia treatment needs to be assessed and the costs for establishing or strengthening these services elucidated.

Because of the level of wasting in Egypt (8 percent), it is proposed that an IMAM program be established to develop the capacity needed for effective treatment of malnutrition. This national program should follow the standard WHO guidelines for the treatment of SAM (WHO 2013b) and include inpatient and outpatient therapeutic feeding programs, as well as treatment of MAM in supplementary feeding programs. Community outreach is a further critical component needed to harness community involvement to support the early detection and referral of cases. Table 3.5 summarizes the proposed treatment of MAM and SAM.

Zinc

Diarrhea is a leading cause of death globally among children under 5. It contributes to nutritional deficiencies, reduced resistance to infections, and impaired

TABLE 3.5 Proposed treatment of moderate acute malnutrition and severe acute malnutrition

INTERVENTION	TARGET BENEFICIARY	DELIVERY CHANNELS	KEY PLAYERS	PARTNERS
Treatment of MAM and SAM	Children 6–59 months	Health units, health centers, public hospital outpatient clinics	Ministry of Health and Population: preventive and hospital services divisions	UN agencies, national and international nongovernmental organizations

Note: MAM = moderate acute malnutrition; SAM = severe acute malnutrition.

growth and development. Zinc supplementation has been shown to reduce the duration and severity of diarrhea and to prevent subsequent episodes. It is also important for supporting growth. A systematic review and meta-analysis of available studies globally have shown that among zinc-treated children there is a 26 percent (95 percent confidence interval: 20–32 percent) reduction in the estimated relative risk of diarrhea lasting beyond three days (Lamberti et al. 2013). Since 2004, WHO and UNICEF have recommended adding zinc to the standard oral rehydration solution (ORS) therapy for infants and children with diarrhea. The current treatment protocol for diarrhea is continued feeding, adequate hydration, and 10–14 days of zinc supplementation—that is, 10 milligrams for infants less than 6 months; 20 milligrams otherwise (WHO and UNICEF 2004).

In Egypt, zinc powder is either incorporated into the ORS sachet or given as a separate tablet in a 10- to 14-day course for children. Accurate estimation of zinc supplementation coverage is therefore challenging and remains suboptimal because only 30 percent of children with diarrhea receive some form of ORS therapy and a meager 1.7 percent receive zinc supplementation (EDHS 2014).

Increasing the number of cases of diarrhea treated with ORS and zinc will require market-based availability (pharmacies) and education of pharmacists and other health care workers because only a fraction of the population seeks care in state-run facilities beyond vaccination. Furthermore, unifying the product for delivery of ORS with zinc so that it easier to administer will make it a more attractive option. Finally, ensuring that the general population understands the potential benefits of zinc through the efforts of health workers, pharmacists, nurses, and other health personnel will be crucial to creating demand and improving coverage. Table 3.6 summarizes the proposed treatment of diarrhea with zinc.

Deworming

When not treated, parasitic infections contribute to suboptimal nutritional status through increased nutrient losses (through blood loss and diarrhea), malabsorption, decreased intake (due to loss of appetite) and increased need (due to fever). To reduce the worm burden of soil-transmitted helminth infection, WHO guidelines recommend that annual or biannual single-dose albendazole (400 milligrams) or mebendazole (500 milligrams) be given to all preschool children 1–4 years of age and to school-age children 5–12 years of age living in areas where the baseline prevalence of any soil-transmitted infection is 20 percent or more among children (WHO 2017b).

For some time, Egypt has had a successful National Bilharziasis Elimination Program (NBEP) in which deworming medication for schistosomiasis and helminth infections is provided at the PHC level. This program has reduced infection rates to historic lows, currently at 0.2 percent, partly because of an ongoing program for mass deworming treatment in primary schools targeting children

TABLE 3.6 Proposed treatment of diarrhea with zinc

INTERVENTION	TARGET BENEFICIARY	DELIVERY CHANNELS	KEY PLAYERS	PARTNERS
Therapeutic zinc supplementation for the management of diarrhea (with oral rehydration solution)	Children 6–59 months	Health units, health centers, general service hospitals, pharmacies	Ministry of Health and Population: primary health care department, Motherhood and Childhood Council	UN agencies

9–12 years of age and mass deworming in highly infected areas of the country, which are now few.

The success of deworming efforts in Egypt highlights the importance of intra- and intersectoral efforts within a comprehensive national scale-up program that could be used as a model for other national scale-up program efforts. Effective collaboration was established between the primary health care and the endemic disease control departments within the MOHP, and the cooperation and coordination of the MOHP, Ministry of Water Resources and Irrigation (MOWRI), Ministry of Agriculture and Land Reclamation (MOALR), and others were secured to ensure success of the program. In addition, the national media campaigns that accompanied the program in the 1980s and 1990s to increase awareness on modes of disease transmission, methods of prevention, and treatment are considered some of the most successful national public health campaigns to date.

Despite its current low prevalence, it is in the national interest to completely eliminate schistosomiasis, while eliminating other types of enteric parasite (helminth) infections. Presently, treatment for schistosomiasis is given only when diagnosed, unless prevalence is found to be greater than 3 percent in an identified area. In that case, mass treatment, snail control, and efforts to ensure clean water and sanitation are undertaken. Therefore, it is likely that many cases go unnoticed in areas where prevalence is less than 3 percent without mass screening. Annual or biannual administration of deworming drugs, particularly for preschool children, would help to eliminate cases of infection and its negative impact on nutrition status. These annual/biannual campaigns can make use of existing delivery platforms such as preschools. Cooperation with MOSS could facilitate reaching the most vulnerable populations. Table 3.7 summarizes the proposed deworming interventions.

Maternal nutrition and adolescent interventions

Two maternal and adolescent nutrition interventions are described in this section: anemia control and prevention and obesity interventions.

Anemia control and prevention
Pregnant women. Accessible, high-quality care before and during pregnancy, childbirth, and the postnatal period is important for the health of the mother and the development of the unborn baby. Antenatal care (ANC), by linking the expectant mother and her family with the formal health system, helps to ensure this continuum of care. ANC prepares pregnant women for birth and parenthood, manages health issues during pregnancy, and provides the appropriate information and advice needed for a healthy pregnancy, safe childbirth, and postnatal recovery. A key component of ANC is anemia detection, treatment, and control during pregnancy because it is associated with increased maternal and newborn complications, including maternal

TABLE 3.7 **Proposed deworming interventions**

INTERVENTION	TARGET BENEFICIARY	DELIVERY CHANNELS	KEY PLAYERS	PARTNERS
Deworming	Children 12–59 months	Health units, health centers, preschools	Ministry of Health and Population, Ministry of Social Solidarity	UN agencies

mortality, low birthweight, and premature birth. WHO (2016a) recommends daily doses of 30–60 millligrams of iron and 400 micrograms of folic acid supplementation for 90 days during pregnancy to prevent maternal anemia, puerperal sepsis, low birthweight, and preterm birth (MOHP and UNICEF 2017b; Sanghvi, Harvey, and Wainright 2010).

In Egypt, the proportion of pregnant women attending antenatal clinics is comparatively high, with over 80 percent attending a minimum of four times during pregnancy and being attended by a trained service provider as recommended by WHO (2016b). And yet, despite the high coverage, more than 15 percent of newborn babies register low birthweight (less than 2.5 kilograms), an indicator of early stunting and inadequate nutrition-related support provided during the pregnancy. ANC services in Egypt are provided by the same public PHC/MCH service system that was described for infants and young children. However, a high proportion (80 percent) of pregnant women prefer to have their ANC checkups in private clinics or hospitals (EDHS 2014). Often, they are using a combination of both types of ANC service providers.

Iron–folic acid supplementation is part of the ANC package provided for pregnant women as outlined in the WHO 2016 guidelines (WHO 2016a). Anemia treatment, prevention, and control efforts during pregnancy are hampered by challenges related to compliance and, according to EDHS 2014, only 36.1 percent of pregnant women took the full (90-day) supplementation during their last pregnancy. This finding highlights the gap between coverage and compliance, the latter often claimed to be the result of the side-effects of iron supplementation (Milman et al. 2016).

Promotion and strengthening of the health care package provided during ANC are key to improving coverage and compliance during pregnancy, and it has already been included in the updated SPANS developed by the MOHP (see case study later in this chapter). Expanding delivery channels to reach pregnant women through community health workers and home visits in remote and rural areas is another potential approach to improving coverage and compliance. This intervention should be viewed as well in the context of an extended package of prenatal care involving appropriate weight gain, behavior change communication, along with a clear referral and management strategy for those clinically diagnosed with anemia.

Adolescent girls

In adolescent girls, menstrual blood losses, accompanied by rapid growth, make them highly vulnerable to iron deficiency, putting them at greater risk of illness and infection, fatigue, and a reduced capacity for physical work and negative outcomes in pregnancy. The WHO (2016a) recommends that adolescent girls take 30-60 milligrams of elemental iron for three consecutive months in every one-year period.

The Ministry of Education (MOE), in collaboration with the School Health Program of the MOHP, has put in place a system to focus on anemia prevention in adolescent girls in secondary schools, although it is not clear how functional it is. This approach aims to initiate iron-folic acid (IFA) supplementation as the adolescent girls enter menarche, thereby aiming to prevent maternal anemia altogether (Aguayo, Paintal, and Singh 2013). Growing evidence is attesting to the potential of pre-pregnancy prevention of anemia to greatly improve the control of anemia during pregnancy. EDHS 2014 reports that 10.9 percent of adolescent girls 15–19 years of age have begun childbearing. Thus this potentially critical

TABLE 3.8 Proposed iron–folic acid interventions

INTERVENTION	TARGET BENEFICIARY	DELIVERY CHANNELS	KEY PLAYERS	PARTNERS
Iron–folic acid supplementation (daily)	Pregnant women	Health units, Health centers, general service hospitals, community nutrition programs, secondary schools, pharmacies	Ministry of Health and Population, Ministry of Education	UN agencies

intervention can be a part of a life cycle strategy that manages and prevents anemia in children and adolescent girls as well as pregnant women. However, it will be important to assess the current status and challenges of this program before considering implementing it at scale. Table 3.8 summarizes the proposed iron–folic acid interventions.

Obesity prevention and control interventions for women of reproductive age

Dietary habits, food consumption patterns, and lack of physical activity all contribute to an increasing prevalence of overweight and obesity, particularly among poorer and rural populations in Egypt. As chapter 2 described, both obesity and overweight in women has increased significantly in Egypt, with more than a third of women overweight and almost half obese. It is a problem not only of the poor but also of the rich and across education levels.

Obesity poses a heavy health and economic burden for both individuals and the society (Global BMI Mortality Collaboration 2016) because it is a major contributor to chronic diseases such as high cholesterol, diabetes, and heart disease and to premature death (Calle 2008; Hu 2008a, 2008b; Kim and Kawachi 2008). The cost of obesity-related health services, in combination with coexisting anemia, can lead to catastrophic spending in poor households or, even worse, may lead individuals to avoid care so they do not become impoverished. Thus the importance of combating obesity cannot be overstated.

Combating obesity requires coordinated efforts from all stakeholders, including the GoE, industry, health care systems, schools, urban planners, the media, communities, and individuals (Hu, Liu, and Willett 2011; Kremers et al. 2010; Malik, Willett, and Hu 2013; Musaiger et al. 2011). Prevention and intervention programs and policies that have been successful in other countries could be tailored to the unique characteristics of the food system and culture in Egypt. Population-based intervention studies in high-income countries have demonstrated the efficacy of several preventive strategies to reduce the risk of chronic diseases in obese women and reduce the obesity risk among the general population (Hutchesson et al. 2015; Kremers et al. 2010; Tobias et al. 2015). However, translating these findings into practice requires changes in health systems and policies (Hu, Liu, and Willett 2011).

The period spanning pregnancy and childbirth is an important window for the prevention of maternal obesity. Egyptian mothers have little awareness of the optimal weight gain during pregnancy and its relation to their food choices, with common misconceptions about foods and eating habits. Meanwhile, health care providers do not routinely weigh women during pregnancy or counsel them on weight gain during pregnancy (Kavle et al. 2014)

At present, programs and interventions to address obesity in Egypt are inadequate. There is little in the way of promotion or awareness of healthy diets or an active lifestyle, as well as a lack of access to healthy foods. Because of weak laws regulating the food industry and lack of a regulating body to enact laws and provisions for the food industry, media advertisements of high sugar and fat content food items continue to target children and adolescents. Currently, there is no oversight mechanism in place to evaluate content or laws enacted banning false health and nutrition messages, prohibiting the targeting of children and adolescents, or promoting unhealthy food and nutrition practices. The Ministry of Youth and Sports has a nationwide program that promotes physical activity under the slogan *Alreyada lel Gami* (Sports for Everyone). Participation in sports, however, is generally low because it traditionally has not been part of the Egyptian culture. The government's NNI and National Research Centre (NRC) have outpatient clinics for the management of obesity, promoting proper nutrition and health messages. However, beyond this there is little capacity within the health system for managing obesity and overweight.

That said, in the last few years the GoE has begun to focus more on noncommunicable diseases (NCDs) in general and obesity in particular. Taking its cue from WHO's development of the Global Action Plan for the Prevention and Control of Noncommunicable Diseases 2013–2020 (WHO 2013a), which aims to achieve the commitments of the UN Political Declaration on Noncommunicable Diseases, the MOHP established an NCD unit in late 2014 and carried out a situational analysis of existing strategies, policies, gaps, and opportunities. Following on from this, the MOHP led a collaborative process in 2017 to develop the Egypt National Multisectoral Action Plan for Prevention and Control of Noncommunicable Diseases 2017–2021. This plan is in line with the Global Action Plan for the Prevention and Control of Noncommunicable Diseases.

A key target of this plan is to halt the rise in obesity by 2021. The plan would implement cost-effective, comprehensive prevention strategies, including promoting healthy diets through health promotion activities in schools, creating national guidelines for promoting physical activity, providing school physical education as part of the national curriculum, improving the detection and management of NCDs, as well as developing strategies to reduce sugar consumption and salt intake. Each relevant sector is expected to incorporate activities to reach the targets set within their sector plans under the guidance of a national NCD committee.

Moving forward, it will be important to ensure that the National Multisectoral Action Plan for the Prevention and Control of Noncommunicable Diseases 2017–2021 is implemented. For this to happen, the national coordination mechanism needs to be fully functional down to the provincial and local level with all identified sectors playing their part. Also, a strong accountability framework should be in place with a national monitoring framework that is in line with the global WHO framework. In the health sector in particular, sufficient numbers of trained and competent professionals are needed to combat obesity, complemented by protocols at the institutional level for the prevention and early detection of overweight and obesity. During and after pregnancy, there is an opportunity through antenatal and postnatal care to improve the practices surrounding pregnancy and childbirth to prevent maternal obesity in Egypt. Another important step in the right direction would be developing national nutrition guidelines to promote healthy eating and promote active living, while enacting legislation banning the promotion of unhealthy food and nutrition practices and prohibiting the targeting of children and adolescents.

Cross-cutting programs: National food fortification

Egypt's mandatory National Wheat Flour Fortification Program to fortify bread with iron and folic acid has the potential to address anemia in women and children. The program was included for national scaling up in the National Food and Nutrition Policy and Strategy (NFNPS) 2007–2017. It was implemented in partnership with the Global Alliance for Improved Nutrition (GAIN) and World Food Programme under the overall leadership of the Ministry of Supply and Internal Trade (MOSIT) in coordination with the MOHP. Under the program, iron (ferrous sulphate) and folic acid were added to all subsidized wheat flour produced of 82 percent extraction rate, providing a daily intake of approximately 12 milligrams of iron and 600 micrograms of folic acid through the consumption of subsidized *baladi* bread.[2] Significant investments were made in infrastructure and capacity building at the institutional level. However, unfortunately the program was interrupted in 2014, and, although no major evaluations were carried out, smaller studies suggested that up to 50 million Egyptians were consuming quality-assured fortified *baladi* bread on a daily basis. In 2011, 6.5 million metric tons of fortified wheat flour were produced by 143 participating public and private sector mills (Elhakim et al. 2012). However, the iron compound and dosage used for fortification do not conform to WHO's current guidelines (WHO, FAO, UNICEF, GAIN, MI, and FFI 2009). The country context also needs to be considered, as many Egyptians consume black tea, a potent inhibitor of iron absorption by 79–94 percent (El-Sahn, El-Masry, and El-Sahn 2003; Hurrell, Reddy, and Cook 1999). Reestablishing a national iron fortification program would have to be preceded by an evaluation study to evaluate the effectiveness of the program and also to follow updated specifications for the iron compound used, dosage, and so forth, as outlined in the WHO guidelines.

Egypt also had a voluntary project that fortifies cooking oil with vitamin A through the National Vegetable Oil Fortification program. This project, implemented with the assistance of GAIN and the WFP, added vitamin A (retinol palmitate) and vitamin D to sunflower oil. The fortified oil was initially sold at a subsidized price to ration card holders. As part of the process, NNI helped to develop national fortification standards of 60 IU of vitamin A and 3 IU of vitamin D per gram of oil, which would deliver approximately 1,000 IU of vitamin A (that is, 35–50 percent of the recommended daily amount for adults and children). Globally, fortification of cooking oil with vitamin A (and vitamin D) has been found to be a very effective approach to controlling these micronutrient deficiencies (Allen et al. 2006). However, like the national wheat flour fortification program, this program was interrupted in 2014. Also, evidence revealed some decay of the vitamin A fortificant from oxidation of the oil (Laillou et al. 2012). Therefore, reinvigorating this program may require further attention to quality control issues at the industry level, as well as storage and light exposure at both the industry and household level.

Finally, to combat iodine-deficiency disorders, the MOHP established a national program of universal salt iodization (USI) in the early 1990s. It partnered with the following stakeholders: the NNI (Secretariat), MOSIT, Ministry of Industry, MOHP, Salt Producers Alliance, Chamber of Food Industries, Salt Alliance Group, Salt Industry Chamber, UNICEF, and WFP. According to EDHS 2014 (MOHP, El-Zanaty and Associates, and ICF International 2015) and the national iodine survey (MOHP, GAIN, and UNICEF 2016), over 90 percent of households in Egypt now use iodized salt, which can be considered at scale. Thus this program can be considered a great achievement. However, the quality assurance and quality control component of the program should be strengthened, particularly at the level of the small- and intermediate-scale producers, to ensure that the level of salt iodization is adequately maintained and that the population is regularly reminded of the need to use iodized salt.

NUTRITION-SENSITIVE INTERVENTIONS

Nutrition-sensitive interventions address the key underlying determinants of nutrition and enhance the coverage and effectiveness of nutrition-specific interventions. Nutrition-sensitive programs draw on committed and accountable collaboration and contributions from sectors such as agriculture, social protection, early child development, education, and water and sanitation to affect the underlying determinants of nutrition, including poverty, food insecurity, and scarcity of access to adequate care resources and health, water, and sanitation services. This section describes nutrition-sensitive interventions related to five areas in Egypt: (1) nutrition-sensitive agriculture and food security; (2) social protection and safety nets; (3) early childhood development; (4) child education; and (5) water, sanitation, and hygiene. Specifically, it describes how these interventions can potentially affect nutrition status, the approach currently being taken, the challenges inherent in making them more nutrition-sensitive, and the potential way forward to ensure that each sector maximizes its impact on nutrition from the relevant programs.

Nutrition-sensitive agriculture and food security

Agricultural interventions have the potential to improve the nutritional status of households through four key pathways: (1) reductions in food prices from greater productivity of nutritious foods, leading to higher consumption; (2) higher incomes from selling the products produced; (3) consumption of one's own production as a result of market imperfections or a focus on home production, including home gardens; and (4) factors linked to gender such as women's social status and empowerment in agriculture, their time, and their health and nutritional status (Ruel and Alderman 2013). A number of studies have found positive relationships between agriculture and nutrition, particularly in terms of greater diet diversity, but less so in terms of nutritional status (Gillespie and van den Bold 2017). However, it is an area in which further research—context-specific—is required.

Whether agricultural interventions increase household income or purchasing power or support household food consumption, agricultural development and food security programs need to focus on improving household food security in terms of both quantity and quality/diversity to achieve the intended nutritional benefits.[3] Various agricultural investment strategies in Egypt are focusing on large-scale production, small-scale farming, as well as the participation of women in agriculture.

Programs to increase agricultural production and productivity
The GoE is investing heavily in national agricultural production and logistics. However, these investments do not have explicit nutrition outcome objectives. Egypt's agriculture sector, largely dependent on the availability of water from the

Nile, is one of the key sources of national income, contributing 19 percent of national merchandise exports, employing 25 percent of the labor force, and representing almost 15 percent of the country's GDP.[4] One of Egypt's major new agribusiness initiatives is the Global Logistics Centre Egypt project, which aims to improves the storage and handling of grains and food commodities and the manufacture and packaging of oilseed crops, unrefined oils, raw sugar, and grains. The initiative will serve a logistics hub that seeks to secure local and regional food markets with a total storage capacity of 20–25 million tons a year. The initiative should consider integrating household food security for vulnerable families as one of the project's secondary outcomes.

Aside from such larger initiatives, programs are seeking to increase the income of small farmers. However, none has been evaluated from a nutrition outcome perspective. Two such programs are supported by the U.S. Agency for International Development (USAID). Food Security and Agribusiness Support is one of the principal activities supported by USAID's Feed the Future initiative. Since 2015, this project has sought to increase the income of 14,000 Egyptian farmers through strengthening the different stages of the agricultural process (value chain). Examples are integrating state-of-the-art technologies into small-scale cold storage infrastructure and irrigation, developing farmers' skills in postharvest processes, and enhancing production and marketing to build the capacity of the fruit and vegetable value chain production for domestic and export markets. Another USAID initiative, Premium Project for Egyptian Small Growers, is also working toward sustainably improving the socioeconomic conditions of farmers by making them internationally competitive. Both approaches have yet to be evaluated from a nutrition perspective, and yet they have the potential to improve nutritional intake and diet diversity by increasing farmers' incomes and enhancing fruit and vegetable production.

Several initiatives in Egypt specifically aim to improve the participation of women (and youth) in agricultural development, but again none has been evaluated from a nutrition perspective. The prevalence of poverty in rural Upper Egypt, compounded by poor infrastructure, illiteracy, and rapid population growth, disproportionately makes women more economically vulnerable, and appears to have a disproportionate impact on nutrition outcomes (see chapter 1). Despite the fact that the share of women in the agriculture labor force has markedly increased since the 1990s, their contributions often remain unpaid and constitute informal "family labor." Customs and gender disparities are at the core of many of the challenges disproportionately faced by women in agriculture. Several USAID-supported projects in Egypt are trying to improve women's participation in agricultural development, and yet none of these programs is used as a "model" for nutrition-sensitive agriculture or intended for national scale-up. Such programs rest on evidence (primarily from elsewhere) that women farmers with access to finance are likely to have more leverage in household decision making, and they are more likely than men to spend their incomes on their families' food, education, and health.

It is important to investigate the effectiveness of the potential linkages between agriculture and nutritional status in the Egyptian context before scaling up the existing programs. Some tentative steps are being taken in this direction by USAID through its Feed the Future approach (2015–20). This approach employs an evaluation component to determine the effects of USAID's agricultural interventions and generate new evidence to inform policy and program design and implementation. This includes examining how to better leverage the links between agriculture and health and nutrition, particularly addressing the challenges of stunting and malnutrition (USAID 2017). In addition to the lessons learned from this evaluation, lessons could be learned for employing similar nutrition evaluation components for other large agricultural programs in Egypt.

Social protection and safety nets

Social protection and safety net programs cover a range of prevention and protection measures that reduce the insecurities arising from income loss, unemployment, illness, and old age. At its core, the provision of social protection should ultimately enhance the capacity of poor and vulnerable groups to address poverty in times of need and uncertainty and promote well-being. By doing so, they can also indirectly affect the immediate and underlying causes of malnutrition through, for example, improving diets via food transfers and school feeding programs and providing access to more diverse and safer sources of food. They also may improve access to and encourage the use of health services or enable households to access safe drinking water and better sanitation. Social protection programs can enhance the ability of household to provide care to young children through, for example, targeted transfers or labor regulations that enable women to breastfeed while working (FAO 2015).

In Egypt, the most widely accessed forms of social protection are employment-based social insurance, health insurance, and noncontributory public social assistance programs (such as the food subsidy program and the Social Fund for Development). A reform process was launched in 2011 to revise the social protection policy put forward in 2010, and there is an urgent need to reform the sector because the main traditional approach of GoE subsidies is rapidly becoming unaffordable and, as is increasingly apparent, ineffective or even counterproductive in terms of nutrition outcomes. The current GoE reform process offers an interesting opportunity to integrate nutrition outcomes as a priority in the different steps of the reform process, along with the necessary monitoring and evaluation tools.

Social and health insurance schemes

Although Egypt has a social insurance program in place, it does not adequately cover women and the poor because of their low labor market participation. The program offers insurance (employment-based) in cases of maternity, retirement, sickness, and disability through the contributions of employers and employees (salary deductions). Under Egyptian labor law, employed women are entitled to three-month paid maternity leave per child (for up to three children) on the condition that these women have paid their social insurance contributions for at least 10 months prior to the maternity leave. All women are also permitted to take a one-hour nursing break (or two half-hours) per day. In large institutions (those with more than 50 employees), women have the right to two years of unpaid childrearing leave per child (for up to two children). However, the low formal labor force participation of women results in truncated social protection coverage, with less than 25 percent of women in any age group of employees. Informal labor markets are also biased against the poorest poor, who lack coverage under the formal social insurance umbrella.

Egypt also has a national health insurance scheme. However, it does not adequately target those most in need. Coverage is highest among public sector workers, with lower levels of coverage found particularly in rural areas and among women because relatively few are working in formal employment (Ameta and Shafie 2015). In addition, women outside the labor force are in general not covered as dependents of beneficiaries. Reforms in 2012 extended health insurance coverage to women heads of households without a source of income or with an income that does not exceed 150 percent of the *ma'ash al daman al-igtima'i* social solidarity pension (see section on conditional and unconditional cash transfers later in this chapter). It was hoped these reforms would reach an estimated 5 million beneficiaries (Sieverding and Selwaness 2012).

However, in January 2018 Egypt approved a new social health insurance law that aims to cover the entire population. The founding principles are based on need rather than ability to pay. The two main pillars of this new approach are compulsory enrollment and subsidization of the poor. To ensure that the reforms will be effective and successful, the approach will also focus on health financing, as well as improving the efficiency, quality, accountability, and responsiveness of the health system to meet an individual's needs.

Food subsidy interventions

Food subsidy interventions have existed for decades in Egypt, but in the past they may have actually contributed to the level of malnutrition in the country rather than preventing it. Created in 1941, the Tamween Food Subsidy System has long consisted of two components: (1) subsidized prices for *baladi* bread, the most consumed staple (and flour), and (2) ration card–based subsidies. In the original program, *baladi* bread was provided at a fixed price, and other GoE regulations ensured quality. Household rations, with fixed monthly quotas dependent on family size, allowed families to buy basic subsidized food items such as cooking oil, sugar, rice, and black tea. However, the lower prices of the calorie-dense and nutrient-poor food items provided through the subsidy program may have encouraged greater consumption at the expense of other, more nutritious food groups, notably in urban Egypt. A recent study suggests that, although these food subsidies have played an important role in protecting the poor from the impact of high food prices in recent crises, they have also contributed to an overreliance on cheap and calorie-dense foods with limited nutrient content. The study finds that when compared with nonbeneficiaries, the probability of mothers being overweight is higher among beneficiary families. Subsidized *baladi* bread also seems to contribute to maternal overweight (Breisinger et al. 2013).

Reforms to the program in 2014 due to budgetary constraints expanded the number of foods that were subsidized but may have increased the potential burden on the poor. The program was reformed into a voucher-like system that replaces subsidized commodity quotas with a monthly cash allotment. The program now combines *baladi* bread with the original subsidized commodities (rice, oil, and sugar) to which many items were added such as pasta, lentils, beans, milk, white cheeses, frozen beef, chicken, and fish. Beneficiaries are, however, now required to make an out-of-pocket co-payment upon purchase of the subsidized commodities, which still limits the poorest families from taking full advantage of the system. Substituting food subsidies for cash transfers (discussed in the sections that follow) has been proposed as an alternative development-oriented strategy for tackling food insecurity and the impacts of poverty on nutrition. Overall, the food subsidy system is not explicitly built to combat malnutrition but to alleviate the burden of poverty and food insecurity.

Thus the consequences for food consumption patterns and therefore nutritional status are not explicitly recognized.

Conditional and unconditional cash transfers

Cash transfers are intended to increase the resilience of poor and vulnerable households to poverty, economic shocks, and social vulnerability. Such resilience can improve a household's ability to obtain food and health care, which are key to ensuring proper nutrition for children. Social protection is therefore recognized as an important strategy for accelerating progress in improving maternal and child nutrition (Ruel and Alderman 2013). Bhutta et al. (2008) estimate that if interventions, including cash transfers, targeted pregnant women and young infants, malnutrition and disease burden could be reduced by 25 percent in the short term. An increasingly popular tool to achieve this is cash transfer programs that target poor and vulnerable groups. Programs may take the form of unconditional cash transfers, in which the cash can be spent as desired, or conditional cash transfers (CCTs), in which funds are given to households on the condition that they comply with certain predefined requirements. Conditions could include regular visits to a health care facility, regular school attendance by children, and compliance with health and nutrition promotion activities.

Although there is evidence that cash transfer programs increase the resources available for food and health care, the evidence is mixed on whether cash transfers have a direct impact on nutrition outcomes, and so further research is required. A study of five CCTs in Latin America found a positive impact on child height but not on micronutrient status (Leroy, Ruel, and Verhofstadt 2009). A second study of CCTs had more mixed results, with programs having a positive impact on child height in Mexico and Nicaragua but not in Brazil and Honduras (Bassett 2008). A World Bank pilot of a CCT in Bangladesh was able to boost household consumption of protein and other nutrition-rich foods and reduce wasting (Ferré and Sharif 2014). The picture elsewhere is decidedly more mixed when it comes to nonconditional cash transfers. A recent study in Kenya finds cash transfers have no impact on nutritional status (Oxford Policy Management 2017), whereas a study in Zambia finds that, although cash transfers improve household consumption, food consumption, diet diversity, and food security, they have no significant impact on nutritional status (Seidenfeld et al. 2014). The lack of consensus in the literature emphasizes the importance of evaluating the effectiveness of the program in the country context.

The GoE runs conditional and unconditional cash assistance programs that could positively affect nutrition outcomes because of the specific conditionalities attached (CCT) and also increase the incomes of the poor. The Takaful (Solidarity) and Karama (Dignity) cash transfer program—eventually split into two subprograms—was developed to offer nationally targeted social safety network subprograms aimed at protecting the poor through income support. In 2015 the program was implemented in nine governorates with poverty rates exceeding 60 percent. Within three years, Takaful and Karama (to September 2018) managed to reach over 2.247 million households and to expand to all districts and governorates nationwide.

Takaful (Solidarity) is a family income support subprogram for poor households with children (0–18 years of age). It was introduced in 2015 under the mandate of MOSS. The amount of the Takaful cash transfer to households depends on the number of children and their school level. Takaful transfers start at LE 325 per household per month, which increases according to the number of children in the household and their education level. Households receive LE 60 for each child under 6 years old, LE 80 per child in primary education, LE 100 per child in preparatory education, and LE 140 per child in secondary education. As of 2019, households can receive benefits for only two children. The recipients of payments, which are made electronically each quarter, are mainly the women caregivers.

At the outset of 2018, conditions were added to the program. They include requiring households in the program to ensure that mothers and children 0–6 years of age participate in MCH clinic visits twice a year, children 6–18 years of age attend school (at least 80 percent attendance), and pregnant women attend antenatal and postnatal care. The introduction of the conditionalities is expected to have significant impacts on both nutrition and children's health in general. In fact, a recent impact evaluation of the program by the International Food Policy Research Institute (IFPRI) found it improves the quality of diets and results in rates of stunting and wasting that are considerably lower than the estimates from EDHS 2014 (Breisinger et al. 2018). It recommended that this finding be further explored. MOSS is currently piloting, together with the WFP, MOHP, and MOSIT, the first 1,000 days program model in three governorates in Upper Egypt. The program is targeting Takaful beneficiaries, including pregnant women and children 0–24 months of age. Recipients receive a food voucher for nutritious foods upon fulfilling the conditionality of receiving regular nutrition services from the PHC units. In addition, women receive nutrition counseling support. This pilot has the potential to affect the key nutrition indicators, but it will be important for partners to evaluate the pilot over a long period to assess the nutritional impact before expanding coverage across the Takaful program with the 1,000 days program model.

Karama (Dignity) is an unconditional income support and social inclusion subprogram that provides unconditional cash payments. Recipients are the elderly and people with disabilities who cannot work and orphans under 18 years of age who are living outside of institutions and are caretakers of extended family members. Elderly persons over 65 years of age and people with disabilities currently receive LE 450 per month, and orphans receive LE 350 per month. Currently, about 306,016 households benefit from the program—82 percent of recipients are elderly and 17 percent are disabled (World Bank 2018b).

Egypt also has a social assistance program designed for households with no male provider. This long-running social safety net program, known as *ma'ash al daman al-igtima'i* (social solidarity pension), was established in 1980 and is administered by the Ministry of Social Affairs (MOSA) and MOSS. It targets households with no male provider capable of earning an income and therefore includes some of the most vulnerable groups in society, including divorced, widowed, and abandoned women, women with no male provider, as well as orphans, the disabled, and households in which the male head is unable to work.

New applicants to this program falling into target categories also covered by *Karama* (such as the elderly, people with disabilities, and orphans) are now directed toward *Karama*, and the social solidarity pension is closed to such new applicants. However, the pension continues to cover some 1.5 million households, although issues with targeting result in a substantial amount of funds going to the nonpoor. Recent new regulations call for updating beneficiaries' information and reviewing their eligibility to ensure the program reaches only those most in need. And yet a review has found that even for the beneficiaries who manage to get into the program, the amount received (ranging from LE 215 for a one-person household to LE 300 for a four-person household) is insufficient to cover the minimum cost of living for the lowest income groups in Egypt (Ameta and Shafie 2015; Korayem 2013; Sieverding and Selwaness 2012).

Early childhood development

Early childhood development is the ongoing process of acquiring the skills and abilities during the early years of life that help a person to think, solve problems, communicate, express emotions, and form relationships. It is also considered the foundation of health, learning, productivity, and well-being and is the building block for future human capital formation. The early childhood period encompasses several quite distinct phases: from conception to birth and from birth to 3 years, with an emphasis on the first 1,000 days (from conception to 24 months), followed by the preschool and preprimary years (from 3 to 5 or 6 years, or the age of school entry) and from 6 to 8 years of age, when the child is transitioning into primary school.

The developing brain needs stimulation, nutrition, and protection. Stimulation sparks connections between brain cells—connections that are also fueled by adequate nutrition. Early brain development also depends on nurturing a protective and healthy environment in which children can grow. However, according to the key indicators, Egypt ranks 88th among the 172 countries ordered from most to least successful in nurturing a healthy environment for their most vulnerable young. These indicators include under-5 mortality, malnutrition that stunts growth, out-of-school children, child labor, early marriage, adolescent births, displacement by conflict. and child homicide (Save the Children 2017).

When children's brains do not reach their potential—in particular, those of the poorest and most disadvantaged children—it perpetuates an intergenerational cycle of disadvantage and inequity. Investing in early childhood development is a challenge, but it is also an opportunity to make substantial, cost-effective progress by investing in relatively simple solutions. Investments in early childhood programs, starting with the youngest, yield more than a 13 percent return in reduced poverty and income gaps and increased prosperity and economic competitiveness. ECD programs are affordable: on average, they cost $0.50 per capita per year when added to the existing health and nutrition service delivery programs (Richter et al. 2017). It has also been found that several existing maternal health and nutrition interventions themselves promote physical and cognitive development during a child's first 1,000 days, such as promotion of optimal infant and young child feeding (Britto et al. 2017).

ECD, a national priority in Egypt, is an integral part of its National Development Plan: Vision 2030. The current legislation is supportive of scaling up early learning opportunities. However, only 8 percent of young children have access to nurseries, and, despite the upward trend in the net enrollment rate for preschool education (from 21 percent to 28 percent between 2010/11 and 2015/16), it is not likely that Egypt will meet the very ambitious target of 80 percent enrollment by 2030. Current national policies also do not allow parents and caregivers to have enough time and resources to care for their children (policies allow only four months of paid maternity leave and no paternity leave). Although there is a long way to go toward ensuring that Egyptian children have a safe and nurturing environment in which to grow up and thrive, progress is being made in some areas.

A countrywide initiative was recently launched to reorganize, revamp, and scale up a comprehensive early childhood development program. Key actors in this process are MOSS, MOE, and MOHP, with overall coordination provided by the National Council for Childhood and Motherhood and support from UNICEF and other partners. The program establishes an institutional support system that will systematically monitor and respond to children's development challenges and opportunities, starting from motherhood through birth and infancy up to preschool and early primary school. This institutional support system is created by linking birth registration and MCH well-baby clinics with the estimated 14,000 nurseries registered under MOSS providing preschool children with day-care and the kindergartens enrolling some 30 percent of children 5–6 years of age. It will take some time to fully develop and scale up this emerging ECD model, and it will be important to ensure that the required capacity and linkages with key sectors, including health and nutrition, are established at an early stage to support the rollout.

Furthermore, UNICEF has begun a new public–private sector initiative on family-friendly policies. This initiative calls on governments and private sector partners to redesign the workplaces of the future to enable parents to give the best start in life to their children while boosting productivity and female empowerment. Specifically, it calls for the introduction of (1) six months of paid parental leave; (2) breastfeeding facilities and remunerated breastfeeding breaks for the first six months; (3) affordable, accessible, and quality child care services; and (4) child grants that support all families with children. This initiative, together with the revamping of the ECD program, have the potential to give children a better start in life, and both programs will be important to ensure that links are established and maintained with key existing nutrition interventions (such as the promotion of optimal infant and young child feeding) and to ensure any new nutrition initiatives implemented through the primary health care system carefully relate to these ECD approaches.

Child education

School-age children are an extremely important group in the population. They are not only soon-to-be-parents but also very important conduits of knowledge and best practice. Nutrition-sensitive education requires gaining a proper understanding of nutrition and the consequences of malnutrition through school health education programs, as well as ensuring that a well-nourished body of students is engaging in their studies and shaping their social values. In addition to other benefits, girls that continue their education through secondary education and beyond are much less likely to undergo teenage pregnancies (related to higher risk of stunting) and have malnourished children in general. Until now, this avenue for nutrition interventions has largely been overlooked in Egypt. A precondition for reaping the benefits of a nutrition-sensitive education system is to ensure that all children are enrolled and are able to complete both their primary and secondary education, and that such an education will benefit them in terms of nutrition.

General access to and quality of education

Although access to basic education in Egypt is substantial, enrollment of the poor is still subpar, and the quality of education in Egypt as well as the nutrition content of the curriculum remain problematic. Overall access to education is substantial—96 percent gross enrollment for primary education and 69 percent for secondary education (CAPMAS and UNICEF 2017). Especially for girls, enrollment in all four levels of education has reached equality. However, the most deprived children from poor families and remote areas are still out of school. The number of children out of school is currently estimated at 0.65 million, with 0.32 million children of primary school age and 0.33 million children of preparatory school age.[5]

The quality of education, however, is problematic. Half of the students in school do not learn foundational skills in mathematics and science. In mathematics, 53 percent of students did not reach the low benchmark in the 2015 Trends in Mathematics and Science Study (TIMSS), and in science 58 percent of students failed to do so (IEA and Boston College 2015). Current school curricula and textbooks do not contain the important nutrition facts that Egyptians in general and Egyptian parents in particular need to know because health education is considered weak overall in the public school curriculum. Physical education is often given low priority by schools and parents alike. It would be particularly beneficial to carry out a review of health education in public primary and secondary schools to ensure that nutrition and healthy lifestyles are being taught.

School feeding programs

Egypt has an effective long-standing National School Feeding Program (NSFP), but its coverage is limited to primary schools. The ministries involved include MOSS, MOE, and MOHP. The program, which currently covers 18 million students, aims to not only provide students with basic nourishment, but also help change behavior and develop the skills children need to choose a healthy meal. It also helps prevent children from entering the labor market too early and encourages school attendance. The meal type differs by school. For daily public schools, a premade or dry meal is supplied, whereas for schools for students with special needs and for boarding and community schools a cooked meal is offered. In public schools, subcontractors are responsible for the distribution of meals under the supervision of MOE and MOSIT. These meals are restricted to primary school students. Although the program is generally considered a success at the primary school level, similar programs do not exist at the kindergarten and secondary level.

The World Food Programme supports components of the NSFP to fill some of the existing gaps. The WFP supports community schools in 16 governorates, with the primary aim of encouraging the enrollment and attendance of children in schools, especially girls. However, the snacks provided (fortified date bars) also help to meet nutritional requirements by providing 25 percent of a child's daily nutritional needs and teachers are trained on adequate nutrition. According to the WFP, it was able to support 636,000 students in 2016, with the majority of beneficiaries being girls (77 percent). In addition, conditional take-home rations were distributed to students with a minimum of 80 percent monthly attendance (WFP 2016). Recently, the Ministry of Education asked to adopt the WFP's fortified date bars for all national schools. The WFP is also providing support for nutrition social and behavioral change in schools and in local communities through community hubs. It is represented on the national school feeding committee, providing strategic support to the GoE on the national school feeding strategy along with MOSS and partners. The Egyptian Food Bank, according to its website,[6] covers community schools in 10 governorates, establishes kitchens in the schools, and trains mothers in adequate nutrition and healthy cooking.

It also provides financial support, covering 21,000 students in 10 governorates in 2014. All meal supplies are contingent upon the availability of funds.

Although the primary aim of school feeding is to encourage enrollment and attendance at schools and support learning by alleviating short-term hunger, it also has the potential to provide nutritional benefits. There is currently little evidence on the cost-benefits of school feeding programs, and the available evidence shows that, although such programs can affect the micronutrient level of targeted children, they have modest effects on health and nutrition outcomes as evaluated by anthropometric measurements (Jomaa, McDonnell, and Probart 2011). Therefore, in the medium term it will be important to ensure that school feeding programs in Egypt are having the desired impact on enrollment, attendance, and nutrition outcomes and can be implemented sustainably before looking to scale up further.

Water, sanitation, and hygiene (WASH)

There is a wealth of evidence linking the lack of sanitation and hygiene with the prevalence of diarrheal diseases among children. It has been estimated that 25 percent of undernourishment in developing countries stems from infectious diseases such as diarrhea, ascariasis, trichuriasis, protozoa, other helminths, and enteric diseases, which are very prevalent in unhealthy environments coupled with unhygienic practices (Caulfield et al. 2004; Humphery 2009; Prüss-Üstün and Corvalán 2006). In Egypt, the lack of proper toilet facilities and open defecation practices are a fertile setting (soil contaminated with feces and wastewater) in which parasitic eggs and larvae can survive and in which these infectious agents can then be easily transmitted back to humans walking through these areas or from the foods grown there. Eventually, the transmission of infectious parasitic diseases affects the intestinal tract of infected individuals and severely undermines digestive health, causing loss of appetite, malabsorption of nutrients, and growth faltering.

The scholarly evidence on the relationship between gastrointestinal infections and malnutrition is overwhelming. Humphery (2009), for example, associates 25 percent of all stunting cases with having five or more repeated episodes of diarrhea in the first 24 months of a child's life. Likewise, based on an analysis of 140 demographic and health surveys, Spears (2013) attributes 50 percent of the variation in children's height across 65 countries to the frequency of open defecation practices. In line with the World Health Organization, Prüss-Üstün and Corvalán (2006) similarly argue that 50 percent of undernourishment in the developing world could be explained by intestinal worm infections. On that point, Fischer Walker et al. (2012) argue that children under 5 in low-income countries tend to experience on average 2.9 episodes of diarrhea a year because of lack of proper water and sanitation facilities. However, systematic reviews of the evidence have demonstrated only marginal improvement in stunting as a result of WASH interventions (Dangour et al. 2013), and more recent efficacy trials have found no benefit of improved household-level WASH on linear growth (Pickering 2019).

In Egypt, similar correlational patterns have been evident. In a study conducted by Ashour and Ahmed (1994) in Dakahliya governorate, the probability of diarrheal infection among children was higher in areas where families disposed of refuse close to dwellings or into nearby water streams. According to WHO, improving access to safe drinking water and sanitation services in Egypt can reduce the total burden of disease by 25.1 percent (Prüss-Üstün et al. 2008). The Second International Conference on Nutrition (ICN2), organized by the Food and Agriculture Organization (FAO) and WHO in November 2014, pinpointed the need to integrate WASH-focused activities into the global nutrition agenda.

Clean water

Access to clean drinking water may have improved for many in Egypt, but it continues to be problematic, particularly for poor communities and some rural governorates. Over the past decades, Egypt has made significant improvements in connecting residential buildings to the water supply. For about 91 percent of buildings, water is piped onto the premises (EDHS 2014). Overall, the access to improved sources of drinking water is very high at 98 percent (EDHS 2014), with little variation between urban and rural areas. However, pockets of the country have poorer access, particularly the frontier governorates (85 percent) and those in the lower wealth quintiles. In addition to the public organizations responsible for clean water, organizations such as UNICEF are working to ensure that the most deprived households have access to clean water.

Although access to improved water sources is high, quality is still a concern. Uninterrupted access to potable water is of paramount importance for the achievement of better nutrition outcomes, and yet many of Upper and Lower Egypt's rural dwellings commonly report stoppages in the supply of water services for several hours a week. The stoppages in turn increase the risk of gastrointestinal infections. On that point, Roushdy, Sieverding, and Radwan (2012), based on the EDHS 2008 results (El-Zanaty and Way 2009), report a statistically significant negative correlation between access to an improved continuous source of drinking water and diarrhea prevalence among children in areas where mothers have little formal education. Therefore, the major issues requiring attention are improving the continuous supply and, linked to this, carrying out regular maintenance of supply systems to ensure safe water is accessible to all.

Improved sanitation

Access to improved sanitation in Egypt remains largely subpar, particularly in rural and remote areas. At the national level, only 49 percent of households have access to public sanitation services, whereas 19 percent are connected to septic tanks, and 23 percent have to dispose of wastewater through pit latrines. Most of the underserved households (74 percent) are located in rural Upper Egypt (EDHS 2014). According to GoE statistics, sewerage coverage in rural areas was a low 12 percent in 2014. Thus some 42 million village dwellers remain underserved. Children in rural areas are also the most deprived. They are 8.5 times more likely to lack toilet facilities, compared with their urban counterparts (UNICEF and WHO 2011). Of greater significance, about 5 percent of Egypt's households, mostly in the rural Nile Delta, still discharge untreated wastewater into nearby canals that feed into the agriculture irrigation system. This situation exacerbates the risk of becoming infected with parasitic and waterborne diseases, even for families who have proper access to public sewer networks because they live close to unsanitary waterways or consume dietary products that have been farmed on polluted land.

The GoE has made improving sanitation a priority and so embarked on a $14 billion National Rural Sanitation Program (NRSP) in 2014, supported by the World Bank and other donors. The NRSP has adopted an investment priority approach that gives priority to areas where the degree of soil contamination and the expected environmental return on investment are the greatest. In doing so, the program initially facilitates the access of more than 800,000 poor Egyptians living in 769 villages in seven governorates[7] to improved sanitation services as well as greater hygiene awareness (World Bank 2018a).

Similar efforts have been replicated by other development partners. USAID, for example, has invested more than $3.4 billion since 1978 in bottom-up participatory sanitation projects to extend access to more than 25 million Egyptians, largely in Cairo, Alexandria, and Suez. Likewise, the German Development Agency (GIZ) has invested since 2004 in decentralized, community-based wastewater treatment facilities, mostly in isolated villages in Lower Egypt. Under the European Union (EU) Neighborhood Investment Facility (NIF), other European donors, such as the Agence Française de Développement (AFD), European Investment Bank (EIB), Swiss Confederation through the State Secretariat for Economic Affairs (SECO), and German Financial Cooperation (KfW), have provided finance and technical assistance for the Improved Water and Wastewater Services Program (IWSP) in eight of Upper and Lower Egypt's governorates: Gharbia, Sharqia, Damietta, Beheira, Qena, Sohag, Asyut, and Minya.

Key challenges and opportunities in the water and sanitation sector

The high cost of providing conventional water and sanitation systems is a key challenge facing the realization of improved coverage. The high cost of construction is further exacerbated by the high operating and maintenance costs and the low tariff fees imposed on water and wastewater treatment services. To that end, the GoE recently announced a new tariff structure that will enable the Holding Company for Water and Waste Water (HCWW) to recover operation and maintenance costs, ration consumption, and ultimately increase the efficiency of service operators. These steps may encourage further investment in water and sanitation services.

The complex institutional arrangement of Egypt's water and sanitation system also poses significant impediments to the improvement of service provision. Strong coordination is needed among the four key ministries responsible for setting the standards and monitoring the quality of delivered services: Ministry of Water Resources and Irrigation (MOWRI), Ministry of Health and Population, Ministry of Environment, and Ministry of Housing, Utilities and Urban Communities (MOHUUC). In addition, the division of responsibilities between the two main operators, the HCWW and the National Organization for Potable Water and Sanitary Drainage (NOPWASD), should be set out more clearly to ensure no duplication in implementation of key projects in the sector. To this end, an overarching integrated strategy should be developed that clearly sets out the main tasks assigned to each player and priorities of the sector. This strategy should in turn foster better intersectoral communication among different actors and enable decision makers to identify in an orderly fashion the real priorities of the sector.

Although WASH interventions in the context of nutrition, particularly water supply and sanitation infrastructure, can positively affect nutrition outcomes by addressing both the immediate and underlying causes of malnutrition, they are usually considered outside of the remit and scope of nutrition scale-up plans because of the large investments required. Moreover, WASH interventions, like all nutrition-sensitive interventions, do not automatically lead to improvements in nutrition, but they are likely to do so in the situations in which WASH factors are indeed the main causes of nutrition problems. Therefore, investments made need to be carefully directed towards the most effective WASH interventions and target those in most need (e.g. deprived households with poor living conditions) with particular WASH interventions part of a multisectoral approach to improving nutritional status. Although the intention may not be building infrastructure from a nutrition perspective, working with the key players in the water and sanitation sector to advocate for improved coverage of water and sanitation services for shared benefits is still important. At the same time, the focus should be on the causal linkages (for example, diarrheal disease and parasitic infections) and extending advocacy to key target groups linked to the critical nutrition life cycle periods, such as 1,000 days). Developing links with the health and education sectors can also help to ensure that the nutrition outcomes of the infrastructure programs are maximized.

Health and hygiene practices

Carried out in parallel with the large-scale interventions just described, the promotion of good hygiene practices can also contribute to the prevention of gastrointestinal infections. Many simple, effective, and cost-efficient practices actually fall under this umbrella, including effective handwashing with soap, proper disposal of young children's feces, safe water conservation and preservation, and good food hygiene behavior. It is argued that seeking behavioral change in this direction is effective in improving nutritional status. On that point, Freeman et al. (2017) claim that health education and hand washing with soap can potentially reduce diarrheal infections by 40 percent. Likewise, in Bangladesh washing at least one hand after defecation and before food preparation was associated with less diarrheal infection (Luby et al. 2011). Prüss-Üstün et al. (2014) also suggest a direct relationship between the unsafe disposal of young children's feces and diarrhea prevalence—children under 5 tend to experience the highest rate of diarrhea, and thus their feces harbor high loads of pathogens that can easily spread into surrounding environments. In fact, EDHS 2014 reveals that the 24 percent of families in Egypt that reported throwing a child's stool into garbage make up about 40.5 percent of those who had diarrhea in the family in the month preceding the EDHS survey. Even more, around 19 percent of them experienced at least three episodes of infection. This finding reflects a real need for raising awareness of the desirability of good hygiene practices to prevent diarrhea prevalence, especially in communities where there is a lack of conviction about the health benefits of these desirable small, doable actions if integrated into everyday activities.

Schools and health clinics can play central roles in improving health and hygiene practices. Between 2007 and 2014, UNICEF Egypt disseminated health information on hygiene, sanitation, and environment-friendly practices to 12,811 families and 200,000 schoolchildren in more than 370 primary schools in Asyut, Sohag, and Qena. In addition, it worked on strengthening the capacity of 2,000 educators to carry out awareness activities. The wide replication of this intervention could enable Egypt to maximize the impact of other nutrition-sensitive programs.

This experience suggests that there are numerous opportunities within schools and health clinics to integrate approaches to improving hygiene. For example, teachers could give brief hygiene talks on fecal contamination and how effective hand washing before food preparation and eating and after the use of toilets can prevent gastrointestinal infections. Schools could also set up hand

TABLE 3.9 Proposed WASH interventions

INTERVENTION	TARGET BENEFICIARY	DELIVERY CHANNELS	KEY PLAYERS	PARTNERS
Use of improved water source	Households	Public and private water and sanitation companies	Ministry of Health and Population (MOHP), Ministry of Water Resources and Irrigation (MOWRI), Ministry of Housing, Utilities and Urban Communities (MOHUUC), Ministry of Agriculture and Land Reclamation, local planning authorities, public water companies	Private water and sanitation companies, UN agencies
Use of water connection in home	Households	Public and private water and sanitation companies	MOHP, MOWRI, MOHUUC, local planning authorities, public water companies	Private water and sanitation companies, UN agencies
Improved excreta disposal (latrine/toilet)	Households	Health units, health centers, schools, public and private water and sanitation companies	MOHP, MOWRI, MOHUUC, Ministry of Environment	Private water and sanitation companies, UN agencies
Hand washing with soap	Households	Health units, health centers, schools, public and private water and sanitation companies	MOHP, MOWRI, MOHUUC, Ministry of Environment	Private water and sanitation companies, UN agencies
Hygienic disposal of children's stools	Households	Health units, health centers, schools, public and private water and sanitation companies	MOHP, MOWRI, MOHUUC, Ministry of Environment	Private water and sanitation companies, UN agencies

Note: WASH = water, sanitation, and hygiene.

washing stations in playgrounds and near food stations as a reminder for students to wash their hands. Written messages could also be placed on corridor walls and school fences. Similarly, health care providers could explain to mothers the importance of the safe disposal of diapers and animal feces, and why they should be kept away of areas where food is prepared and served. In fact, attendance at regular health checkups, a conditionality of the Takaful conditional cash transfer program, could serve as a platform for health professionals to reinforce these hygiene messages. Table 3.9 summarizes the proposed WASH interventions.

RECOMMENDATIONS: POTENTIAL HIGH-IMPACT NUTRITION POLICY AND PROGRAM OPTIONS TO CONSIDER FOR EGYPT

The following briefly summarizes the nutrition-specific and nutrition-sensitive interventions and programs to be considered for scale-up in Egypt in the context of 1,000 days, the *Lancet* high-impact interventions, and the Egyptian context as outlined and discussed in chapter 1 and the earlier parts of this chapter.

Which key focus areas and why?

Focusing on interventions during the 1,000-day period from a child's conception until second birthday to ensure the nutritional status of a woman at conception and during pregnancy and of the child through the first two years of life so that the child has every opportunity to grow and thrive is critical. Malnutrition starts in utero and thus adequate maternal nutrition is critical for the growth of the fetus in utero and, later on, the nutrient content of breast milk, thereby ensuring the proper growth and development of the newborn. Later, proper complementary feeding of the child (from the age of 6 months) along with micronutrient supplementation are also important to support the growth of the child. However, currently in Egypt there are gaps in coverage of the relevant interventions, resulting in suboptimal IYCF practices and reduced micronutrient status. Fully implementing SBCC for expectant and lactating mothers through antenatal care and growth monitoring and promotion, as well as scaling up the provision of key micronutrient supplements for pregnant women (IFA) and children (vitamin A and iron) will help to ensure that the child advances into childhood adequately nourished.

Currently, the IMCI strategy in Egypt lacks specific protocols for the effective management of malnutrition, which is a major cause of mortality in children under 5. The treatment of malnourished children at home and by health staff and CHWs at the PHC unit level, as well as at referral hospitals at the district and governorate level, is currently not taking place at scale. Because of the level of wasting (8 percent), it is proposed that the capacity to enable effective treatment of malnutrition be developed by establishing an IMAM program for the treatment of SAM and MAM cases.

A whole range of childhood disease prevention and treatment activities are needed to safeguard the continued healthy growth and development of children. During childhood, the vicious cycle of repeated infections and malnutrition hinders growth, resulting in both acute and chronic malnutrition. Many childhood prevention and treatment activities are included in the well-established IMCI strategy used at the PHC level in Egypt, but a few complementary and critical nutrition interventions need to be more systematically implemented as part of this IMCI protocol—namely, therapeutic zinc supplementation in cases of diarrhea, deworming (if indicated), and ensuring proper sanitation and hygiene practices to control intestinal infections during infancy and childhood.

Finally, ensuring a safe and clean environment by scaling up WASH interventions, particularly in rural areas where coverage is lower, can reduce the number of cases of infectious diseases such as diarrhea, reducing the prevalence of malnutrition among pregnant women and children in Egypt. Table 3.10 summarizes the 16 interventions recommended for scale-up.

Nutrition-relevant interventions and programs not included for scale-up

Some interventions discussed in this chapter in the context of Egypt are not included in the suggested list for scale-up. These include some of the evidence-based, high-impact nutrition-specific interventions from the *Lancet* and other interventions and programs that are currently, or have the potential to be, nutrition-sensitive. A summary of the rationale for these decisions, discussed more extensively in the previous section, is outlined in this section.

Provision of complementary foods. The provision of nutrient-dense complementary foods for children has not been implemented in Egypt. Although it could be an option for children living in impoverished conditions to ensure that their nutritional needs are met, it would have to be tested as part of the wider IYCF strategy and evaluated before being considered for scale-up.

Flour fortification with iron and folic acid and oil fortification with vitamin A. If the national flour fortification program is to be reestablished, it would be necessary to use the WHO– recommended iron compound, NaFeEDTA

TABLE 3.10 Nutrition interventions recommended for scale-up in Egypt

INTERVENTION	DESCRIPTION	TARGET POPULATION
Infant and young child feeding (IYCF) and micronutrients		
1. Promotion and support of breastfeeding	Communication of optimal breastfeeding practices	Pregnant women and mothers of children 0–6 months
2. Complementary feeding promotion	Communication of complementary feeding practices (excluding provision of food)	Mothers of children 6–23 months
3. Growth monitoring and promotion (GMP)	Systematic strengthening of GMP guidelines and operational procedures, training, and scale-up	Children 0–59 months
4. Vitamin A supplementation	Biannual supplementation of vitamin A capsules	Children 6–59 months
5. Iron supplementation	Weekly supplementation for three months with iron drops, followed by three months of no supplementation, and repeated until child is 5 years of age	Children 6–59 months
Curative interventions (SAM/MAM)		
6. Treatment of moderate acute malnutrition (MAM)	Treatment of MAM in supplementary feeding programs	Children 6–59 months
7. Management of severe acute malnutrition (SAM)	Admission of severely malnourished children to either inpatient or outpatient therapeutic feeding programs	Children 6–59 months
Disease prevention and management		
8. Treatment of diarrhea (ORS)	Management of mild and moderate diarrhea with oral rehydration solution (ORS)	Children 6–59 months
9. Therapeutic zinc supplementation	As part of diarrhea management with ORS	Children 6–59 months
10. Deworming	Annual or biannual single-dose albendazole (400 milligrams) or mebendazole (500 milligrams) to reduce the worm burden of soil-transmitted helminth infection	Children 12–59 months
Maternal nutrition		
11. Iron–folic acid supplementation	Three months supplementation of iron–folic acid during pregnancy	Pregnant women
Water, sanitation, and hygiene (WASH)		
12. Use of improved water source	Regulation and advocacy activities to ensure access to water supply services from an "improved" source within 1 kilometer of the user's dwelling. An improved source is one that is likely to provide "safe" water.	All households
13. Use of water connection in home	Regulation and advocacy activities to ensure access to safe water from a household connection	All households
14. Improved excreta disposal (latrine/toilet)	Promotional activities to ensure access to improved/hygienic excreta disposal (access to improved latrine or flush toilet)	All households
15. Hand washing with soap	Promotional activities for "appropriate" hand washing behavior	All households
16. Hygienic disposal of children's stools	Promotional activities for the proper disposal of children's stools	All households

Note: GMP = growth monitoring and promotion; MAM = moderate acute malnutrition; ORS = oral rehydration solution; SAM = severe acute malnutrition; WASH = water, sanitation, and hygiene.

(Aaron et al. 2012), in the most commonly consumed staples among the target age groups, with consideration of the higher premix price. In addition, a pilot study is needed to collect data on coverage and clinical outcomes at the baseline and endline (at least) before taking this intervention to scale. If deemed cost-effective, flour fortification should be incorporated into a multi-intervention strategy for the treatment, prevention, and awareness of iron deficiency anemia among the targeted age groups. Similarly, for the national oil fortification program, evaluation of the following is necessary prior to considering scale-up: verification of the amount of vitamin in the oil, stability of vitamin A at the point of consumption, and coverage and clinical outcomes among target populations. Before scaling up, it will be necessary to address the gaps and challenges that existed in those programs. Moving forward, public education campaigns and advocacy efforts would have to be incorporated in future plans to reinstate these programs.

Salt iodization. For the scale-up and costing of nutrition interventions, the common assumption is 90 percent coverage rather than 100 percent coverage because the marginal cost rises substantially for the remaining 10 percent (SUN Movement 2010). National coverage of iodized salt is 91 percent, and thus the intervention could be considered at scale.

Obesity prevention and control. Obesity and overweight are critical issues in Egypt, particularly among women of reproductive age. More than a third are overweight, and close to half are obese. Dietary habits, food consumption patterns, and lack of physical activity all contribute to the increasing prevalence of overweight and obesity in both the adolescent and the adult population. The GoE recognized the potential consequences of this phenomenon by developing the Egypt National Multisectoral Action Plan for Prevention and Control of Noncommunicable Diseases 2017–21, whose target is to halt the rise in obesity by 2021. With the focus currently on ensuring that the necessary structures and processes are in place to implement the action plan, it will be important to establish at this stage that nutrition is maintained as a key focal area of the plan and that the key interventions are implemented.

Nutrition-sensitive agriculture and food security. None of the current programs has been evaluated from a nutrition perspective. Therefore, it will be important to investigate the potential linkages between agriculture and improved nutritional status in the Egyptian context before seeking to scale up the existing programs.

Social protection and safety nets. A large number of social protection schemes and safety nets are in place in Egypt, covering a large proportion of the population. However, only the conditional cash transfer program, Takaful, focuses on improving the health and nutrition outcomes (along with education) of poor households. A recent evaluation by Breisinger et al. (2018) suggests that the program is already having some impact on nutrition outcomes, and the current pilot in three governorates in Upper Egypt aims to improve nutrition outcomes further. Once the pilot is finalized and the program further evaluated, the scope to scale up nationwide can be assessed.

Early childhood development. A countrywide initiative was recently launched to reorganize, revamp, and scale up a comprehensive early childhood development program, starting from motherhood through birth and infancy and up to preschool and early primary school. However, because it will take some time to fully develop, assess, and scale up this emerging ECD model, it is too early to understand whether it will have an impact on nutrition outcomes.

Child education. Evidence suggests that health education in public schools in Egypt currently does not focus on nutrition and healthy lifestyles and therefore is unlikely to have any impact on nutrition outcomes. School feeding is primarily aimed at encouraging enrollment and attendance at school and supporting learning by alleviating short-term hunger. Thus it is likely having only modest effects on health and nutrition outcomes. There is also the question of cost-effectiveness in relation to other alternatives.

APPROACHES TO SCALING UP THE IDENTIFIED INTERVENTIONS

The interventions identified in this chapter could be scaled up in various ways. This section considers the alternative options of (1) scale-up by intervention to full national coverage, (2) scale-up by region, and (3) scale-up by prioritizing interventions.

Scale-up by intervention to full national coverage

A full scale-up of the complete intervention package outlined in this chapter would take time, depending on when the capacities and resources needed to expand the whole package nationwide are made available. However, they would also result in the most comprehensive coverage and, based on the evidence in the *Lancet* series (Lancet 2008 and 2013) and the current Egyptian context, the would have the greatest impact on stunting through the existing delivery platforms. The advantages and disadvantages of this approach are outlined in table 3.11.

Scale-up by region

First tackling the nutrition issues in regions with a higher prevalence of malnutrition (for example, where stunting rates are higher) and then extending efforts to other regions with lesser prevalence are often considered desirable for equity and to have the biggest impact in the shortest time. This report has shown that certain geographic areas in Egypt see a higher prevalence of many nutrition problems. And many of these areas, but not all of them, are pockets of poverty. The advantages and disadvantages of this method are summarized in table 3.12.

Scale-up by prioritizing interventions

For several reasons, policy makers may be inclined to prioritize the scale-up of certain interventions in a nutrition package. For example, when a single effective intervention is available for the control of a particular disorder, such as salt iodization for iodine deficiency. This intervention has been implemented as a stand-alone and effective intervention in many countries. However,

TABLE 3.11 **Advantages and disadvantages of scaling up by intervention to full national coverage**

ADVANTAGES	DISADVANTAGES
• Targets the most vulnerable populations across the whole country for the key interventions.	• Not suited to dealing with all of the current nutritional priorities in Egypt (such as obesity).
• Likely to have the largest impact on stunting.	• Determinants for certain nutritional issues can vary by region.
• National media promotion and awareness campaigns can be carried out concurrently as the corresponding services and activities become available nationwide.	• The highest cost of all three approaches to scale-up and sufficient funding may not be forthcoming in the short term.
• Scaling up to full national coverage (rather than by region or intervention) may facilitate speedier legislative and policy action.	• Need for rapid scale-up in implementation capacity.
• This approach could benefit from cross fertilization and synergy of interventions.	

TABLE 3.12 Advantages and disadvantages of scaling up package of interventions by region

ADVANTAGES	DISADVANTAGES
• Targets the most vulnerable populations.	• Not suitable when nutrition issues have widespread prevalence.
• A (minimum) package of essential nutrition interventions can demonstrate important synergies and the need for a multisectoral approach.	• Not suitable if the data available are not representative of regions (for example, data are nationally representative, but not representative at governorate level).
• Could serve as its own pilot and facilitate subsequent scaling up.	• National media promotion and awareness campaigns usually not suitable if corresponding services and activities are only available in limited areas.
• Highest return on investment can be used to showcase the importance of nutrition investment.	• Can create political problems if resources for scaling up are not forthcoming.
• May be possible to spread out investment costs and to focus on oversight and management capacity.	• Difficult to champion for speedy legislative and policy action.
	• Determinants of certain nutrition issues can vary by region.

TABLE 3.13 Advantages and disadvantages of scaling up by intervention

ADVANTAGES	DISADVANTAGES
• Draws national attention and efforts toward a unified goal (such as the schistosomiasis campaigns in the 1980s).	• Not suited to dealing with all of the current nutrition priorities in Egypt (stunting, anemia, and obesity).
• Can potentially demonstrate efficacy and effectiveness, thereby facilitating funding for additional interventions.	• Takes a longer time to achieve complete scale-up of a national nutrition package.
• Efficacy will help gain the support of stakeholders involved in other nutrition-sensitive interventions.	• Other nutrition problems may worsen.
• Can adopt a life cycle sequence, starting with interventions targeting pregnant women, then infants, etc.	• Undermines the multidimensional nature of nutrition.
• Government can continue building capacity as resources become available.	• Does not benefit from cross-fertilization and synergy of interventions.
• Lessons learned for future interventions can benefit from the different regional contexts across Egypt.	
• Mass media campaigns for promotion and awareness can be more focused.	
• Quicker legislative and policy action.	

in most developing nations a sole nutrition problem seldom exists. The fact that nutrients are delivered to bodies through foods in different variations and combinations makes a sole nutrient deficiency fairly uncommon. The different determinants of anemia and the vicious cycle of malnutrition and infection are other examples of how different interventions are often needed to combat a single problem. Thus the decision of what should be prioritized warrants careful consideration. Another approach is to prioritize scale-up of interventions in the package by their perceived cost-effectiveness—that is, which ones will potentially have the biggest impact on reducing stunting, for example, for the lowest cost. This may be an appropriate approach in resource-constrained settings.

Several criteria could be used to determine which interventions should be given priority such as (1) the severity of the public health problem at hand; (2) the estimated costs and benefits; (3) the duration and complexity of the intervention; (4) the infrastructure and human capacity needed; and (5) the speed and feasibility by which a program can be scaled up. The advantages and disadvantages of scale-up by intervention are summarized in table 3.13.

ELEMENTS CRITICAL TO SCALE-UP SUCCESS

Strengthening the health system

Because the majority of the nutrition interventions proposed are delivered through the health system, strengthening of this system is fundamental to the success of a nutrition scale-up plan. The most prominent health platforms in Egypt that deliver the majority of nutrition interventions are antenatal care, well-baby clinic visits, community-based nutrition programs (presently usually child-oriented but can be extended to women), and child health days.

Egypt is set to undergo major health care system reform and health sector restructuring, which is expected to improve public health care dramatically in terms of quality and equity. All the goals associated with improving and strengthening the health system directly affect nutrition, and thus this reform is yet another opportunity to integrate the plan to improve, scale up, and strengthen nutrition programs and interventions (WHO 2007). For example, the health workforce should be trained regularly to conduct routine nutrition screening, documentation of nutrition service delivery, and education and counseling of patients and families. Similarly, the information system should incorporate nutrition indicators and outcomes in routine health services. The WHO health systems framework outlines the necessary health system building blocks and the path to achieving overall goals through quality and safe services. Coverage and access are not sufficient for achieving the outcomes of the WHO strategy if Egyptians do not use the available services and programs. The beneficiary is a key participant in the access/coverage/utilization triangle, and thus advocacy and the sensitization of the community to these services are fundamental.

Multisectoral involvement of ministries and partners

The MOHP is intricately involved in all the interventions selected and particularly the nutrition-specific interventions. However, other ministries will be closely involved and even lead when the health sector is not the main partner. The critical roles and contributions of nonhealth ministries should not be ignored. For example, adequate complementary feeding practices, including the consumption of diverse diets rich in iron and vitamin A, are not translatable into practices if the targeted populations are food-insecure. This demonstrates the role that ministries such as MOALR and MOSS can play. Complementary feeding practices, WASH, and deworming interventions would not be effective without the involvement of MOE, MOALR, and MOWRI. These are only a few examples that illustrate the need for an interministerial nutrition coordinating committee at the national level and multisectoral management committees at the lower administrative levels.

Positioning a multisectoral coordinating committee under the MOHP, as in many African countries, will usually lead to difficulties in convening with other line ministries. This should be avoided, but it is likewise not advisable to marginalize the role of the health sector while health-based nutrition services are still serving as the frontline in preventing and treating the most severe forms of malnutrition. However, they also do not address the whole life cycle of malnutrition nor the underlying and basic causes. This factor demonstrates the need to give the health sector strong support and recognition, while establishing strong leadership across ministries by, for example, having the prime minister serve as the chair of the National Nutrition Coordinating Committee. Work is presently ongoing to update the national nutrition policy and programming frameworks, and it is anticipated that multisectoral and multistakeholder nutrition coordination and management structures and mechanisms will be reviewed and defined as part of this process.

The integration of nutrition indicators across sectors will be critical to developing a common results framework and granting a sense of ownership, responsibility, and eventual accountability. This effort calls for the involvement of the various ministries early in the planning phase and will help identify resource and capacity gaps and prevent shortcomings in the implementation phase. In addition, a broader interagency committee should involve stakeholders from the private sector, civil society organizations (CSOs), international agencies, and NGOs.

NOTES

1. Growth monitoring and promotion is normally not considered a highly effective nutrition intervention, but growth monitoring—if done properly—is normally a good tool to enhance the effectiveness of IYCF and other growth promotion efforts because it will allow the child caretaker and the nurse or nutrition counsellor to jointly see the success of their efforts to safeguard the healthy growth of the child. In Egypt, GMP is still the term preferred for this combined monitoring and promotion activity.
2. *Baladi* bread is the most consumed staple in Egypt and is part of its long-standing food subsidy program. However, it is nontargeted and so operates on a first-come, first-served basis. According to the WFP Analysis of Consumer Profiles and Behaviour Patterns, 80 percent of urban households and 65 percent of rural households consume this bread.
3. The Egypt Strategy Support Program (Egypt SSP) of the International Food Policy Research Institute (IFPRI) is a policy research, capacity strengthening, and communication program that seeks raise the incomes of the rural poor and improve food and nutrition security in Egypt.
4. World Bank, Country Data—Egypt. https://data.worldbank.org/country/egypt-arab-rep.
5. UNICEF Middle East and North Africa Out-of-School Children Initiative, http://www.oosci-mena.org.
6. https://www.egyptianfoodbank.com/en/program/school-feeding-program.
7. Beheira, Dakahliya, Sharkiya, Damietta, Menoufiya, Gharbiya, and Giza.

REFERENCES

Aaron, G. J., A. Laillou, J. Wolfson, and R. Moench-Pfanner. 2012. "Fortification of Staple Cereal Flours with Iron and Other Micronutrients: Cost Implications of Following World Health Organization–Endorsed Recommendations." *Food and Nutrition Bulletin* 33: S336–43.

Aguayo, V. M., K. Paintal, and G. Singh. 2013. "The Adolescent Girls' Anaemia Control Programme: A Decade of Programming Experience to Break the Inter-generational Cycle of Malnutrition in India." *Public Health Nutrition* 16 (9): 1667–76.

Al-Jawaldeh, A., and A. Abul-Fadl. 2018. "Assessment of the Baby Friendly Hospital Initiative Implementation in the Eastern Mediterranean Region." *Children* 5 (3): 41. https://pdfs.semanticscholar.org/e761/a597cdd9be4786caf9d332761a72b3b949bc.pdf.

Allen, L., B. de Benoist, O. Dary, and R. Hurrell, eds. 2006. *Guidelines on Food Fortification with Micronutrients.* Geneva and Rome: WHO (World Health Organization) and FAO (Food and Agriculture Organization).

Ameta, D., and H. El Shafie. 2015. "Social Protection and Safety Nets in Egypt." Institute of Development Studies for the World Food Programme.

Ashour, S., and M. Ahmed. 1994. "Logistic Regression for Social-economic and Cultural Factors Affecting Diarrhea Diseases in Children under Two Years in Egypt." *Egypt Population and Family Planning Review* 28 (1): 1–18.

Bassett, L. 2008. "Can Conditional Cash Transfer Programs Play a Greater Role in Reducing Child Undernutrition?" Social Protection Discussion Paper 0835, World Bank, Washington, DC.

Bhutta, Z. A., T. Ahmed, R. E. Black, S. Cousens, K. Dewey, E. Giugliani, B. A. Haider, B. Kirkwood, S. S. Morris, H. P. S. Sachdev, and M. Shekar. 2008. "What Works? Interventions for Maternal and Child Undernutrition and Survival." *Lancet* 371 (9610): 417–40.

Bhutta, Z. A., J. K. Das, A. Rizvi, M. F. Gaffey, N. Walker, S. Horton, P. Webb, A. Lartey, and R. E. Black. 2013. "Evidence-Based Interventions for Improvement of Maternal and Child Nutrition: What Can Be Done and at What Cost?" *Lancet* 382 (9890): 452–77.

Black, R. E., L. H. Allen, Z. A. Bhutta, L. E. Caulfield, M. de Onis, M. Ezzati, C. Mathers, and J. Rivera. 2008. "Maternal and Child Undernutrition: Global and Regional Exposures and Health Consequences." *Lancet* 371 (9608): 243–60.

Black, R. E., C. G. Victora, S. P. Walker, Z. A. Bhutta, P. Christian, M de Onis, M. Ezzati, S. Grantham-McGregor, J. Katz, R. Martorell, and R. Uauy. 2013. "Maternal and Child Undernutrition and Overweight in Low-Income and Middle-Income Countries." *Lancet* 382 (9890): 427–51. doi:10.1016/S0140-6736(13)60937-X.

Breisinger, C., P. Al-Riffai, O. Ecker, R. Abuismail, J. Waite, N. Abdelwahab, A. Zohery, H. El-Laithy, and D. Armanious. 2013. "Tackling Egypt's Rising Food Insecurity in a Time of Transition." Joint IFPRI-WFP Country Policy Note. IFPRI and WFP, Washington, DC, and Rome.

Breisinger, C., D. Gilligan, N. Karachiwalla, S. Kurdi, H. El-Enbaby, A. H. Jilani, and G. Thai. 2018. "Impact Evaluation Study for Egypt's *Takaful and Karama* Cash Transfer Program: Part 1: Quantitative Report." MENA RP Working Paper 14. Washington, DC, and Cairo, Egypt: International Food Policy Research Institute (IFPRI). http://ebrary.ifpri.org/cdm/ref/collection/p15738coll2/id/132719.

Britto, P. R., S. J. Lye, K. Proulx, A. K. Yousafzai, S. G. Matthews, T. Vaivada, R. Perez-Escamilla, N. Rao, P. Ip, L. C. H. Fernald, H. MacMillan, M. Hanson, T. D. Wachs, H. Yao, H. Yoshikawa, A. Cerezo, J. F. Leckman, Z. A. Bhutta, and Early Childhood Development Interventions Review Group. 2017. "Nurturing Care: Promoting Early Childhood Development." *Lancet* 389 (10064): 91–102.

Calle, E. E. 2008. "Obesity and Cancer." In *Obesity Epidemiology*, edited by F. B. Hu, 196–215. New York: Oxford University Press.

CAPMAS (Central Agency for Public Mobilization and Statistics) and UNICEF (United Nations Children's Fund). 2017. *Children in Egypt 2016: A Statistical Digest.* Cairo: UNICEF.

Caulfield, L. E., M. De Onis, M. Blössner, and R. E. Black. 2004. "Undernutrition as an Underlying Cause of Child Deaths Associated with Diarrhea, Pneumonia, Malaria, and Measles." *American Journal of Clinical Nutrition* 80 (1): 193–98.

Dangour, A. D., L. Watson, O. Cumming, S. Boisson, Y. Che, Y. Velleman, S. Cavill, E. Allen, and R. Uauy. 2013. "Interventions to Improve Water Quality and Supply, Sanitation and Hygiene Practices, and Their Effects on the Nutritional Status of Children." *Cochrane Database of Systemic Reviews* (8): CD009382.

De-Regil, L. M, P. S. Suchdev, G. E. Vist, S. Walleser, and J. P. Peña-Rosas. 2011. "Home Fortification of Foods with Multiple Micronutrient Powders for Health and Nutrition in Children under Two Years of Age." *Cochrane Database of Systemic Reviews* (9): CD008959. doi: 10.1002/14651858.CD008959.pub2.

Elhakim, N., A. Laillou, A. El Nakeeb, R. Yacoub, and M. Shehata. 2012. "Fortifying Baladi Bread in Egypt: Reaching More than 50 Million People through the Subsidy Program." *Food and Nutrition Bulletin* 33: S260–71.

El-Sahn, F. F., A. G. El-Masry, and A. A. El-Sahn. 2003. "Anemia, Parasitic Infections and Some Risk Factors among Physical Education Female Students in Alexandria." *Journal of the Egypt Public Health Association* 78 (3–4):191–207.

El-Zanaty, F., and A. Way. 2009. *Egypt Demographic and Health Survey 2008.* Cairo, Egypt: Ministry of Health Egypt, El-Zanaty and Associates, and Macro International. https://dhsprogram.com/pubs/pdf/FR220/FR220.pdf.

FAO (Food and Agriculture Organization). 2015. *Social Protection and Nutrition in the Food and Agriculture Sector: Suggestions for Programme Designers and Implementers on How to Maximize the Positive Impact of Social Protection Policies and Programmes on Nutrition.* FAO, Rome.

Ferré, C., and I. Sharif. 2014. "Can Conditional Cash Transfers Improve Education and Nutrition Outcomes for Poor Children in Bangladesh? Evidence from a Pilot Project." Policy Research Working Paper 7077, World Bank, Washington, DC.

Fischer Walker, C. L., J. Perin, M. J. Aryee, C. Boschi-Pinto, and R. E. Black. 2012. "Diarrhea Incidence in Low- and Middle-Income Countries in 1990 and 2010: A Systematic Review." *BMC Public Health* 12: 220.

Freeman, M. C., J. V. Garn, G. D. Sclar, S. Boisson, K. Medlicott, K. T. Alexander, G. Penakalapati, D. Anderson, A. G. Mahtani, J. E. T. Grimes, E. A. Rehfuess, and T. F. Clasen. 2017. "The Impact of Sanitation on Infectious Disease and Nutritional Status: A Systematic Review and Meta-analysis" *International Journal of Hygiene and Environmental Health* 220 (6): 928–49.

Gillespie, S., and M. van den Bold. 2017. "Agriculture, Food Systems, and Nutrition: Meeting the Challenge." *Global Challenges* 1 (3). https://doi.org/10.1002/gch2.201600002.

Global BMI Mortality Collaboration. 2016. "Body-Mass Index and All-Cause Mortality: Individual-Participant-Data Meta-analysis of 239 Prospective Studies in Four Continents." *Lancet* 388 (10046): 776–86.

Horta, B. L., C. Loret de Mola, and C. G. Victora. 2015. "Long-term Consequences of Breastfeeding on Cholesterol, Obesity, Systolic Blood Pressure and Type 2 Diabetes: A Systematic Review and Meta-analysis." *Acta Paediatrica* 104 (467): 30–37. doi:10.1111/apa.13133.

Horton, S., and J. Ross. 2003. "The Economics of Iron Deficiency." *Food Policy* 28 (1): 51–75.

Hu, F. B. 2008a. "Metabolic Consequences of Obesity." In *Obesity Epidemiology*, edited by F. B. Hu, 149–73. New York: Oxford University Press.

———. 2008b. "Obesity and Cardiovascular Diseases." In *Obesity Epidemiology*, edited by F. B. Hu, 174–95. New York: Oxford University Press.

Hu, F. B., Y. Liu, and W. C. Willett. 2011. "Preventing Chronic Diseases by Promoting Healthy Diet and Lifestyle: Public Policy Implications for China." *Obesity Reviews* 12 (7): 552–59.

Humphery, J. 2009. "Child Undernutrition, Tropical Enteropathy, Toilets, and Handwashing." *Lancet* 374 (9694): 1032–35.

Hurrell, R. F., M. Reddy, and J. D. Cook. 1999. "Inhibition of Non-haem Iron Absorption in Man by Polyphenolic-Containing Beverages." *British Journal of Nutrition* 81 (4): 289–95.

Hutchesson, M. J., M. E. Rollo, R. Krukowski, L. Ells, J. Harvey, P. J. Morgan, R. Callister, R. Plotnikoff, and C. E. Collins. 2015. "eHealth Interventions for the Prevention and Treatment of Overweight and Obesity in Adults: A Systematic Review with Meta-analysis." *Obesity Reviews* 16 (5): 376–92.

IEA (International Association for the Evaluation of Educational Achievement) and Boston College. 2015. "TIMSS 2015 International Reports." http://timss2015.org/timss-2015 /mathematics/performance-at-international-benchmarks/.

Jomaa, L. H., E. McDonnell, and C. Probart. 2011. "School Feeding Programs in Developing Countries: Impacts on Children's Health and Educational Outcomes." *Nutrition Reviews* 69 (2): 83–98. https://doi.org/10.1111/j.1753-4887.2010.00369.x.

Kavle, J., S. Mehanna, G. Khan, M. Hassan, G. Saleh, and R. Galloway. 2014. "Cultural Beliefs and Perceptions of Maternal Diet and Weight Gain during Pregnancy and Postpartum Family Planning in Egypt." U.S. Agency for International Development, Washington, DC.

Kim, D., and I. Kawachi. 2008. "Obesity and Health-Related Quality of Life." In *Obesity Epidemiology*, edited by F. B. Hu, 234–60. New York: Oxford University Press.

Korayem, K. 2013. "Food Subsidy and the Social Assistance Program in Egypt: Targeting and Efficiency Assessment." *Topics in Middle Eastern and North African Economies* 15.

Kremers, S., A. Reubsaet, M. Martens, S. Gerards, R. Jonkers, M. Candel, I. de Weerdt, and N. de Vries. 2010. "Systematic Prevention of Overweight and Obesity in Adults: A Qualitative and Quantitative Literature Analysis." *Obesity Reviews* 11 (5): 371–79.

Laillou, A., S. A. Hafez, A. H. Mahmoud, M. Mansour, F. Rohner, S. Fortin, J. Berger, N. A. Ibrahim, and R. Moench-Pfanner. 2012. "Vegetable Oil of Poor Quality Is Limiting the Success of Fortification with Vitamin A in Egypt." *Food and Nutrition Bulletin* 33 (3): 186–93.

Lamberti, L. M., C. L. Walker, K. Y. Chan, W.-Y. Jian, and R. E. Black. 2013. "Oral Zinc Supplementation for the Treatment of Acute Diarrhea in Children: A Systematic Review and Meta-Analysis." *Nutrients* 5 (11): 4715–40. doi:10.3390/nu5114715.

Lancet. 2008. *Maternal and Child Undernutrition Series.* https://www.thelancet.com/series /maternal-and-child-undernutrition.

Lancet. 2013. *Maternal and Child Nutrition Series.* https://www.thelancet.com/series/maternal -and-child-nutrition.

Leroy, J. L., M. Ruel, and E. Verhofstadt. 2009. "The Impact of Conditional Cash Transfer Programmes on Child Nutrition: A Review of Evidence Using a Programme Theory Framework." *Journal of Development Effectiveness* 1 (2): 103–29.

López, M. A., and F. C. Martos. 2004. "Iron Availability: An Updated Review." *International Journal of Food Sciences and Nutrition* 55 (8): 597–606.

Luby S., A. Halder, H. Tarique, L. Unicomb, and R. Johnston. 2011. "The Effect of Handwashing at Recommended Times with Water Alone and with Soap on Child Diarrhea in Rural Bangladesh: An Observational Study." *PLOS Medicine* 8 (6).

Malik, V. S., W. C. Willett, and F. B. Hu. 2013. "Global Obesity: Trends, Risk Factors and Policy Implications." *National Review of Endocrinology* 9 (1): 13–27.

Milman, N., T. Paszkowski, I. Cetin, and C. Castelo-Branco. 2016. "Supplementation during Pregnancy: Beliefs and Science." *Gynecological Endocrinology* 32 (7): 509–16.

MOHP (Ministry of Health and Population), El-Zanaty and Associates, and ICF International. 2015. *Egypt Demographic and Health Survey 2014.* Cairo, Egypt and Rockville, MD: Ministry of Health and Population and ICF International. https://dhsprogram.com/pubs/pdf /FR302/FR302.pdf.

MOHP (Ministry of Health and Population), GAIN (Global Alliance for Improved Nutrition), and UNICEF (United Nations Children's Fund). 2016. *Egypt Iodine Survey 2014–2015 Summary Report.* Cairo.

MOHP (Ministry of Health and UNICEF (United Nations Children's Fund). 2017a. *Nutrition Stakeholder and Action Mapping Report.* Cairo: UNICEF. https://www.unnetworkforsun. org/sites/default/files/2018-08/Nutrition%20Stakeholder%20%26%20Action%20 Mapping%20Report-Egypt.pdf.

——. 2017b. *The Integrated Perinatal Health and Nutrition Programme.* Cairo.

Musaiger, A. O., H. M. Al Hazzaa, A. Al-Qahtani, J. Elati, J. Ramadan, N. A. AboulElla, N. Mokhtar, and H. A. Kilani. 2011. "Strategy to Combat Obesity and to Promote Physical Activity in Arab Countries." *Diabetes, Metabolic Syndrome, and Obesity: Targets and Therapy* 4: 89–97.

Oxford Policy Management. 2017. *Evaluation of the Kenya Hunger Safety Net Programme Phase 2: Impact Evaluation Final Report.* Oxford, U.K.: Oxford Policy Management.

Peters, S. A. E., Y. T. van der Schouw, A. M. Wood, M. J. Sweeting, K. G. M. Moons, E. Weiderpass, L. Arriola, V. Benetou, H. Boeing, F. Bonnet, S. T. Butt, F. Clavel-Chapelon, I. Drake, D. Gavrila, T. J. Key, E. Klinaki, V. Krogh, T. Kühn, C. Lassale, G. Masala, G. Matullo, M. Merritt, E. Molina-Portillo, C. Moreno-Iribas, T. H. Nøst, A. Olsen, N. C. Onland-Moret, K. Overvad, S. Panico, M. L. Redondo, A. Tjønneland, A. Trichopoulou, R. Tumino, R. Turzanski-Fortner, I. Tzoulaki, P. Wennberg, A. Winkvist, S. G. Thompson, E. Di Angelantonio, E. Riboli, N. J. Wareham, J. Danesh, and A. S. Butterworth. 2016. Parity, Breastfeeding and Risk of Coronary Heart Disease: A Pan-European Case-Cohort Study. *European Journal of Preventive Cardiology* (16): 1755–65. https://doi.org/10.1177 /2047487316658571.

Pickering, A. J., C. Null, P. J. Winch, G. Mangwadu, B. F. Arnold, A. J. Prendergast, S. M. Njenga, M. Rahman, R. Ntozini, J. Benjamin-Chung, C. P. Stewart, T. M. N. Huda, L. H. Moulton, J. M. Colford, S. P. Luby, J. H. Humphrey. 2019. "The WASH Benefits and SHINE Trials: Interpretation of WASH Intervention Effects on Linear Growth and Diarrhoea." *Lancet Global Health* 7 (8): e1139–46.

Prüss-Ustün, A., J. Bartram, T. Clasen, J. M. Colford, Jr., O. Cumming, V. Curtis, S. Bonjour, A. D. Dangour, J. De France, L. Fewtrell, M. C. Freeman, B. Gordon, P. R. Hunter,

R. B. Johnston, C. Mathers, D. Mäusezahl, K. Medlicott, M. Neira, M. Stocks, J. Wolf, and S. Cairncross. 2014. "Burden of Disease from Inadequate Water, Sanitation and Hygiene in Low- and Middle-Income Settings: A Retrospective Analysis of Data from 145 Countries." *Tropical Medicine and International Health* 19 (8): 894–905. doi: 10.1111/tmi.12329.

Prüss-Üstün A., R. Bos, F. Gore, and J. Bartram. 2008. "Safer Water, Better Health: Costs, Benefits and Sustainability of Interventions to Protect and Promote Health." World Health Organization, Geneva.

Prüss-Üstün, A., and C. Corvalán. 2006. *Preventing Disease through Healthy Environments. Towards an Estimate of the Environmental Burden of Disease.* Geneva: World Health Organization.

Richter, L. M., B. Daelmans, J. Lombardi, J. Heymann, F. Lopez Boo, J. R. Behrman, C. Lu, J. E. Lucas, R. Perez-Escamilla, T. Dua, Z. A. Bhutta, K. Stenberg, P. Gertler, G. L. Darmstadt, the Paper 3 Working Group, and the Lancet Early Childhood Development Series Steering Committee. 2017. "Investing in the Foundation of Sustainable Development: Pathways to Scale Up for Early Childhood Development." *Lancet* 389 (10064): 103–18.

Roushdy, R., M. Sieverding, and H. Radwan. 2012. "The Impact of Water Supply and Sanitation on Child Health: Evidence from Egypt." Poverty, Gender, and Youth Working Paper 24, Population Council, Washington, DC.

Ruel, M. T., and H. Alderman. 2013. "Nutrition-Sensitive Interventions and Programmes: How Can They Help to Accelerate Progress in Improving Maternal and Child Nutrition?" *Lancet* 382 (9891): 536–51. https://doi.org/10.1016/S0140-6736(13)60843-0.

Sanghvi, T. G., P. W. J. Harvey, and E. Wainwright. 2010. "Maternal Iron–Folic Acid Supplementation Programs: Evidence of Impact and Implementation." *Food and Nutrition Bulletin* 31: S100-7.

Save the Children. 2017. *Stolen Childhoods: End of Childhood Report 2017.* Fairfield. https://campaigns.savethechildren.net/sites/campaigns.savethechildren.net/files/report/EndofChildhood_Report_2017_ENGLISH.pdf.

Seidenfeld, D., S. Handa, G. Tembo, S. Michelo, C. Harland Scott, and L. Prencipe. 2014. "The Impact of an Unconditional Cash Transfer on Food Security and Nutrition: The Zambia Child Grant Programme." IDS Special Collection. Institute of Development Studies, University of Sussex, Brighton, U.K. https://core.ac.uk/download/pdf/29135318.pdf.

Sieverding, M., and I. Selwaness. 2012. "Social Protection in Egypt: A Policy Overview." Gender and Work in the MENA Region Working Paper 23, Population Council, Cairo.

Spears, D. 2013. "How Much International Variation in Child Height Can Open Defecation Explain?" Policy Research Working Paper 6351, World Bank, Washington, DC.

SUN Movement. 2010. "Scaling Up Nutrition: A Framework for Action." https://scalingupnutrition.org/wp-content/uploads/2013/05/SUN_Framework.pdf.

Tobias, D. K., M. Chen, J. E. Manson, D. S. Ludwig, W. Willett, and F. B. Hu. 2015. "Effect of Low-Fat Diet Interventions Versus Other Diet Interventions on Long-Term Weight Change in Adults: A Systematic Review and Meta-analysis." *Lancet Diabetes and Endocrinology* 3 (12): 968–79.

UNICEF (United Nations Children's Fund). 2011. *Infant and Young Child Feeding: Programming Guide.* New York. https://www.unicef.org/aids/files/hiv_IYCF_programmingguide_2011.pdf.

UNICEF (United Nations Children's Fund), MOHP (Ministry of Health and Population), and USAID (U.S. Agency for International Development). 2017. "Integrated Perinatal Health and Nutrition (IPHN) in Disadvantaged Areas of Egypt (2012–2017)." Review and Documentation of Program Evolution and Learning, UNICEF, Egypt.

UNICEF (United Nations Childen's Fund) and WHO (World Health Organization). 2011. *Drinking Water: Equity, Safety and Sustainability.* JMP Thematic Report on Drinking Water. New York/Geneva.

USAID (U.S. Agency for International Development). 2015. "WASH and Nutrition Water Development Strategies." Implementation Brief. https://www.usaid.gov/sites/default/files/documents/1865/WASH_Nutrition_Implementation_Brief_Jan_2015.pdf.

——. 2017. "Egypt Programme Overview—Agriculture." https://www.usaid.gov/sites/default/files/documents/1883/5_USAIDEgypt_Agriculture_Fact_Sheet_Sep2017_EG_OK.pdf.

Victora, C. G., M. de Onis, P. C. Hallal, M. Blössner, and R. Shrimpton. 2010. "Worldwide Timing of Growth Faltering: Revisiting Implications for Interventions." *Pediatrics* 125 (3): e473–e480. doi:10.1542/peds.2009-1519.

WFP (World Food Programme). 2016. "Egyptian Government to Expand National School Feeding Programme to Reach All Public Schools." News Release. https://www.wfp.org /news/news-release/egyptian-government-expand-national-school-feeding-programme -reach-all-public-scho.

WHO (World Health Organization). 2005. *Handbook: IMCI Integrated Management of Childhood Illness.* Geneva: WHO. https://apps.who.int/iris/handle/10665/42939.

WHO (World Health Organization), FAO (Food and Agriculture Organization), UNICEF (United Nations Children's Fund), GAIN (Global Alliance for Improved Nutrition), MI (Micronutrient Initiative), and FFI. 2009. "Recommendations on Wheat and Maize Flour Fortification. Meeting Report: Interim Consensus Statement." WHO, Geneva. http://www .who.int/nutrition/publications/micronutrients/wheat_maize_fort.pdf.

WHO (World Health Organization) and UNICEF (United Nations Children's Fund). 2003. *Global Strategy for Infant and Young Child Feeding.* Geneva: WHO.

——. 2004. "Clinical Management of Acute Diarrhea." WHO/UNICEF Joint Statement (2004), Geneva and New York, May.

——. 2007. *Everybody's Business: Strengthening Health Systems to Improve Health Outcomes: WHO's Framework for Action.* Geneva: WHO. http://www.who.int/healthsystems/strategy /everybodys_business.pdf.

——. 2009. *Baby Friendly Hospital Initiative: Revised, Updated and Expanded for Integrated Care.* Geneva/New York. http://www.who.int/nutrition/publications/infantfeeding/bfhi_ trainingcourse_s1/en/.

——. 2011a. *Guideline: Intermittent Iron Supplementation for Preschool and School-Age Children.* Geneva: WHO. http://apps.who.int/iris/bitstream/10665/44648/1/9789241502009_eng.pdf.

——. 2011b. *Guideline: Vitamin A Supplementation in Infants and Children 6–59 Months of Age.* Geneva: WHO.

——. 2013a. *Global Action Plan for the Prevention and Control of Noncommunicable Diseases 2013–2020.* Geneva: WHO.

——. 2013b. *Guideline: Updates on the Management of Severe Acute Malnutrition in Infants and Children.* Geneva: WHO.

——. 2016a. *Guideline: Daily Iron Supplementation in Infants and Children.* Geneva: WHO.

——. 2016b. *WHO Recommendations on Antenatal Care for a Positive Pregnancy Experience.* Geneva: WHO.

——. 2017a. *National Implementation of the Baby-Friendly Hospital Initiative 2017.* Geneva: WHO.

——. 2017b. *Guideline: Preventive Chemotherapy to Control Soil-Transmitted Helminth Infections in At-risk Population Groups.* Geneva: WHO.

WHO (World Health Organization), UNICEF (United Nations Children's Fund), and WFP (World Food Programme). 2014. "Global Nutrition Targets 2025: Wasting Policy Brief." WHO/NMH/NHD/14.8, Geneva.

World Bank. 2018a. "Egypt—Sustainable Rural Sanitation Services Program: Additional Financing." Environmental and Social Systems Assessment (English), World Bank, Washington, DC. http://documents.worldbank.org/curated/en/174281528990876317 /Environmental-and-social-systems-assessment.

——. 2018b. "The Story of Takaful and Karama Cash Transfer Program." November 15. https:// www.worldbank.org/en/news/feature/2018/11/15/the-story-of-takaful-and-karama-cash -transfer-program.

Yan, J., L. Liu, Y. Zhu, G. Huang, and P. P. Wang. 2014. "The Association Between Breastfeeding and Childhood Obesity: A Meta-analysis." *BMC Public Health* 14: 1267.

4 Cost-Effectiveness of Potential Scale-Up Scenarios in Egypt

DAVIDE DE BENI

KEY MESSAGES

- This chapter analyzes the three scale-up scenarios outlined in chapter 3, calculating the cost, expected cost-benefits, and cost-effectiveness to determine which will bring the greatest returns.
- Because of the methodology used (LiST Model), only 13 of the 16 chosen interventions could be modeled against the three scale-up scenarios (full national coverage, interventions by region, prioritization of interventions).
- To reach the highest number of stunted children, Egypt should prioritize funding the most cost-effective interventions, which achieves the same result as full coverage: infant and young child feeding (especially promoting complementary feeding), iron–folic acid supplementation, vitamin A supplementation of children, and promotion of hygienic disposal of children's stools (421,360 cases of stunting averted).
- When comparing costs and benefits, if the main priority is the reduction of stunting, delivering only the most cost-effective interventions to reduce stunting provides better value for the money (cost per death prevented, $19,412; cost per stunting case prevented, $196).
- Giving priority to implementation of the most cost-effective interventions for stunting reduction is estimated to translate into and return the highest economic benefits over the productive lives of children who receive the interventions (a return of $17.87 in economic benefits for each dollar invested).
- However, focusing only on those interventions that are most effective in reducing stunting will not have any impact on the current levels of wasting and will only prevent 4,249 additional deaths (30 percent of the full national coverage scenario).

INTRODUCTION

This chapter analyzes the three scenarios for scaling up selected nutrition interventions described in chapter 3 and calculates the cost, expected cost-benefits (including possibly the social returns on investments), and cost-effectiveness. The objectives of this analysis are as follows:

- To estimate the costs of a set of nutrition interventions that have the potential to be scaled up through tested delivery mechanisms in Egypt
- To conduct a basic economic analysis to calculate the potential benefits and cost effectiveness associated with the proposed scale-up
- To estimate the economic benefits of scaling up nutrition interventions in Egypt
- To propose a series of scenarios for a costed scale-up plan that rolls out this package of nutrition interventions in phases, based on considerations of impact, geography, implementation capacity, and costs.

METHODOLOGY

Scope of the analysis and description of the interventions

The following estimates of the costs and benefits of scaling up a set of selected nutrition-specific and nutrition-sensitive interventions are based on those discussed in chapter 3. Table 3.10 in chapter 3 outlines the 16 elected interventions, which are mostly supported by scientific evidence on their potential impact on stunting, particularly from the 2008 and 2013 *Lancet* series on maternal and child nutrition, and which have the potential to be scaled up rapidly in Egypt using the existing mechanisms and infrastructure. As for other interventions discussed in chapter 3, either evidence is lacking on their effectiveness to reduce child malnutrition, or in some cases potentially effective programs are still being developed, such as those targeting overweight, or are being evaluated, such as the Takaful conditional cash transfer (CCT) program.

Furthermore, of the 16 interventions that could effectively be scaled up, not all can be modeled using the impact tool adopted for this study. The Lives Saved Tool (LiST) estimates the global health impacts of scaling up key interventions by modeling outcomes around neonatal, child, and maternal mortality and birth outcomes and nutrition outcomes, among others. Its wide range of interventions include periconceptual, pregnancy, childbirth, breastfeeding, preventive, vaccines, and curative.

Of the 16 selected interventions, 13 are modeled in LiST as shown in table 4.1 with the associated target groups. These interventions are grouped into four separate packages that are in line with the groups of key interventions in the LiST model that can have an impact on specific outcomes: (1) infant and young child feeding (IYCF) and micronutrients; (2) curative interventions; (3) disease prevention and management; and (4) water, sanitation, and hygiene (WASH). The three interventions not modeled in LiST are growth monitoring and promotion, iron supplementation for children 6–59 months of age, and deworming. The associated drawbacks of this methodological limitation are discussed later in this chapter.

The expenditures estimated in this model are the financial costs of the goods and services required to deliver each of the interventions from a supply-side prospective.[1] They do not reflect the full economic and social value of how resources could be used differently, such as the opportunity costs (for example, lost wages) of the time spent by beneficiaries seeking and accessing health services.

TABLE 4.1 **Nutrition-specific and nutrition-sensitive interventions included in the analysis**

INTERVENTION	DESCRIPTION	TARGET POPULATION
Infant and young child feeding (IYCF) and micronutrients		
1. Promotion and support of breastfeeding	Communication of optimal breastfeeding practices	Pregnant women and mothers of children 0-6 months
2. Promotion of complementary feeding	Communication of complementary feeding practices (excluding provision of food)	Mothers of children 6–23 months
3. Iron–folic acid supplementation	Three months supplementation of iron–folic acid during pregnancy	Pregnant women
4. Vitamin A supplementation (children)	Biannual supplementation of vitamin A capsules[a]	Children 6–59 months
Curative interventions (MAM/SAM)		
5. Treatment of moderate acute malnutrition (MAM)	Treatment of MAM in supplementary feeding programs	Children 6–59 months
6. Management of severe acute malnutrition (SAM)	Severely malnourished children admitted to either inpatient or outpatient therapeutic feeding programs	Children 6–59 months
Disease prevention and management		
7. Treatment of diarrhea (ORS)	Management of mild and moderate diarrhea with oral rehydration solution (ORS)	Children 6–59 months
8. Therapeutic zinc supplementation	As part of diarrhea management with ORS	Children 6–59 months
Water, sanitation, and hygiene (WASH)		
9. Use of improved water source	Regulation and advocacy activities to ensure access to water supply services from an "improved" source within 1 kilometer of the user's dwelling. An improved source is one that is likely to provide "safe" water	All households
10. Use of water connection in home	Regulation and advocacy activities to ensure access to safe water from a household connection	All households
11. Improved excreta disposal (latrine/toilet)	Promotional activities to ensure access to improved/hygienic excreta disposal (access to improved latrine or flush toilet)	All households
12. Hand washing with soap	Promotional activities for "appropriate" hand washing behavior	All households
13. Hygienic disposal of children's stools	Promotional activities for the proper disposal of children's stools	All households

a. The cost-effectiveness analysis of vitamin A supplementation is based on optimal implementation of the biannual protocol as recommended by World Health Organization (WHO) guidelines: one-time vitamin A (100,000 international units, IU) for infants 6–11 months (one dose) per first year and one-time vitamin A (200,000 IU) for children 12–59 months every four to six months. At the time of writing this report, the 200,000 IU dose is given in Egypt only once, at 18 months, instead of two times as per the WHO recommendations.

Scale-up scenarios and coverage levels

This economic analysis of the three scale-up scenarios for increasing coverage of selected nutrition interventions uses 2017 as a baseline year and considers the five-year time frame 2018–22. The three scenarios are defined as follows:

1. *Scale up by intervention to full national coverage:* 90 percent of currently implemented interventions—80 percent for moderate acute malnutrition (MAM)/severe acute malnutrition (SAM) interventions, (scenario 1)

2. *Scale up by region:* prioritize full package only in region group with highest burden of stunting (scenario 2)

3. *Scale up by prioritizing interventions:* scale up to full national coverage the most cost-effective interventions to reduce stunting (scenario 3).

An additional scenario would consist of simply maintaining the current coverage of the existing interventions.

The analysis assumes that coverage for each intervention increases linearly at a constant rate from the baseline year (2017) to the target coverage rates over the five-year period to 2022, as described in table 4.2. The current baseline coverage levels were obtained from different sources. In the absence of most recent data, the 2014 Egypt Demographic and Health Survey (EDHS 2014) was maintained as the primary official reference (MOHP, El-Zanaty and Associates, and ICF International 2015), and the *Nutrition Stakeholder and Action Mapping Report* was used as an additional resource where necessary (MOHP and UNICEF 2017).

Methodology for calculating unit costs for each intervention

The default treatment inputs and prices used in this analysis are global standards not specific to Egypt. Unit costs for each intervention were obtained from the OneHealth Tool[2] costing module, which provides a way to estimate the financial and human resources required to deliver nutrition services to beneficiaries.

Intervention unit costs include the required drugs and consumable supplies (such as gloves and syringes), direct staff time, and number of inpatient days and outpatient visits needed to effectively provide an intervention. These factors are drawn from the intervention assumptions developed for the OneHealth Tool,

TABLE 4.2 Baseline and target coverage rates per intervention

INTERVENTION	BASELINE COVERAGE (2017)	SOURCE	FULL NATIONAL COVERAGE
Infant and young child feeding (IYCF) and micronutrients			
1. Breastfeeding promotion and support	62.0%	Nutrition Stakeholder and Action Mapping Report, 2017	90.0%
2. Complementary feeding promotion	62.0%	Nutrition Stakeholder and Action Mapping Report, 2017	90.0%
3. Iron-folic acid supplementation (pregnant women)	36.1%	Egypt Demographic and Health Survey (EDHS) 2014	90.0%
4. Vitamin A supplementation (children)	75.0%	Nutrition Stakeholder and Action Mapping Report, 2017	90.0%
Curative interventions (SAM/MAM)			
5. Treatment of moderate acute malnutrition (MAM)	0.0%	New intervention	80.0%
6. Management of severe acute malnutrition (SAM)	0.0%	New intervention	80.0%
Disease prevention and management			
7. Treatment of diarrhea (ORS)	28.4%	EDHS 2014	90.0%
8. Therapeutic zinc supplementation	0.3%	UNICEF, Egypt	90.0%
Water, sanitation, and hygiene (WASH)			
9. Use of improved water source	97.8%	EDHS 2014	97.7%
10. Use of water connection in home	90.9%	EDHS 2014	90.9%
11. Improved excreta disposal	90.1%	EDHS 2014	90.1%
12. Hand washing with soap	96.1%	UNICEF, Egypt	96.1%
13. Hygienic disposal of children's stools	60.8%	EDHS 2014	90.0%

Sources: EDHS 2014 (MOHP, El-Zanaty and Associates, and ICF International 2015); *Nutrition Stakeholder and Action Mapping Report* (MOHP and UNICEF 2017).
Note: ORS = oral rehydration solution.

based on the World Health Organization (WHO) norms and guidelines where available, and from expert input where explicit guidance was not available. Drugs and consumable supply prices are extracted from international sources such as the MSH Drug Price Indicator Guide, UNICEF supply catalogue, and the Global Price Reporting Mechanism. Staff cost data are based on assumptions for salaries, benefits, and time utilization drawn from WHO-CHOICE (Choosing Interventions that Are Cost-Effective).[3] These data points are used to estimate a cost per minute for delivering the various interventions.

Program costs are added to unit costs as a percentage of direct costs (such as for drugs and supplies and staff time), and they are intended to capture the service delivery costs associated with the interventions. These costs include those for training, supervision, monitoring and evaluation, equipment, advocacy and communication, and media and outreach. Default program cost categories and percentages have been provided based on the Scaling Up Nutrition (SUN) nutrition plan costing exercises, the Education Program for Immunization Competencies (EPIC) immunization studies, and WHO (see details in table 4.3).

The unit costs for the 13 interventions analyzed in this study appear in table 4.4.

Methodology for calculating total and annual scale-up costs

The analysis estimates the costs of increasing coverage of a set of nutrition interventions in Egypt from the current coverage rates to target rates defined for each scale-up scenario. The total scale-up costs per intervention (or set of interventions) over the five-year period are obtained by the product of the unit costs and the number of cases (beneficiaries) per intervention per year

$$total \ scale\text{-}up \ costs = UC * NC$$

TABLE 4.3 **Default program cost categories and percentages**

CATEGORY	PERCENTAGE	SOURCE
Program-specific human resources	1	Lives Saved Tool (LiST)
Training	1	EPIC studies
Supervision	2	EPIC studies
Monitoring and evaluation	2	EPIC studies
Infrastructure	2	NASA
Transport	2	Comprehensive vaccine planning (WHO)
Communication, media, and outreach	1	SUN-costed nutrition plans
Advocacy	1	EPIC studies
General program management	2	EPIC studies
Community health worker training	1	Expert estimates (no data)
Total	**15**	

Note: EPIC = Education Program for Immunization Competencies; NASA = National AIDS Spending Assessment; SUN = Scaling Up Nutrition; WHO = World Health Organization.

TABLE 4.4 Unit costs per average case by intervention

INTERVENTION	TARGET POPULATION	UNIT COST (US$)
Promotion and support of breastfeeding	Pregnant women and mothers of children 0–6 months	8.47
Promotion of complementary feeding	Mothers of children 6–23 months	3.45
Iron–folic acid supplementation	Pregnant women	3.36
Vitamin A supplementation (children)	Children 6–59 months	1.68
Treatment of moderate acute malnutrition (MAM)	Children 6–59 months	53.89
Management of severe acute malnutrition (SAM)	Children 6–59 months	201.47
Treatment of diarrhea (oral rehydration solution)	Children 6–59 months	1.43
Therapeutic zinc supplementation	Children 6–59 months	4.26
Use of improved water source	All households	0.51
Use of water connection in home	All households	0.51
Improved excreta disposal (latrine/toilet)	All households	0.51
Hand washing with soap	All households	0.51
Hygienic disposal of children's stools	All households	0.51

Source: Unit costs: WHO OneHealth Tool, http://www.who.int/choice/onehealthtool/en/.

where *UC* is the unit cost of the intervention, and *NC* is the number of cases per intervention each year.

The *number of cases per intervention each year* is based on the size of the target population, population in need, and coverage rates as expressed by

number of cases = size of target population * population in need (%) * coverage (%)

where *target population* is defined as the population that could possibly receive the intervention. Examples of target populations include pregnant women and children 6–59 months of age. *Population in need (%)* is the share of the target population requiring the intervention per year. For most preventive care interventions, the share will be 100 percent. For example, daily iron and folic acid supplementation will be required for all pregnant women. The population in need can be interpreted as the incidence and prevalence of conditions for interventions such as treatment of MAM or SAM. *Coverage (%)* refers to how many people in the population in need are receiving the intervention. It indicates the baseline intervention coverage of the population in need and targeted scale-up over the selected five-year period.

Estimating benefits and cost-effectiveness

LiST (version 5.61) is used to calculate the expected effects of each scale-up scenario on the under-5 mortality rate, number of lives saved, prevalence of stunting and wasting among children under 5, prevalence of exclusive breastfeeding, prevalence of anemia in pregnant women, and disability-adjusted life years (DALYs) saved. LiST is an epidemiological model created as part of the work undertaken for the 2003 *Lancet* child survival series. It estimates the impact of expanding coverage of maternal and child health and nutrition interventions on the mortality, morbidity, and nutritional status of children under 5. The estimation of DALYs averted for each intervention and scale-up scenario is based on Bhutta et al. (2008): one life saved equals 33 DALYs averted; one case of stunting averted equals 0.23 DALYs averted.

Cost-effectiveness analysis is used to identify the interventions and scale-up scenarios that produce the most impact for the least cost. Ratios of costs to estimates of impact are calculated for (1) deaths prevented in children under 5 (Lives Saved), (2) cases of stunting averted, and (3) number of DALYs averted. The scale-up scenario with the lowest cost per benefit is considered to be the most cost-effective among the alternatives under analysis. The evaluation of the cost-effectiveness ratio in absolute terms is based on the categorization used by WHO-CHOICE.[4]

Estimating economic benefits

The cost-benefit analysis is based on the estimated economic value of the benefits attributable to the reductions in under-5 mortality and stunting prevalence, which in turn are attributable to scaling up the nutrition interventions contained in each scenario. LiST is used to estimate the number of lives saved and the reduction in stunting prevalence. Following established practice, a life year saved is valuated as equivalent to gross domestic product (GDP) per capita (current U.S. dollars, 2015). This is a conservative measure because it accounts only for the economic and not the social value of a year of life. To estimate the economic benefits generated from the reductions in stunting prevalence, the methodology used in Hoddinott et al. (2013) is applied, which valuates a year of life lived without stunting as a 21 percent increase in wage earnings.

Limitations of the methodology used

The cost estimates presented in this study are highly dependent on the assumptions made in terms of health status, nutrition indicators, and current coverage of the interventions. In the absence of more recent data, EDHS 2014 is maintained as the primary official reference even though it does not reflect the latest nutrition programs in Egypt (MOHP, El-Zanaty and Associates, and ICF International 2015). The *Nutrition Stakeholder and Action Mapping Report* of 2016 is used for coverage data not available in EDHS 2014 (MOHP and UNICEF 2017).

Unit costs for each intervention are obtained from the OneHealth Tool costing module and are not specific to the Egyptian context. These costs are drawn from intervention assumptions developed for the OneHealth Tool, adopting the so-called ingredient approach, and based on WHO norms and guidelines. This methodology has the disadvantage of potentially underestimating the real cost of implementing the programs in Egypt and potentially omitting wastages or inefficiencies. Furthermore, the study team added program costs as a fixed percentage of direct costs. It is then not possible to account for the potential economy of scale or the need to expand capital costs to account for significant scaling up of program activities over a relatively short period.

As described in the introduction to this chapter, this analysis only estimates the costs and benefits of those interventions currently modeled in LiST, which includes only 13 of the 16 interventions outlined in chapter 3 as having the most potential to be scaled up in the short to medium term to substantially improve the nutrition situation in Egypt. Therefore, because of data and methodological shortcomings, this analysis cannot produce the full scale of the potential benefits of scaling up the packages of nutrition interventions described and discussed in this report.

FINDINGS

Cost of scaling up nutrition in Egypt

Estimation of spending at current coverage level (2017)

The total estimated resources required for maintaining current coverage of the existing interventions for the period 2018–22 is $561 million, or an average of $112 million a year (table 4.5). The high cost required to implement the WASH package ($54 million a year) is driven by the high coverage assumptions used for this set of interventions. IYCF and micronutrients cost $39 million a year, of which $16 million is required to maintain the current coverage of vitamin A supplementation for children—estimated at 75 percent in the *Nutrition Stakeholder and Action Mapping Report* (MOHP and UNICEF 2017). Despite the relatively low coverage of therapeutic zinc supplementation (0.3 percent, according to UNICEF Egypt) because of its relatively high unit cost ($4.26 to treat one child a year), $14 million a year is required to maintain the current coverage. The management of acute malnutrition (MAM/SAM) is currently not implemented at scale in Egypt, and therefore no costs are included in the table.

Figure 4.1 shows the breakdown of the current annual requirements by governorate. About 50 percent of the estimated annual resources are allocated to seven governorates (Giza, Cairo, Beheira, Sharqia, Dakahlia, Asyut, and Qalyubia) because of the large size of their populations of children under 5 and pregnant women and their high burden of stunting and coverage of interventions. The significant allocation of resources for Beheira and Asyut is driven by high coverage of disease prevention and management interventions, particularly those for the treatment of diarrhea.

TABLE 4.5 Total and annual costs for current coverage scenario

CURRENT COVERAGE SCENARIO	TOTAL COST (LE, MILLIONS)	ANNUAL COST (LE, MILLIONS)	TOTAL COST (US$, MILLIONS)	ANNUAL COST (US$, MILLIONS)
Infant and young child feeding (IYCF) and micronutrients	**3,550**	**710**	**197**	**39**
Promotion and support of breastfeeding	857	171	48	10
Promotion of complementary feeding	1,077	215	60	12
Iron–folic acid supplementation	219	44	12	2
Vitamin A supplementation (children)	1,397	279	78	16
Management of acute malnutrition	—	—	—	—
Treatment of moderate acute malnutrition (MAM)	—	—	—	—
Management of severe acute malnutrition (SAM)	—	—	—	—
Disease prevention and management	**1,679**	**336**	**93**	**19**
Treatment of diarrhea (oral rehydration solution)	422	84	23	5
Therapeutic zinc supplementation	1,257	251	70	14
Water, sanitation, and hygiene (WASH)	**4,867**	**973**	**270**	**54**
Use of improved water source	1,092	218	61	12
Use of water connection in home	1,016	203	56	11
Improved excreta disposal (latrine/toilet)	1,007	201	56	11
Hand washing with soap	1,074	215	60	12
Hygienic disposal of children's stools	679	136	38	8
Total current coverage scenario	**10,096**	**2,019**	**561**	**112**

Source: Based on unit costs from the WHO OneHealth Tool, http://www.who.int/choice/onehealthtool/en/.
Note: Because the management of acute malnutrition (MAM/SAM) is currently not implemented at scale in Egypt, no costs are included in the table. LE = Egyptian pound.

FIGURE 4.1

Estimated annual expenditure by governorate of maintaining interventions at current coverage

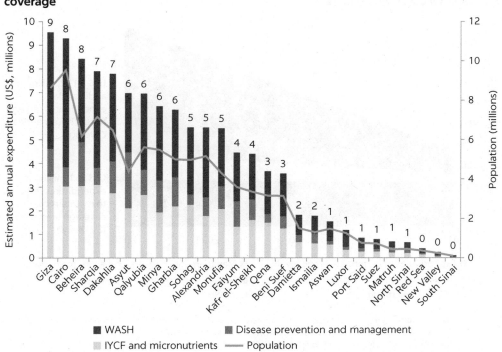

Source: Estimated annual expenditures based on unit costs obtained from the WHO OneHealth Tool, http://www.who.int/choice/onehealthtool/en/. Population: UN 2017.
Note: Percentage of annual expenditures by governorate appears above bars. IYCF = infant and young child feeding; WASH = water, sanitation, and hygiene.

Estimation of costs for full coverage (scenario 1)

Scaling up the existing package of nutrition interventions to full national coverage (90 percent) and implementing the treatment of MAM and SAM nationwide to 80 percent coverage will require an additional $1,132 million over the period 2018–22 (figure 4.2).

For this scenario, disease prevention and management and the treatment of acute malnutrition would account for the biggest expenditure increase (table 4.6). The cost rise for the disease prevention and management category is explained by the scaling up of zinc supplementation, from 0.3 percent to 90 percent coverage, because of the high number of beneficiaries to reach and the relatively high unit cost of this intervention ($4.26). For the same reasons, MAM/SAM treatment would require significant financial resources ($61 million a year).

WASH's financial requirement will not change substantially over current coverage because it is already implemented at scale throughout the nation (according to current coverage rates). Reaching 90 percent coverage nationwide for IYCF and micronutrient interventions would require an additional $52 million per year.

Ensuring full national coverage is based on the anticipated increases in capacity levels as the interventions are implemented. To ensure that adequate capacity is developed, 15 percent of the additional cost of interventions ($30 million a year) is added to invest in strengthening the health system to address malnutrition across sectors.

FIGURE 4.2

Annual financing requirements of maintaining current interventions and expanding to full national coverage by 2022

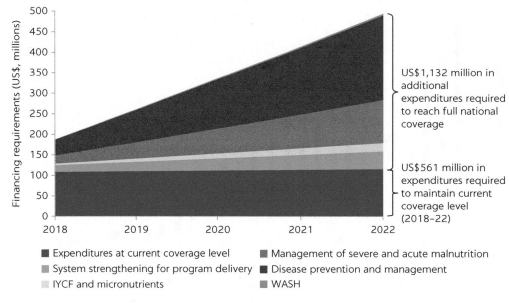

US$1,132 million in additional expenditures required to reach full national coverage

US$561 million in expenditures required to maintain current coverage level (2018–22)

- ■ Expenditures at current coverage level
- ■ System strengthening for program delivery
- ■ IYCF and micronutrients
- ■ Management of severe and acute malnutrition
- ■ Disease prevention and management
- ■ WASH

Source: Financing requirements based on unit costs obtained from the WHO OneHealth Tool, http://www.who .int/choice/onehealthtool/en/, and population projections from UN 2017.
Note: IYCF = infant and young child feeding; WASH = water, sanitation, and hygiene.

TABLE 4.6 Total and annual costs for full national coverage scenario

FULL NATIONAL COVERAGE SCENARIO	TOTAL COST (LE, MILLIONS)	ANNUAL COST (LE, MILLIONS)	TOTAL COST (US$, MILLIONS)	ANNUAL COST (US$, MILLIONS)
Infant young child feeding and micronutrients	**4,643**	**929**	**258**	**52**
Promotion and support of breastfeeding	1,176	235	65	13
Promotion of complementary feeding	1,489	298	83	17
Iron–folic acid supplementation	419	84	23	5
Vitamin A supplementation (children)	1,559	312	87	17
Management of acute malnutrition	**5,527**	**1,105**	**307**	**61**
Treatment of moderate acute malnutrition (MAM)	701	140	39	8
Management of severe acute malnutrition (SAM)	4,826	965	268	54
Disease prevention and management	**12,587**	**2,517**	**699**	**140**
Treatment of diarrhea (oral rehydration solution)	3,163	633	176	35
Therapeutic zinc supplementation	9,424	1,885	524	105
Water, sanitation, and hygiene (WASH)	**5,065**	**1,013**	**281**	**56**
Use of improved water source	1,092	218	61	12
Use of water connection in home	1,016	203	56	11
Improved excreta disposal (latrine/toilet)	1,007	201	56	11
Hand washing with soap	1,074	215	60	12
Hygienic disposal of children's stools	877	175	49	10
System strengthening for program delivery	**2,659**	**532**	**148**	**30**
Total, full national coverage scenario	**30,481**	**6,096**	**1,693**	**339**

Source: Based on unit costs from the WHO OneHealth Tool, http://www.who.int/choice/onehealthtool/en/.
Note: LE = Egyptian pound.

Benefits of scaling up nutrition in Egypt

Estimating health and nutrition impacts using the Lives Saved Tool (LiST)

Using LiST, the expected benefits of the nutrition interventions contained in each scale-up scenario are assessed in terms of the (1) under-5 mortality rate; (2) number of lives saved; (3) cases and prevalence of stunting; (4) prevalence of wasting among children under 5; (5) prevalence of anemia in pregnant women; and (6) exclusive breastfeeding prevalence. LiST predicts changes for each of these rates and prevalence using changes in coverage of each intervention for the period considered in the analysis, 2018–22. Expected benefits are computed using a deterministic mathematical model based on the best available scientific evidence of the cause-specific effectiveness estimates for each intervention. For each of the packages of interventions modeled in this analysis, the specific pathways and the relationships between interventions and outcomes used in LiST are shown in figures 4.3, 4.4, 4.5, and 4.6.

FIGURE 4.3

LiST underlying model for estimating impacts of nutrition preventive interventions: IYCF and micronutrients

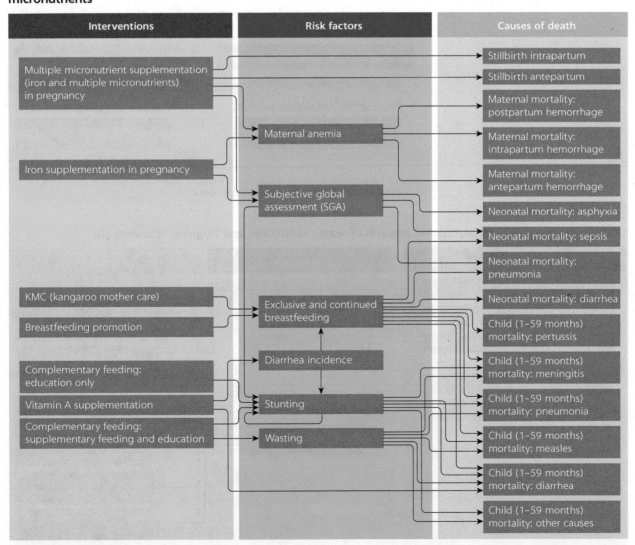

Source: https://listvisualizer.org/, © Lives Saved Tool (LiST). Reproduced with permission from Lives Saved Tool (LiST); further permission required for reuse.
Note: IYCF = infant and young child feeding.

FIGURE 4.4

LiST underlying model for estimating impacts of nutrition curative interventions: MAM and SAM

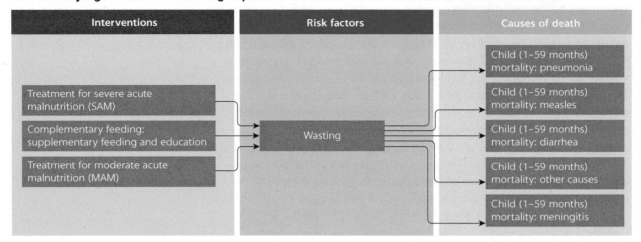

Source: https://listvisualizer.org/, © Lives Saved Tool (LiST). Reproduced with permission from Lives Saved Tool (LiST); further permission required for reuse.
Note: MAM = moderate acute malnutrition; SAM = severe acute malnutrition.

FIGURE 4.5

LiST underlying model for estimating impacts of maternal, neonatal, and child health interventions

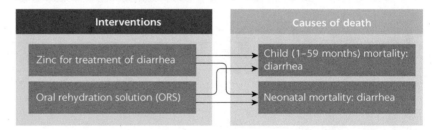

Source: https://listvisualizer.org/, © Lives Saved Tool (LiST). Reproduced with permission from Lives Saved Tool (LiST); further permission required for reuse.

FIGURE 4.6

LiST underlying model for estimating impacts of water, sanitation, and hygiene interventions

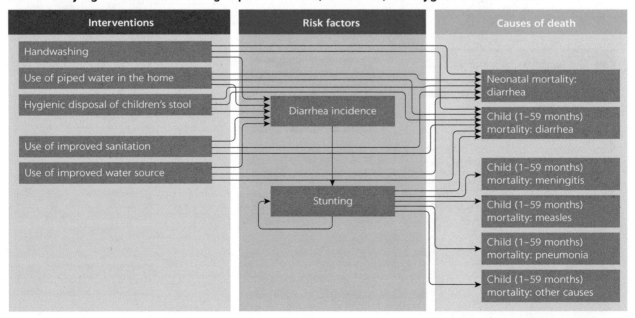

Source: https://listvisualizer.org/, © Lives Saved Tool (LiST). Reproduced with permission from Lives Saved Tool (LiST); further permission required for reuse.

In LiST, the nutrition preventive interventions (including IYCF and micronutrients) have an impact on child and neonatal mortality through their effect on stunting, diarrhea incidence, and maternal anemia. The following risk factors are thought to have a direct impact on several child (1–59 months) and neonatal causes of morbidity and mortality: measles, meningitis, pneumonia, diarrhea, sepsis, congenital anomalies, and other causes[5] (figure 4.3). As mentioned earlier in this chapter, GMP, salt iodization, and deworming are not currently modeled in LiST. Thus estimates of the real impacts of implementing the full preventive package on nutritional status and child mortality may be underestimated.

The package of curative interventions includes the treatment of moderate and severe acute malnutrition (MAM/SAM). According to the LiST model, these interventions have an indirect positive effect on reduction of child mortality through wasting (Bhutta et al. 2013; Lenters et al. 2013). Complementary feeding (supplementation of food and education), which is included in the package of nutrition preventive interventions, also appears in figure 4.3 because of its impact on wasting. In the LiST model, wasting increases a child's risk of dying from five specific causes of mortality: pneumonia, meningitis, measles, diarrhea, and other causes (figure 4.4). This also means that children wasted will be much more likely to die in a country or region where the incidence of diarrhea, pneumonia, and measles is high than in an area where the prevalence of those diseases is low.

The maternal, neonatal, and child health (MNCH) interventions considered in this analysis—oral rehydration solution (ORS) and zinc for the treatment of diarrhea—have a direct impact on the reduction of diarrhea as a cause-specific mortality condition for children 0–59 months of age. In Egypt, diarrhea is one of the leading causes of death in children under 5 (11 percent of child deaths are from diarrhea).[6] Therefore, in this model the treatment of diarrhea with ORS and zinc is particularly effective in the reduction of child mortality (figure 4.5).

The two leading causes of mortality among children under 5 in Egypt, pneumonia and diarrhea, are closely linked to poor water, sanitation, and hygiene. For the WASH interventions, the LiST model assumes an indirect effect on stunting through a direct reduction of diarrhea incidence for the five interventions included in this analysis: use of improved water source, use of water connection in home, improved excreta disposal, handwashing with soap, and hygienic disposal of children's stools (Cairncross et al. 2010; Cairncross and Valdmanis 2006). In the model, as for the package of curative nutrition interventions, stunting and diarrhea incidence increase a child's risk of dying from five specific causes of mortality: pneumonia, meningitis, measles, diarrhea, and other causes (figure 4.6).

Current evidence suggests that WASH can also bring significant gains in tackling childhood undernutrition (Cumming and Cairncross 2016). Studies that specifically address maternal and child environmental exposures are currently under way, and they will permit the quantification of both the independent effect of WASH interventions on stunting and the combined effect of WASH and food supplementation interventions—the so-called Sanitation, Hygiene, Infant Nutrition Efficacy (SHINE) and WASH Benefits (Humphrey 2013).

Benefits of scaling up to full national coverage (scenario 1)
Under-5 mortality

Using LiST to project scaling up the package of interventions to full national coverage shows a reduction of under-5 mortality rate from 30.0 per 1,000 live births in 2017 to 28.1 per 1,000 live births by 2022 (figure 4.7).

FIGURE 4.7

Under-5 mortality rates: current and full national coverage, 2017–22

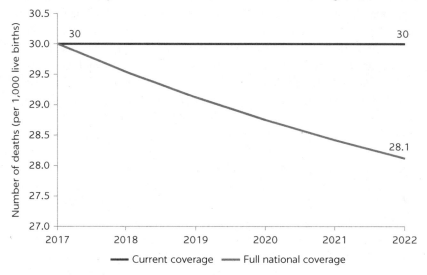

Source: EDHS 2014 (MOHP, El-Zanaty and Associates, and ICF International 2015).
Projections performed using Lives Saved Tool (LiST), https://listvisualizer.org/.

FIGURE 4.8

Additional deaths of children 0–59 months of age prevented by scaling up interventions to full national coverage

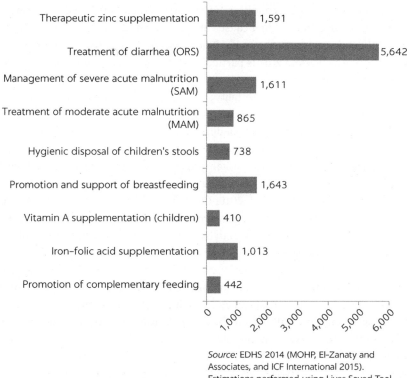

Source: EDHS 2014 (MOHP, El-Zanaty and Associates, and ICF International 2015). Estimations performed using Lives Saved Tool (LiST), https://listvisualizer.org/.
Note: ORS = oral rehydration solution.

Figure 4.8 depicts the additional number of lives saved by scaling up the package of interventions to full national coverage. Over the period 2018–22, 13,955 more deaths would be prevented than in the current coverage scenario (assuming the same level of coverage for all interventions throughout the period).

Almost half of deaths prevented would result from scaling up the treatment of diarrhea with ORS from 28 percent to 90 percent coverage nationwide (5,642 lives saved). The reasons are the direct effect of this intervention on the reduction of diarrhea as a cause-specific mortality condition, and in Egypt diarrhea is one of the leading causes of death in children under 5 (as noted, 11 percent of child deaths are due to diarrhea).[7]

Stunting

Experience has shown that stunting in Sub-Saharan Africa can be reduced at an average annual rate of 1.5 percent (Teller and Alva 2008).[8] Bhutta et al. (2013) estimated that scaling up 10 highly effective nutrition interventions to 90 percent coverage over a period of 10 years would reduce stunting in 34 countries by 20 percent. Furthermore, a recent study by the World Bank estimates that scaling up some essential nutrition-specific and -sensitive interventions to 90 percent coverage over a 10-year period would lead to about a 40 percent decline in the number of stunted children in 37 high-burden countries by 2025 (Shekar et al. 2017). The Bank's finding is in line with the target for stunting endorsed by the Sixty-fifth World Health Assembly (WHA).[9]

This analysis shows that the current level of stunting can be reduced by only 1.5 percentage points over five years by scaling up all interventions to full national coverage (figure 4.9). However, because stunting in previous age cohorts affects the future level of stunting, assuming that the same level of coverage will be maintained beyond 2022, the prevalence will drop, reaching 18.9 percent by 2026 from the current baseline level of 21.2 percent.

If stunting is analyzed in terms of the number of stunted children in absolute terms, the full national coverage scenario would ensure a 15 percent decline in the number of children under 5 stunted by 2030 compared with 2017 (figure 4.10). This reduction in stunting will not ensure the 40 percent decline in the number of stunted children endorsed as a target for stunting by the Sixty-fifth WHA.

Figure 4.10 also shows the initial increase in the number of stunted children from 2017 to 2018. The increase was driven by two main factors: (1) because being stunted while in the previous age cohort is itself a risk factor for stunting, stunting rates take time to drop; and (2) the reduction in the under-5 mortality

FIGURE 4.9

Prevalence of stunting of children 0–59 months of age: current and full national coverage, 2017–30

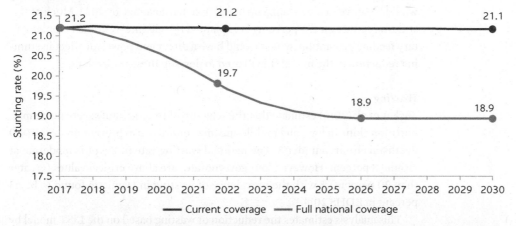

Source: EDHS 2014 (MOHP, El-Zanaty and Associates, and ICF International 2015). Projections performed using Lives Saved Tool (LiST), https://listvisualizer.org/.

FIGURE 4.10

Number of stunted children 0–59 months of age: current and full national coverage, 2017–30

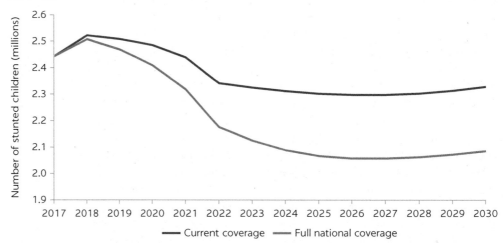

Source: EDHS 2014 (MOHP, El-Zanaty and Associates, and ICF International 2015). Projections performed using Lives Saved Tool (LiST), https://listvisualizer.org/.

FIGURE 4.11

Additional cases of stunting averted for children 0–59 months of age

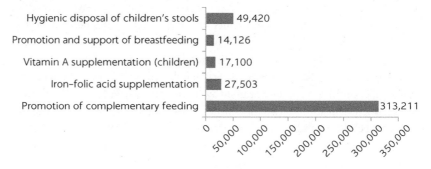

Source: EDHS 2014 (MOHP, El-Zanaty and Associates, and ICF International 2015). Estimations performed using Lives Saved Tool (LiST), https://listvisualizer.org/.

rate spurred by this package of interventions partially outweighs the stunting reduction effect as more children 0–59 months remain alive and can potentially become stunted. Figure 4.11 shows that 421,360 additional cases of stunting would be prevented by scaling up to full national coverage by 2022. Much of this stunting reduction (74 percent) is explained by one intervention, complementary feeding promotion, which would have a direct and powerful effect in stunting reduction in the model (LiST) used to develop these projections.

Wasting

Shekar et al. (2016) estimate that the scale-up of treatment of severe acute malnutrition alone in low- and middle-income countries can prevent up to 860,000 deaths in children under 5. The national wasting rate in Egypt is moderate at around 8 percent. However, four governorates are above critical values (greater than 20 percent),[10] with the prevalence of wasting in Damietta found to be 63 percent in EDHS 2014.

This analysis estimates the reduction of wasting based on the LiST model by scaling up both treatment of MAM/SAM and promotion of complementary feeding. The combined effect of scaling up promotion of complementary feeding from 62 percent in 2017 to 90 percent in 2022 and MAM/SAM from 0 to 80 percent over the same period nationwide will reduce the wasting rate from 8.7 percent in 2017 to 6 percent in 2022 (figure 4.12). Although this projection is conducted using national averages, the critical high values of wasting reported by EDHS 2014 for Damietta (63 percent), Monufia (22.6 percent); Asyut (32.5 percent), and New Valley (35.4 percent) suggest that these governorates should be given priority in the implementation of treatment of MAM/SAM and promotion of complementary feeding.

Anemia in pregnant women

In the LiST model, iron–folic acid supplementation, the intervention that prevents anemia in pregnant women, is considered in the full national package. Remarkably, this analysis shows that scaling up this intervention from 36 percent to 90 percent coverage would reduce anemia in pregnant women by almost 50 percent, from 18 percent in 2017 to 9.5 percent by 2022 (figure 4.13).

Exclusive breastfeeding prevalence

In this analysis, the promotion and support of exclusive breastfeeding are included in the first package of nutrition-specific preventive interventions (IYCF and micronutrients). Promotion of breastfeeding requires providing

FIGURE 4.12

Prevalence of wasting in children 0–59 months of age: current and full national coverage, 2017–22

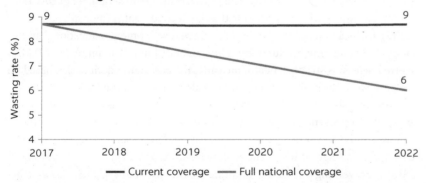

Source: EDHS 2014 (MOHP, El-Zanaty and Associates, and ICF International 2015). Projections performed using Lives Saved Tool (LiST), https://listvisualizer.org/.

FIGURE 4.13

Percentage of pregnant women with iron-deficiency anemia: current and full national coverage, 2017–22

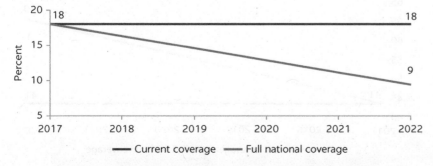

Source: EDHS 2014 (MOHP, El-Zanaty and Associates, and ICF International 2015). Projections performed using Lives Saved Tool (LiST), https://listvisualizer.org/.

mothers with education and counseling, campaigns to promote optimal breast-feeding practices, as well as development of the appropriate policies and legislation to protect exclusive breastfeeding. The World Health Assembly set the target for increasing exclusive breastfeeding for infants up to 6 months of age from 37 percent in 2012 to 50 percent in 2025 (Shekar et al. 2017).

Figure 4.14 shows that scaling up the promotion of exclusive breastfeeding to full national coverage from 62 percent in 2017[11] to 90 percent coverage in 2022 would ensure an increase of exclusive breastfeeding prevalence of 9 percentage points (from 41 percent in 2017 to 50 percent in 2022). This result would comply with the 50 percent target set by the World Health Assembly for 2025.

Cost-effectiveness analysis of full national coverage (scenario 1)

The cost per benefit is based on three key indicators: lives saved, number of cases of stunting averted, and disability-adjusted life years averted. DALYs averted is a key measure used in health economics to evaluate and compare the cost-effectiveness of health programs and interventions. DALY combines mortality and morbidity in a single metric. It captures the number of years of a person's life saved by a given intervention and adjusts it by the health status that person is expected to have during those years. For example, if an intervention saves a person's life and that person is expected to live in perfect health for next 30 years, the intervention would avert 30 DALYs. In this analysis, the number of DALYs averted is calculated using Bhutta et al. (2008) as a reference: one life saved equals 33 DALYs averted; one case of stunting averted equals 0.23 DALYs. Thus because of the way this metric is computed, interventions that affect mortality generate the greatest impact in terms of DALYs (that is, avert the greatest number of DALYs).

Preventing stunting has benefits that go beyond health (mortality and morbidity); it has an impact on a child's cognitive development, educational attainment, and economic productivity. Thus, in addition to the number of DALYs averted, which is strictly a health measure, the cost per benefit is also based on the number of cases of stunting averted (calculated using the LiST model).

This analysis suggests that scaling up all the interventions to full national coverage would prevent over 13,955 child deaths and 421,360 cases of stunting in children under 5 over the course of five years and avert 55,743 DALYs (table 4.7). Using the package of interventions, preventing one death would cost about $81,154; preventing one case of stunting would cost about $2,688; and averting one DALY would cost about $20,317.

FIGURE 4.14

Percentage of children under 6 months of age exclusively breastfed: current and full national coverage, 2017–22

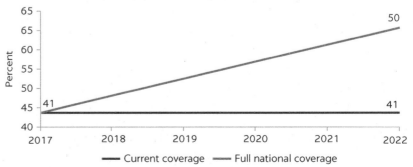

Source: EDHS 2014 (MOHP, El-Zanaty and Associates, and ICF International 2015). Projections performed using Lives Saved Tool (LiST), https://listvisualizer.org/.

TABLE 4.7 Costs and benefits for full national coverage scenario

INTERVENTIONS FOR FULL NATIONAL COVERAGE	EXPECTED BENEFITS			COST PER BENEFITS (US$)		
	ADDITIONAL DEATHS PREVENTED	ADDITIONAL CASES OF STUNTING AVERTED[a]	DALYS AVERTED	COST PER ADDITIONAL DEATH AVERTED	COST PER ADDITIONAL CASE OF STUNTING AVERTED	COST PER DALY AVERTED
IYCF and micronutrients	**3,508**	**371,940**	**20,131**	**17,312**	**163**	**3,017**
Promotion and support of breastfeeding	1,643	14,126	5,747	10,772	1,253	3,080
Promotion of complementary feeding	442	313,211	8,662	51,819	73	2,644
Iron–folic acid supplementation	1,013	27,503	3,975	10,968	404	2,795
Vitamin A supplementation (children)	410	17,100	1,746	21,992	527	5,163
Management of acute malnutrition	**2,476**	**—**	**8,171**	**124,020**	**—**	**37,582**
Treatment of moderate acute malnutrition	865	—	2,855	45,033	—	13,646
Management of severe acute malnutrition	1,611	—	5,316	166,431	—	50,434
Disease prevention and management	**7,233**	**—**	**23,869**	**83,781**	**—**	**25,388**
Treatment of diarrhea (oral rehydration solution)	5,642	—	18,619	26,993	—	8,180
Therapeutic zinc supplementation	1,591	—	5,250	285,160	—	86,412
Water, sanitation, and hygiene (WASH)[b]	**738**	**49,420**	**3,572**	**14,897**	**222**	**3,078**
Hygienic disposal of children's stools	738	49,420	3,572	14,897	222	3,078
Total	**13,955**	**421,360**	**55,743**	**81,154**	**2,688**	**20,317**

Source: Expected benefits estimated using the Lives Saved Tool (LiST), https://listvisualizer.org/. Estimated costs based on unit costs obtained from the WHO OneHealth Tool, http://www.who.int/choice/onehealthtool/en/.

Note: DALY = disability-adjusted life year; IYCF = infant and young child feeding; — = zero.

a. IYCF and micronutrients and WASH interventions are the only interventions that have an impact on the risk of stunting, according to the LiST model.

b. Hygienic disposal of children's stools is the only WASH intervention with baseline coverage in 2017 below full coverage (60 percent). No scale-up was modeled for the remaining WASH interventions because they are already at over 90 percent coverage.

To reduce child mortality, the most cost-effective interventions in terms of cost per life saved are promotion and support of breastfeeding ($10,772), iron–folic acid supplementation ($10,968), vitamin A supplementation for children ($21,992), and hygienic disposal of children's stools ($14,987). In terms of stunting, the most cost-effective interventions are promotion of complementary feeding ($73), iron–folic acid supplementation ($404), vitamin A supplementation for children ($527), and hygienic disposal of children's stools ($222).

The most cost-effective interventions to avert DALYs are promotion of complementary feeding ($2,644), iron–folic acid supplementation ($2,795), promotion and support of breastfeeding ($3,080), and hygienic disposal of children's stools ($3,078), and vitamin A supplementation for children ($5,163). All these interventions are considered cost-effective according to the categorization used by World Health Organization–Choosing Interventions That Are Cost-Effective (WHO-CHOICE).[12]

The treatment of severe acute malnutrition and therapeutic zinc supplementation for the treatment of diarrhea are overall the least cost-effective interventions in the package in terms of lives saved and DALYs averted. The reason is that high additional costs are required to scale up these interventions to full national coverage ($307 million for MAM/SAM; $453 million for zinc over five years).

Prioritized scale-up options

Chapter 3 describes the options for scaling up nutrition programs in Egypt. The financing resources needed to expand to full national coverage by 2022 are significant, and fiscal and capacity constraints render this option not viable in the short term. Furthermore, expanding the complete package of interventions nationwide will take time, and it does not take into consideration the geographical disparities between governorates in terms of nutrition and poverty indicators.

This section analyzes two additional scale-up scenarios that consider the burden of stunting, geography, and implementation capacity:

- *Scale up by region (scenario 2):* prioritize the full package only in region groups with the highest burden of stunting
- *Scale up by prioritizing interventions (scenario 3):* scale up to full national coverage the most cost-effective interventions aimed at reducing stunting.

Scale up by region (scenario 2)

Scenario 2 targets resources by geography and demography, focusing on governorates with the highest prevalence of stunting and number of stunted children. Using these criteria, eight governorates with the highest stunting prevalence in Egypt account for 50 percent of all stunted children: Giza, Sharqia, Cairo, Sohag, Minya, Gharbia, Beni Suef, and Faiyum (figure 4.15).

For this scenario, it is projected that all nutrition interventions will be scaled up to full national coverage in the eight priority governorates, and current coverage throughout the five-year period is assumed for the remaining governorates.

Scale up by intervention (scenario 3)

This scenario scales up to full national coverage only those interventions that have the highest impact on stunting. Analysis of the cost-effectiveness of the nutrition interventions performed for the full national coverage scenario demonstrated that the most cost-effective interventions measured based on cases of stunting and DALYs averted are IYCF[13] and micronutrients and hygienic disposal of children's stools.

FIGURE 4.15

Prevalence of stunting and population by governorate

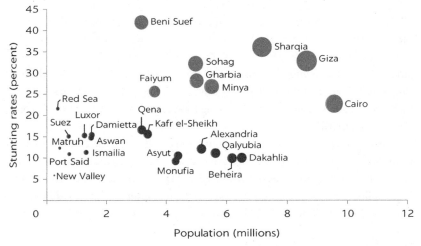

Source: EDHS 2014 (MOHP, El-Zanaty and Associates, and ICF International 2015).
Note: Size of bubble is indicative of number of stunted children.

These interventions are also those that can be scaled up quickly either with existing capacity or with relatively small investments. Therefore, this scale-up scenario excludes treatment of acute malnutrition (MAM/SAM) for children and pregnant women. These interventions are given lowest priority in the context of this analysis because (1) their impact on the prevalence of wasting but not on stunting is known; (2) their unit costs are significantly higher than those of other interventions, and they are linked to supply chain and logistics challenges associated with the large-scale distribution of food; and (3) their cost-effectiveness is low compared with that of other nutrition preventive interventions (Shekar et al. 2017).

Cost-effectiveness analysis of prioritized scale-up options versus full coverage

Figure 4.16 shows the total additional costs by scenario to scale up the package of nutrition interventions over the period 2018–22. The expected resources requirement for scaling up the existing package of nutrition interventions to full national coverage (90 percent) and implementing the treatment of MAM and SAM nationwide to 80 percent coverage will be an additional $1,132 million over the period.

The additional cost of scaling up to 90 percent coverage only in the region group with the highest burden of stunting between 2018 and 2022 will be $556 million. By focusing on the eight governorates with the highest stunting rates and number of stunted children, the financial requirement will generally decrease proportionally compared with that for the full national coverage scenario. WASH interventions will remain close to full scale, with the exception of

FIGURE 4.16

Total and additional costs by scenario, 2018–22

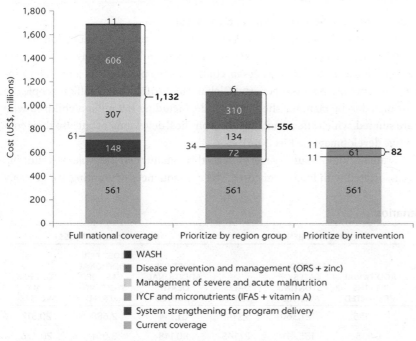

Source: Estimated costs based on unit costs obtained from the WHO OneHealth Tool, http://www.who.int/choice/onehealthtool/en/.
Note: IFAS = iron–folic acid supplementation; IYCF infant and young child feeding; ORS = oral rehydration solution; WASH = water, sanitation, and hygiene.

hygienic disposal of children's stools (which will rise from 60 percent to 90 percent coverage in the eight governorates only).

Delivery of only the most cost-effective interventions in stunting reduction (IYCF and micronutrients and hygienic disposal of children's stools) will require an additional $82 million over the period 2018–22: $61 million for IYCF and micronutrients, $11 million for hygienic disposal of children's stools, and $11 million for system strengthening. The savings gained by adopting this strategy stems from prioritizing those interventions having the highest impact on stunting reduction and therefore not considering MAM/SAM and maintaining ORS and zinc at the current coverage levels.

When comparing the costs and benefits of all three scenarios included in this analysis (table 4.8), prioritizing by intervention (scenario 3) is the most cost-effective strategy of implementation by all parameters: cost per additional life saved ($19,412), cost per additional case of stunting averted ($196), and cost per DALY averted ($3,478). For stunting, this scenario would prevent the same number of stunted children as ensured by scaling up to full national coverage (421,360), but at a significantly lower additional cost ($82 million) because it delivers those interventions that are the most cost-effective in stunting reduction. Treatment of acute malnutrition and maintaining implementation of ORS and zinc at current coverage levels throughout the country would therefore be excluded. Scenario 3 would also allow setting aside some strategic funding for scaling up implementation in vulnerable areas and populations of the country.

Focusing only on those interventions that are most effective in reducing stunting will not have any impact on the current levels of wasting and will prevent only 4,249 additional deaths (30 percent of the full national coverage scenario).

Cost-benefit analysis

Socioeconomic benefits of investing in nutrition

Current estimates suggest that all forms of malnutrition (undernutrition, micronutrient deficiencies, and overweight) cost the global economy an estimated $3.5 trillion a year, or $500 a person, compromising productivity and undermining any attempt to reduce poverty (Global Panel 2016). Over 2 billion people are estimated to be malnourished worldwide, including 159 million children who are stunted, which affects not only their physical development but also their cognitive development (IFPRI 2016).

Stunted children suffer severe effects throughout their life cycle, and stunting is associated with long-term costs. The consequences of stunting are not only

TABLE 4.8 **Costs and benefits for all scenarios**

SCALE-UP SCENARIO	ADDITIONAL SCALE-UP COSTS (US$, MILLIONS)	EXPECTED BENEFITS			COST PER BENEFIT (US$)		
		ADDITIONAL DEATHS PREVENTED	ADDITIONAL CASES OF STUNTING AVERTED	DALYS AVERTED	COST PER ADDITIONAL DEATH AVERTED	COST PER ADDITIONAL CASE OF STUNTING AVERTED	COST PER DALY AVERTED
1. Full national coverage	1,132	13,955	421,360	55,743	81,154	2,688	20,317
2. Prioritize by region group	556	6,935	185,211	27,145	80,148	3,001	20,476
3. Prioritize by intervention	82	4,249	421,360	23,713	19,412	196	3,478

Source: Expected benefits estimated using the Lives Saved Tool (LiST), https://listvisualizer.org/. Estimated costs based on unit costs obtained from the WHO OneHealth Tool, http://www.who.int/choice/onehealthtool/en/.
Note: DALY = disability-adjusted life year.

FIGURE 4.17

Investments in nutrition build human capital and boost shared prosperity

SCHOOLING

Early nutrition programs can increase school completion by one year

EARNINGS

Early nutrition programs can raise adult wages by 5–50%

POVERTY

Children who escape stunting are 33% more likely to escape poverty as adults

ECONOMY

Reduction in stunting can increase GDP by 4–11% in Asia and Africa

Source: Shekar et al. 2017, based on Hoddinott et al. 2008, 2011; Horton and Steckel 2013; Martorell et al. 2010.

higher risk of death and disability, but also loss of creative and intellectual energy (Lye 2016). Stunting is the root cause of adverse outcomes in youth and adulthood, such as delayed schooling, poorer performance in school, fewer years of education, lower incomes, greater risk of poverty, and higher costs for the economy. The costs of stunting are mainly associated with two factors: (1) reduced cognitive capacity and educational attainment and (2) higher health care costs.

Widespread evidence indicates that being stunted in early childhood is associated with a delayed start at school (Daniels and Adair 2004), reduced schooling attainment (Fink et al. 2016; Martorell et al. 2010), and substantially lower adult wages when measured at both the individual and country level (Fink et al. 2016). One study found that young children who were stunted were 33 percent less likely to escape poverty as adults (Shekar et al. 2017). As described in figure 4.17, these consequences add up to overall GDP losses of 4–11 percent in Africa and Asia (Horton and Steckel 2013).

Nutrition interventions that can mitigate the burden of stunting are consistently identified as being among the most cost-effective development and global health actions (Horton and Hoddinott 2014). Benefit-cost ratios across nutrition interventions and programs reveal very high economic returns to investing in nutrition (Alderman, Behrman, and Puett 2016; Copenhagen Consensus Center 2015; Hoddinott et al. 2013). Several economic analyses have calculated benefit-cost ratios well above 1, the break-even point, with the benefits of investments aimed at reducing stunting as high as $15 in return for every $1 invested (Shekar et al. 2017; Galasso et al. 2017).

Cost-benefit analysis of scale-up priorities

Scaling up the interventions to full national coverage (scenario 1) would result in total net benefits from increases in economic productivity of about $547 million over the productive lives of the children who benefited from the interventions. Under this scenario, the benefit-cost ratio would be 0.54, which means that every dollar invested in nutrition would bring $0.54 in economic benefits. The estimated internal rate of return (IRR) for this investment would be 1.09 percent.

The benefit-cost ratio for scaling up to full national coverage in eight governorates only (scenario 2) would be 0.40, with economic benefits of about $201 million and an estimated rate of return of 0.85 percent (table 4.9).

TABLE 4.9 Cost, benefits, and benefit-cost ratios

SCALE-UP SCENARIO	DISCOUNT RATE (%)	TOTAL NET ADDITIONAL COST (US$, MILLIONS)	NET BENEFITS (US$, MILLIONS)	BENEFIT-COST RATIO	INTERNAL RATE OF RETURN (DISCOUNTED COSTS AND BENEFITS, %)
1. Full national coverage	3	1,017	547	0.54	1.09
2. Prioritize by region group	3	499	201	0.40	0.85
3. Prioritize by intervention	3	74	1,326	17.87	9.80

Source: Expected benefits estimated using LiST Lives Saved Tool (LiST), https://listvisualizer.org/. Estimated costs based on unit costs obtained from the WHO OneHealth Tool, http://www.who.int/choice/onehealthtool/en/.

The highest benefit-cost ratio would be ensured by scenario 3, which prioritizes implementation of the most cost-effective interventions in stunting reduction. Adopting this strategy in Egypt would return $17.87 in economic benefits for each dollar invested, and $1,326 million in productivity gains, indicating that the benefits of adopting this strategy significantly outweigh the costs. The rate of return from investing in this scenario is 9.80 percent, well above the IRR for scenarios 1 and 2.

CONCLUSIONS

The case for investing in child and maternal nutrition globally and in Egypt is strong. The analytical approach used in this economic analysis combines costs with estimates of impact and makes a case for investing in nutrition in Egypt even stronger, helping policy makers to identify and prioritize the most cost-effective packages of interventions in a context in which financing is constrained.

To maximize the number of nonstunted children, Egypt should prioritize funding the most cost-effective interventions: IYCF (especially promotion of complementary feeding), iron–folic acid supplementation, vitamin A supplementation for children, and promotion of hygienic disposal of children's stools. When comparing the costs and benefits, if the main priority is reduction of stunting, focusing on delivering only the most cost-effective interventions in stunting reduction (scenario 3) provides better value for the money.

The expected additional resources required for implementing scenario 3 over the five-year period from 2018 to 2022 is $82 million. Compared with current coverage levels, the estimates presented in this economic analysis indicate that this investment would prevent 4,249 additional deaths and 421,360 additional cases of stunting and save 23,713 DALYs.

The significant cost savings for scenario 3 stem from prioritizing those interventions that are better able to reduce stunting. This means maintaining only supplementation of ORS and zinc for the treatment of diarrhea at current coverage levels and not considering treatment of acute malnutrition (MAM/SAM). By doing so, however, scenario 3 will not have any impact on the current level of wasting, and it will only prevent 30 percent of additional deaths (4,249), compared with the full national coverage scenario.

This analysis shows that adopting the strategy described for scenario 3 would result in substantial economic benefits and the best value for the money for Egypt. Scenario 3, which prioritizes implementation of the most cost-effective interventions for stunting reduction, is estimated to translate into and return the highest economic benefits over the productive lives of the children who receive the interventions. The estimated benefit-cost ratio for implementing this scenario in Egypt is 17.87 and suggests that every dollar invested would result in about $18 in economic returns and $1,326 million in productivity gains, indicating that the benefits of investing in nutrition significantly outweigh the costs.

NOTES

1. A supply-side analysis means that demand has not been explicitly addressed in terms of accessibility and quality of care for those with poor health care–seeking behavior.
2. http://www.who.int/choice/onehealthtool/en/.
3. http://www.who.int/choice/.
4. http://www.who.int/choice/costs/CER_levels/en/.it.
5. In the LiST model, "other causes" indicates a specific category of mortality.
6. LiST: WHO estimates (2000–2015); http://www.who.int/healthinfo/global_burden _disease/estimates_child_cod_2015/en/.
7. LiST: WHO estimates (2000–15), http://www.who.int/healthinfo/global_burden_disease /estimates_child_cod_2015/en/.
8. Six countries in Sub-Saharan Africa—Senegal, Namibia, Togo, Uganda, Eritrea, and Tanzania—reduced stunting among children under 3 with declines of at least 2 percentage points a year.
9. In 2012 the Sixty-fifth World Health Assembly endorsed a target for stunting: reduce the number of stunted children under 5 by 40 percent by 2025. This target has been adopted for Sustainable Development Goal 2: end hunger, achieve food security and improved nutrition, and promote sustainable agriculture.
10. Monufia 22.6 percent; Asyut, 32.5 percent; New Valley, 35.4 percent; Damietta, 63 percent (EDHS 2014).
11. Based on data from the *Nutrition Stakeholder and Action Mapping Report* (MOHP and UNICEF 2017).
12. http://www.who.int/choice/costs/CER_levels/en/. Threshold values for intervention cost-effectiveness: less than GDP per capita, very cost-effective; 1–3 times GDP per capita, cost-effective; less than 3 times GDP per capita, not cost-effective. For Egypt: very cost -effective: cost per DALY is less than GDP per capita ($3,548); cost-effective: cost per DALY is less than 1–3 times GDP per capita ($3,548–$10,644); not cost-effective: cost per DALY is greater than 3 times GDP per capita ($10,644).
13. Within IYCF, promotion and support of breastfeeding is the intervention less cost-effective in terms of reduction of stunting. However, because it is normally implemented during IYCF sessions together with the promotion of complementary feeding, it is advisable to consider the two interventions to be practically indistinguishable.

REFERENCES

Alderman, H., J. R. Behrman, and C. Puett. 2016. "Big Numbers about Small Children: Estimating the Economic Benefits of Addressing Undernutrition." *World Bank Research Observer* 31 (2).

Bhutta, Z. A., T. Ahmed, R. E. Black, S. Cousens, K. Dewey, E. Gugliani, B. A. Haider, B. Kirkwood, S. S. Morris, H. P. S. Sachdev, and M. Shekar. 2008. "What Works? Interventions for Maternal and Child Undernutrition and Survival." *Lancet* 371 (9610): 417–40.

Bhutta, Z. A., J. K. Das, A. Rizvi, M. F. Gaffey, N. Walker, S. Horton, P. Webb, A. Lartey, and R. E. Black. 2013. "Evidence-Based Interventions for Improvement of Maternal and Child Nutrition: What Can Be Done and at What Cost?" *Lancet* 382 (9890): 452–77.

Cairncross, S., C. Hunt, S. Boisson, K. Bostoen, V. Curtis, I. C. Fung, and W. P. Schmidt. 2010. "Water, Sanitation and Hygiene for the Prevention of Diarrhoea." *International Journal of Epidemiology* 39 (Suppl. 1): i93–i205. http://www.ncbi.nlm.nih.gov/pubmed/20348121.

Cairncross, S., and V. Valdmanis. 2006. "Water Supply, Sanitation, and Hygiene Promotion." In *Disease Control Priorities in Developing Countries,* 2nd ed., edited by D. T. Jamison,

J. G. Breman, A. R. Measham, G. Alleyne, M. Claeson, D. B. Evans, P. Jha, A. Mills, and P. Musgrove, 771–92. Washington, DC: World Bank; New York: Oxford University Press. http:// www.ncbi.nlm.nih.gov/books/NBK11728/.

Copenhagen Consensus Center. 2015. *Smart Development Goals: The Post-2015 Consensus*. http://www.copenhagenconsensus.com/sites/default/files/ outcomedocument_col.pdf.

Cumming, O., and S. Cairncross. 2016. "Can Water, Sanitation and Hygiene Help Eliminate Stunting? Current Evidence and Policy Implications." *Maternal and Child Nutrition* 12 (Suppl. 1): 91–105. doi: 10.1111/mcn.12258.

Daniels, M. C., and L. S. Adair. 2004. "Growth in Young Filipino Children Predicts Schooling Trajectories through High School." *Journal of Nutrition* 134(6): 1439–46.

Fink, G., E. Peet, G. Danaei, K. Andrews, D. C. McCoy, C. R. Sudfeld, M. C. Smith Fawzi, M. Ezzati, and W. W. Fawzi. 2016. "Schooling and Wage Income Losses Due to Early-Childhood Growth Faltering in Developing Countries: National, Regional, and Global Estimates." *American Journal of Clinical Nutrition* 104 (1): 104–12.

Galasso, E., A. Wagstaff, S. Naudeau, and M. Shekar. 2017. "The Economic Costs of Stunting and How to Reduce Them." Policy Research Note, World Bank, Washington, DC. http://pubdocs .worldbank.org/en/536661487971403516/PRN05-March2017-Economic-Costs-of -Stunting.pdf.

Global Panel (Global Panel on Agriculture and Food Systems for Nutrition). 2016. *The Cost of Malnutrition: Why Policy Action Is Urgent*. Technical Brief No. 3. London, UK: Global Panel on Agriculture and Food Systems for Nutrition. https://glopan.org/cost-of-malnutrition.

Hoddinott, J., H. Alderman, J. R. Behrman, L. Haddad, and S. Horton. 2013. "The Economic Rationale for Investing in Stunting Reduction." *Maternal and Child Nutrition* 9 (Suppl. 2): 69–82.

Horton, S., and J. Hoddinott. 2014. "Benefits and Costs of the Food and Nutrition Targets for the Post-2015 Development Agenda: Post-2015 Consensus." Food Security and Nutrition Perspective Paper, Copenhagen Consensus Center.

Horton, S., and R. Steckel. 2013. "Malnutrition: Global Economic Losses Attributable to Malnutrition 1900–2000 and Projections to 2050." In *The Economics of Human Challenges*, edited by B. Lomborg, 247–72. Cambridge, UK: Cambridge University Press.

Humphrey, J. 2013. "SHINE Sanitation, Hygiene, Infant Nutrition Efficacy Project." https:// clinicaltrials. gov/ct2/show/ NCT01824940.

IFPRI (International Food Policy Research Institute). 2016. "Global Nutrition Report 2016: From Promise to Impact: Ending Malnutrition by 2030." Washington, DC.

Lenters, L. M., K. Wazny, P. Webb, T. Ahmed, and Z. A. Bhutta. 2013. "Treatment of Severe and Moderate Acute Malnutrition in Low- and Middle-Income Settings: A Systematic Review, Meta-analysis and Delphi Process." *BMC Public Health* 13 (Suppl 3): S23. http:// www.ncbi .nlm.nih.gov/pmc/articles/PMC3847503/.

Lye, S. J. 2016. "The Science of Early Development: Investing in the First 2000 Days of Life to Enable All Children, Everywhere to Reach Their Full Potential." Presentation at World Bank Early Childhood Development Meeting, Washington, DC, April 2016.

Martorell, R., B. L. Horta, L. S. Adair, A. D. Stein, L. Richter, C. H. D. Fall, S. K. Bhargava, S. K. Dey Biswas, L. Perez, F. C. Barros, C. G. Victora, and Consortium on Health Oriented Research in Transitional Societies Group. 2010. "Weight Gain in the First Two Years of Life Is an Important Predictor of Schooling Outcomes in Pooled Analysis from 5 Birth Cohorts from Low- and Middle-Income Countries." *Journal of Nutrition* 140: 348–54.

MOHP (Ministry of Health and Population), El-Zanaty and Associates, and ICF International. 2015. *Egypt Demographic and Health Survey 2014*. Cairo, Egypt and Rockville, MD: Ministry of Health and Population and ICF International. https://dhsprogram.com/pubs/pdf /FR302/FR302.pdf.

MOHP (Ministry of Health and Population) and UNICEF (United Nations Children's Fund). 2017. *Nutrition Stakeholder and Action Mapping Report*. Cairo: UNICEF. https://www .unnetworkforsun.org/sites/default/files/2018-08/Nutrition%20Stakeholder%20%26%20 Action%20Mapping%20Report-Egypt.pdf.

Shekar, M., J. Kakietek, J. Dayton Eberwein, and D. Walters. 2017. *An Investment Framework for Nutrition: Reaching the Global Targets for Stunting, Anemia, Breastfeeding, and Wasting*.

Directions in Development. Washington, DC: World Bank. https://openknowledge
.worldbank.org/handle/10986/26069.

Teller, C. H., and S. Alva. 2008. "Reducing Child Malnutrition in Sub-Saharan Africa: Surveys
Find Mixed Progress." Population Reference Bureau, Washington, DC. https://www.prb
.org/stuntingssa/.

UN (United Nations). 2017. *World Population Prospects 2017—Data Booklet*. New York: United
Nations, Department of Economic and Social Affairs, Population Division. https://www.un
.org/development/desa/publications/world-population-prospects-the-2017-revision.html.

5 Fiscal Space to Scale Up Nutrition in Egypt

HELEN C. CONNOLLY

KEY MESSAGES

- This chapter examines the extent to which the existing and projected fiscal space will be conducive to absorbing the additional costs of implementing the scale-up scenarios discussed in chapter 4.
- According to World Bank estimates, total nutrition expenditures are a little over $150 million a year in Egypt, which is 0.33 percent of the total government expenditure and 0.81 percent of the total health expenditure. However, according to the National Health Accounts for 2012, the proportion specifically spent on nutritional deficiencies is only $11 million.
- Egypt relies little on foreign assistance for funding nutrition programs. The reported overseas development assistance funding for nutrition represents only 2.33 percent of the estimated $152.6 million total expenditure on domestic nutrition.
- This analysis found that out of the five pillars of fiscal space, improved macroeconomic conditions in the long run as well as medium-run efficiency gains are two areas with good prospects of generating significant additional resources for nutrition.
- Other potential sources are more limited in opportunity. Increased funding through the health budget is not likely because of the competing priorities for finite resources and the highly centralized decision making in Egypt. Raising further funds in the health sector through, for example, taxes earmarked for health (or nutrition) face difficulties because of the evolving and multisectoral nature of nutrition and the potential negative impacts of such taxes. And foreign assistance is not likely as well because Egypt does not rely on external funding for nutrition.
- In the long run, it is reasonable to expect significant economic growth from the higher productivity of Egypt's workforce stemming from a reduction in stunting. Lower levels of stunting and consequent improved health will also reduce the reliance on social programs and cut stunting-related health costs.
- Aside from economic growth, government revenue could also increase if tax revenue increases through an expanded tax base, new taxes, or more efficient tax collection.

- This discussion relies heavily on public information available for the health sector in Egypt. A more in-depth analysis of fiscal space for nutrition that includes both health and other key sectors would depend on expanding the specifics in the pillars discussed here to include information from all of these sectors.

This chapter examines the extent to which the existing and projected fiscal space in Egypt will be conducive to absorbing the additional costs of implementing the scale-up scenarios discussed in chapter 4.

ESTIMATING THE CURRENT LEVEL OF SPENDING ON NUTRITION IN EGYPT

This section describes the methods and sources used for estimating the current level of spending on nutrition in Egypt through domestic financing from the government of Egypt (GoE), official development assistance (ODA), and other sources. Current estimates are identified where they are available.

Domestic government financing

In Egypt, information is available from the Ministry of Finance (MOF) for fiscal year 2016 on the actual expenditure of each central administration (ministry) for all sectors. The expenditures for the eight (of the 34) ministries[1] with the most nutrition-related programming totaled $46.5 billion in 2016. Little information is available on the current level of GoE spending on nutrition because there are no clear budget lines for nutrition in ministry budgets, making it difficult to quantify the actual expenditures. However, estimates provided by the World Bank and shown in table 5.1 show that the total nutrition expenditure (TNE) for 2016 was $152.6 million, or 0.33 percent of the total government expenditure (TGE) and 0.81 percent of the total health expenditure (THE). A full estimate of nutrition spending requires a broader look at all ministries contributing to the nutrition agenda.

TABLE 5.1 **Estimated fiscal space indicators: Egypt, 2016**

INDICATOR		ANNUAL
General	Population (2017, millions)	94.8
	Gross domestic product (GDP) (2016; US$, millions)	336,300
	Total government expenditure (TGE) (2016; US$, millions)	46,251.3
Health	Total health expenditure (THE) (2016; US$, millions)	18,832.8
	THE as % of GDP	5.6%
	THE as % of TGE	40.7%
	THE per capita (US$)	198.7
Nutrition	Total nutrition expenditure (TNE), estimated (2016; US$, millions)	152.6
	TNE as % of GDP	0.05%
	TNE as % of TGE	0.33%
	TNE as % of THE	0.81%
	TNE per capita (US$)	1.61
	Private nutrition spending per capita	0.77

Source: World Development Indicators (database) , World Bank, Washington, DC, http://datatopics .worldbank.org/world-development-indicators/.

The cost analysis in chapter 4 finds that the costs of current coverage using unit costs established in the OneHealth tool for the 13 (primarily nutrition-specific) interventions prioritized for scale-up total $112 million a year. Although this calculation is broadly in line with the TNE estimate (which includes the 13 prioritized interventions), this analysis would be better informed by a broader understanding of the Egypt-specific costs associated with nutrition programming.

Key sources for understanding government expenditures on nutrition

Budget analysis. A full budget analysis of nutrition programming across all ministries is a relatively quick and easy method for identifying where current funding (public and external funding included in the budget) is supporting nutrition programming of all kinds. By 2018, 47 Scaling Up Nutrition (SUN) movement countries had conducted an analysis of their government budgets for nutrition, with 26 countries having done it for a second time.[2] A nutrition budget analysis, framed in the country context using the relevant policy documents to define nutrition and identify nutrition interventions, would help to identify Egypt-specific (and potentially governorate-specific) unit costs for the 13 prioritized interventions. This would give a more accurate reflection of the actual costs of scale-up in the Egyptian context.

Public expenditure review. A more detailed source of information on spending is a public expenditure review (PER). A PER assesses the level and composition of actual public expenditures against a predetermined set of policy goals and outputs in the relevant national strategy or plan (as well as elements of the efficiency and effectiveness of those expenditures). Existing reporting and data monitoring systems are used, including budgets, National Health Accounts, or the OECD/DAC (Development Assistance Committee) CRS (Creditor Reporting System) database.[3] Like budget analyses, PERs are usually restricted to government expenditure and external funding that is in the budget. PERs provide a snapshot in time (repeated only every three to five years) and so does not allow a dynamic assessment of changes over time. As with budget analyses, a meaningful, efficient PER for nutrition would need to be framed in the country context using the relevant policy documents to define nutrition and identify nutrition interventions.

The World Bank is currently undertaking a PER for health in Egypt, which may help clarify nutrition-related health expenditures. This review could be enhanced to ensure that nutrition expenditures are identified separately within health expenditures. Alternatively (or in addition), a PER for nutrition (outside of the health sector) could also be undertaken that specifically examines programs with nutrition outcomes across all relevant ministries.

Health accounts. The globally standardized National Health Accounts (NHAs) are used to track health spending. The result is a standard set of tables summarizing health expenditures. NHAs track actual expenditures across sources (public, private, and external) through the perspective of function, providers, and financing mechanisms. However, they apply only to the health sector and so provide little information on nutrition-sensitive spending.

The System of Health Accounts (SHA)[4] is the framework used to implement the NHA method. Implementation of the SHA framework is country-driven and not always produced on a regular basis. The framework allows for the identification of expenditures by disease and condition (OECD, Eurostat, and WHO 2011), including public domestic and external sources of spending on treatment of nutrition deficiencies. Although the classification for diseases and conditions is only recently available and not used in all implementing countries, by using SHA 2011 one could potentially identify nutrition-related expenditures by matching interventions to the relevant NHA codes. However, this analysis is still limited to the health sector.

Table 5.2 provides the latest available information on GoE and external funding for health in Egypt in 2012 and 2015 (2012 is the only year in which data are

TABLE 5.2 National Health Accounts indicators of health expenditure: Egypt, 2012 and 2015

INDICATOR		2012	2015
General	Population (millions)		
	Total	87.81	93.78
	Less than 5 years of age	91.39	
	Females, 15–49 years of age	31.35	32.86
	Gross domestic product (GDP) (US$, millions)	254,671	352,127
	General government expenditure (GGE) (US$, millions)	84,964	105,672
Health	Current health expenditure (CHE)	12,591	14,689
	CHE as % of GDP	4.9%	4.2%
	CHE as % of GGE	14.8%	13.9%
	CHE per capita (US$)	143.38	156.64
	Domestic health expenditure (DHE) (US$, millions)	12,542	14,652
	DHE as % of GDP	4.9%	4.2%
	DHE as % of GGE	14.8%	13.9%
	DHE as % of CHE	99.6%	99.7%
	CHE per capita (US$)	142.82	156.24
	Domestic general government health expenditure (GGHE-D)	3,740	4,419
	GGHE-D as % of DHE	29.8%	30.2%
	GGHE-D per capita (US$)	42.59	47.12
	Domestic private health expenditure (PVT-D)	8,802	10,233
	PVT-D as % of DHE	70.2%	69.8%
	PVT-D per capita (US$)	100.24	109.12
	Out-of-pocket (OOP)	7,930	9,101
	OOP as % of PVT-D	90.1%	88.9%
	OOP per capita (US$)	90.31	97.05
	External health expenditure (EHE)	49	37
	EHE as % of CHE	0.4%	0.3%
	EHE per capita (US$)	0.56	0.40
	External health expenditure channeled through government (EHE-G)	36	24
	EHE-G as % of EHE	73%	64%
Nutrition	Public domestic sources of spending on nutrition deficiencies (NUT-D)	11	
	NUT-D as % of GDP	0.00%	
	NUT-D as % of GGE	0.01%	
	NUT-D as % of CHE	0.09%	
	NUT-D as % of DHE	0.09%	
	NUT-D as % of GGHE-D	0.30%	
	NUT-D per capita (US$)	0.13	

Source: Global Health Expenditure Database (GHED), World Health Organization, Geneva, http://apps.who.int/nha/database/Select/Indicators/en.

available on nutrition deficiencies). Public spending on treatment of nutrition deficiencies in Egypt was reported to be $11 million in 2012, as compared with the 2016 cost of coverage for micronutrient deficiencies (iron–folic acid and vitamin A) of $18 million calculated in chapter 4. This estimate is limited to the treatment of specific nutrition deficiencies and so does not include the prevention of poor nutrition outcomes as a whole.

A major drawback of NHAs is that they require specialized expertise, and the exercise is extremely resource-intensive. Reported public spending on nutrition deficiencies captures only 10 percent of the calculated costs of current coverage for the 13 priority interventions. Better use of the detailed function, provider, and funding mechanism data available in the NHAs to examine fiscal space for nutrition requires a number of assumptions to estimate health sector spending on nutrition programs that do not focus on treatment of nutrition deficiencies.

Nongovernmental expenditures

Official development assistance and other flows

The Creditor Reporting System[5] (CRS) of the Organisation for Economic Co-operation and Development (OECD) includes data on the value of commitments and disbursements for all official development assistance (ODA) and other official flows (including nonconcessional loans) recorded from participating Development Assistance Committee (DAC) members as well as multilateral and non-DAC donors.[6] These data can be accessed through the OECD website.[7]

The CRS includes "purpose codes" that make it possible to identify the amounts each contributor assigns to funding streams associated with the specific purpose code. The "basic nutrition" code (12240) is often used to identify nutrition-specific funding.[8] In Egypt in 2016, total committed ODA was $2,891 million, whereas $3,553 million was actually disbursed. Of that, only $2.07 million (0.07 percent) was committed to programs identified under the nutrition purpose code, while $3.56 million (0.10 percent) was actually disbursed. Reported ODA funding on nutrition represents only 2.33 percent of the estimated $152.6 million total domestic nutrition expenditure (table 5.3).

TABLE 5.3 **Committed and disbursed external funding, total and basic nutrition: Egypt, 2007–16**

| | TOTAL ALLOCATION (US$, MILLIONS) | | | | | | 12240: BASIC NUTRITION ALLOCATION (US$, MILLIONS) | |
| | COMMITMENT | | | GROSS DISBURSEMENT | | | COMMITMENT | GROSS DISBURSEMENT |
YEAR	ODA	OOF	PRIVATE GRANTS	ODA	OOF	PRIVATE GRANTS	ODA	ODA
2007	1,697	306	—	1,549	1,805	—	0.08	0.08
2008	1,957	1,444	—	1,760	628	—	1.08	0.05
2009	1,264	1,854	—	1,626	1,099	—	0.00	0.72
2010	2,481	2,784	—	1,460	1,117	—	0.09	0.27
2011	1,498	1,078	—	1,231	608	—	0.09	0.17
2012	2,896	946	—	2,130	823	—	1.12	0.14
2013	7,630	1,325	—	5,916	803	—	0.00	0.00
2014	2,651	3,034	—	4,495	1,107	—	7.55	0.49
2015	4,260	4,378	—	3,569	5,887	—	0.52	5.21
2016	2,891	4,352	—	3,553	3,538	16.57	2.07	3.56

Source: DAC CRS Database, OECD, Paris, https://stats.oecd.org/Index.aspx?ThemeTreeID=3&lang=en.
Note: — = none reported; 12240 = "basic nutrition" code; ODA = official development assistance; OOF = other official flows.

Tracking funds for nutrition by means of the CRS database using only the "basic nutrition" purpose code has several limitations. The basic nutrition code includes many of the nutrition-specific priority interventions identified for scale-up in Egypt, but currently it also contains other interventions without evidence that they have a significant impact on nutrition outcomes. To determine the specific intervention being reported, it is necessary to review each relevant project description. These descriptions are not completed at the same level of detail by all donors.

To capture other high-impact or nutrition-sensitive interventions in the CRS, one must investigate descriptions of other projects assigned to other codes[9] to assess their alignment with the available nutrition policy documents in Egypt, including the National Food and Nutrition Policy and Strategy 2007–2017 (NFNPS) and the *Nutrition Agenda for Action* 2017. Many interventions may be assigned to other codes, such as other health categories. Furthermore, nutrition-sensitive interventions, such as those implemented through water, sanitation, and hygiene (WASH) or education, will not be found under nutrition, even if nutrition is a defined outcome. Therefore, investigation of project descriptions is required to identify all nutrition-relevant projects.

Because nutrition is a multisectoral issue, nutrition-relevant programs would likely be identified across many purpose codes. However, because of lack of standardization across donors, other difficulties may arise. Although some donors will disaggregate programs with multiple purposes across multiple codes, others will assign these larger activities to a single purpose code, meaning that the relevant nutrition programs may be attached to unexpected purpose codes requiring careful investigation of the project descriptions.

Relevant projects can be identified by checking the detail of projects known to be or expected to be relevant to nutrition outcomes. This can be guided at a country level when donor activities are known. Another option is to use a keyword search of project descriptions, understanding that the level of detail in project descriptions will vary and keywords should be chosen to capture a variety of relevant projects. Once projects are identified, an assessment will be required to determine what proportion of the project should be considered relevant to nutrition.

An approach recently developed for the SUN Donor Network tracks aid in the CRS that supports nutrition targets (D'Alimonte, Heung, and Hwang 2016). This methodology is meant to improve comparability across donors, recipients, and time; complement ongoing efforts to change the way in which the CRS tracks and codes for nutrition; and align with global nutrition-specific cost estimates. If this approach is adapted by CRS, tracking of donor nutrition estimates could be significantly simplified.

Other sources of expenditure

Funding for nutrition from civil society organizations (CSOs), nongovernmental organizations (NGOs), philanthropic organizations, and other sources is not easily captured and could be substantial. These sources are normally not tracked through donor reporting or through the national accounts. In fact, this kind of primarily off-budget funding can be very difficult to track. Some country CSO networks track these investments. If NGOs provide significant resources for nutrition programming, these expenditures should be considered. Otherwise, these data may be excluded from the analysis.

IDENTIFYING FISCAL SPACE FOR NUTRITION: THE FIVE PILLARS

Fiscal space is defined as the room in a government's budget that allows it to provide resources for a desired purpose without jeopardizing the sustainability of its financial position or the stability of the economy (Heller 2005).

Domestic revenue for nutrition spending is a function of several factors: economic growth, tax collection, and the allocation of revenues to social programs. Domestic public revenue can be increased for additional spending in several ways, including increasing the tax base (the number of organizations and individuals that pay taxes); increasing the tax rates (tax as a share of economic output); and improving the efficiency of the tax administration (effectively and efficiently collecting revenue). ODA allocated to nutrition or to the general government budget or borrowing are additional sources of revenue that should be counted and potentially leveraged to increase spending for nutrition programs.

The potential for increasing fiscal space and mobilizing the additional resources required to finance the priority scale-up scenarios described in chapter 4 can be identified using Heller et al.'s 2006 framework examining five primary sources of change:

1. Conducive macroeconomic conditions

2. Reprioritization of expenditures within the government budget

3. Increase in sector-specific resources

4. Sector-specific grants or foreign aid

5. Increased efficiency of the existing sector outlay.

Conducive macroeconomic conditions

Conducive macroeconomic conditions include sustained economic growth, improved revenue generation, and low levels of fiscal deficits and debt. High levels of economic growth can result in an increase in space for nutrition funding if all spending rises proportionately and price changes for nutrition interventions are in line with overall price changes in the country. According to Central Bank of Egypt figures, overall inflation in Egypt has been high in recent years, but fell considerably, to 14.4 percent in 2018, after peaking at over 30 percent in 2017 (figure 5.1). Because nutrition is a multisectoral issue, further investigation is required to understand the effects on fiscal space of changes in prices across sectors aligned with nutrition interventions.

Figure 5.2 shows the change in the GDP growth rate over the past decade. Foreign direct investment (FDI) was a contributing factor in economic growth prior to 2010, with net inflows reaching 9.3 percent of GDP in 2006. The 2011 revolution produced an economic slowdown, which was again followed by expansion after 2012, with economic growth in 2017 at just over 4 percent and net inflows of FDI climbing steadily back up to reach 3.4 percent of GDP. Economic growth is forecast to remain relatively steady through 2020 (World Bank 2018).

From 2012 to 2015, the domestic general government health expenditure responded less than proportionately to GDP growth, with an elasticity of 0.47,[10] which is very low compared with the estimated average of low-income countries

FIGURE 5.1

Core Consumer Price Index (year-on-year percentage change): Egypt, 2011–18

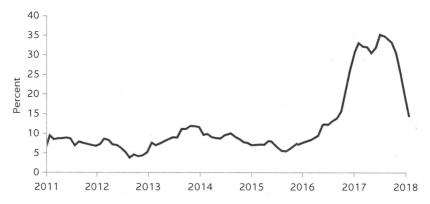

Source: Central Bank of Egypt, Economic Research Statistics: Inflation, http://www.cbe.org.eg /en/EconomicResearch/Statistics/Pages/Inflationhistorical.aspx.
Note: All index values are for January of the year shown.

FIGURE 5.2

GDP growth rate: Egypt, 2008–18

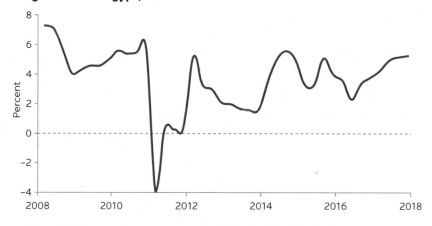

Source: Tradingeconomics.com representation of data from Central Bank of Egypt.

of 1.16. However, the analysis conducted in chapter 4 demonstrates that scaling up cost-effective stunting reduction interventions to full national coverage would result in significant internal returns (9.80 percent) on the initial five-year investment. This outcome results from the higher economic productivity of children, who do not become stunted because of the scaled-up interventions.

Although forecasting future GDP growth attributable to improvement in nutrition outcomes is outside the scope of this analysis, it is reasonable to expect a degree of economic growth from the increased productivity of Egypt's workforce able to escape stunting and the reduced reliance on social programs such as health. The reduction of stunting in Asia and Africa is estimated to increase GDP by 4–11 percent (Horton and Steckel 2013). Assuming an annual growth rate for Egypt at the low end of 4 percent and based on the 2015 GDP and current elasticity (0.47), the stunting reduction in Egypt could potentially increase the available resources for health by $33.4 million over a five-year period. This additional fiscal space is sufficient to finance the scale-up of more than half of the IYCF and micronutrient programs to full national coverage (estimated to cost a total of $61 million for the period 2018–22—see chapter 4).

Health, however, is only one element of the package of interventions for scaling up nutrition in Egypt. Consistent estimates of nutrition expenditures across sectors and years would depend on whether nutrition spending in all sectors is trending with health spending. If nutrition-related spending is targeting WASH, as suggested in the scenarios discussed in chapter 4, then changes in expenditures in the health sector alone would not be an accurate reflection of changes in nutrition investments and would not be sufficient to predict future expansion in the fiscal space for nutrition. Expenditures reflecting all nutrition programming should be collected over time to get a better overall picture.

Aside from economic growth, government revenue could also increase if tax revenue increased through an expanded tax base, new taxes, or more efficient tax collection. Revenue was 12.4 percent of GDP in 2012 and 12.5 percent of GDP in 2015, but it fluctuated between 13.5 percent in 2013 and 12.2 percent in 2014 (figure 5.3). The median tax revenue as a percentage of GDP for lower-middle-income countries has exceeded 15 percent each year since 2004 (IMF 2016), suggesting there is some room for a moderate increase in fiscal space through improved revenue generation. Revenue share in GDP tends to rise with income, but only slightly for lower-income countries. Without substantive tax policy and administration reforms, revenue increases tend not to be sustainable and are generally no more than half a percentage point of GDP per year (Bevan 2005).

Economic growth and increased revenue provide a larger pool of resources. Additional fiscal space for nutrition, however, requires government prioritization. Multisectoral strategies can utilize greater fiscal capacity to access growth across sectors. However, nutrition could be overlooked or crowded out if ownership and focus do not accompany growth.

Reprioritization of nutrition within the government budget

Another source of expansion of fiscal space is through reprioritization of nutrition in the overall government budget. Raising the overall share of nutrition spending, particularly in health, is often a challenge in Egypt because of the competing priorities for finite resources and the country's highly centralized budget allocation decisions, leaving little space to advance a nutrition agenda. In Egypt,

FIGURE 5.3

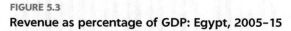

Revenue as percentage of GDP: Egypt, 2005–15

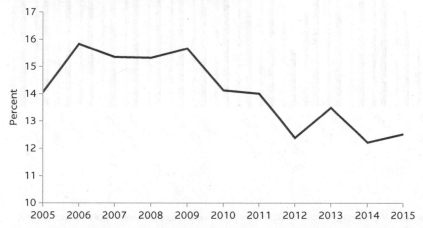

Source: World Bank, https://data.worldbank.org/indicator/GC.TAX.TOTL.GD.ZS?locations=EG.

health expenditure as a percentage of GDP was 5.6 percent in 2014 as reported by the World Bank.[11] This share falls below the median (6.1 percent) and mean (6.8 percent) for lower-middle-income countries in the Middle East and North Africa, Sub-Saharan Africa, and South Asia in the same time period (see figure 5.4). There is an opportunity, therefore, for an increase in fiscal space for nutrition through health.

Nutrition strategies, however, are multisectoral and require prioritization and coordination at a high level to achieve common goals. Egypt's nutrition policy is mainly divided among eight ministries: Health and Population; Agriculture and Land Reclamation; Industry, Trade and Small Industries; Supply and Internal Trade; Social Solidarity; Local Development (representing governorates); Higher Education and Scientific Research; and Education.

Effective organization and management across these sectors are needed to set common goals, prioritize interventions across sectors, and coordinate activities to promote efficiencies and build on synergistic activities. Prioritization of a multisectoral issue such as nutrition requires agreement and buy-in from all participating ministries. No interministerial or intraministerial committees exist in Egypt to aid in coordination or joint accountability. In addition, complementary

FIGURE 5.4

Health expenditure share of GDP: selected countries, 2008–14

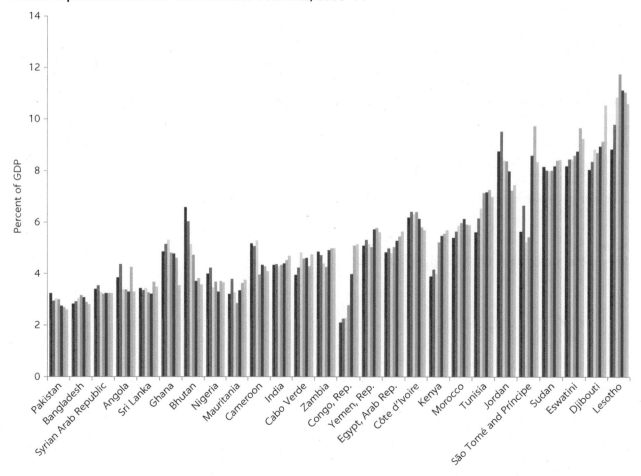

Source: World Development Indicators (database), World Bank, Washington, DC, current health expenditure (percent of GDP) indicator SH.XPD. TOTL.ZS, https://data.worldbank.org/indicator/.

Note: Bars represent (from left to right) the years 2008–14. GDP = gross domestic product.

areas of interest result in overlapping efforts, wasted resources, and competing management and control. Chronic weakness in cross-ministerial coordination, a lack of clear roles and responsibilities, and the absence of a results-based accountability framework for such cross-sectoral policies make aligning priorities and implementing a common results framework challenging.

Increase in sector-specific resources

Although the multisectorality of nutrition presents challenges across sectors, there may be an opportunity to increase fiscal space through a broader range of sectoral options. Nutrition programming involves diverse dimensions and entities. Even with agreement across sectors, interest and commitment within sectors vary. Understanding the variation in commitment as well as the potential for improving nutrition outcomes resulted in the prioritization of the 13 interventions for scale-up, leaving health as the main sector of implementation in the short term.

New resources could be collected within the health sector through programs such as taxes earmarked for health (or nutrition), mandatory fee-bearing programs (such as insurance), or user fees for public health facilities. Earmarking is effective in that it specifies where funding must be directed, thereby protecting nutrition programming in years when it is not as highly prioritized. Such an approach takes political will and a commitment to guaranteeing long-term funding, but it can be inefficient if nutrition priorities change and the earmarking does not align with new interventions. This is complicated in multisectoral environments where it is not simple to define or identify "nutrition interventions," especially in a changing environment and within evolving understanding of evidence-based practices. Furthermore, it is important to ensure that earmarking is not used simply to shift resources and that the earmarked funds do not replace the existing flows of funding.

Increasing taxes specifically on goods that are known to have adverse impact nutrition outcomes, such as sugary drinks and junk food, is another option. In addition to raising revenue, this approach can also reduce the types of behaviors that nutrition programming seeks to change, providing both public health and economic benefits. Even if the funds are not specifically earmarked for nutrition programs, improved public health and expansion of the general revenues should both benefit nutrition programs and outcomes.

Care must be taken when implementing such taxes, however, to ensure that the taxed goods are not disproportionately affecting the poor and that healthier substitutes are available when prices faced by consumers rise. A detailed benefit-incidence analysis is needed to ensure a tax is not regressive, that increasing taxes will raise total tax revenue (and by what amount), and to determine if the tax will affect employment.

In Egypt, sugar subsidies have increased consumption of sugar at the expense of the government budget. Removing subsidies has the same general effect as raising taxes both in benefits and detriments. Consideration must be given to secondary markets and employment.

Nutrition-specific grants or foreign aid

External assistance for health, and more recently nutrition, can be an important element of overall fiscal space for improving nutrition. However, Egypt is not heavily reliant on aid in this area. According to the NHA, external funding as a proportion of the current health expenditure in 2015 was only 0.3 percent, down from 0.4 percent in 2012, with no external sources of funding for treatment of nutrition deficiencies identified (table 5.2). The CRS data show that $5.2 million in ODA was disbursed for basic nutrition in 2015, with a further $3.6 million disbursed in 2016 by donors (table 5.3). The 2016 figure represents 3.2 percent of the $112 million required for current coverage of the 13 prioritized nutrition interventions.

The low level of reliance on external funding sources at a time when health and nutrition-specific aid programs have increased significantly since the adoption of the Millennium Development Goals (MDGs) suggests there may be room to expand donor funding in Egypt. However, the unpredictability of aid flows may increase the risk of losing sustainable prioritized programming. Requesting aid for specific programs or start-up costs for programs may be a way to mitigate the uncertainty of external funds. It is important to ensure that external aid does not replace domestic resources and that a withdrawal plan is in place. This is, however, less of an issue in countries such as Egypt where overall donor funding is a small percentage of health expenditures and where domestic funding can supplement programs.

How funds are distributed is also important to the effectiveness of applying funds to activities in national-level nutrition plans. Where donor assistance is off-budget, donors can control how resources are used, possibly ignoring government priorities. The method of funding in Egypt has become more important in light of the law Regulating the Work of Associations and Other Institutions Working in the Field of Civil Work issued in 2017, which requires a rigorous process of state approval for all NGO operations. Domestic organizations need prior permission before they "cooperate with, join, affiliate with, or participate with" any foreign organization. Authorization is also required before receiving any foreign funds or funds from Egyptians abroad, conducting field research, or collecting data. This law could severely curtail the ability of donors to support programs within Egypt. On the other hand, if the law is well implemented, the GoE would have a much better understanding of the flow of funds and would be better able to ensure that funds align with priorities and to redirect resources where there are overlaps and inefficiencies.

Increased efficiency of the existing sector outlays

Efficiency—technical or allocative—is achieved by maximizing outputs with a given level of inputs. Technical efficiency is achieved when maximum output (for example, the number of children reached) is achieved for a given level of inputs. Allocative efficiency refers to the choice of an appropriate mix of inputs to achieve the outputs needed (for example, the appropriate targets are reached). Nutrition programming in Egypt can benefit through changes in both.

The cost-effectiveness analysis in chapter 4 identifies the package of interventions and scale-up scenarios that produces the most impact (in terms of deaths prevented in children under 5, cases of stunting averted, and DALYs averted) for the least cost (scenario 3). The intervention package includes IYCF programs (breastfeeding and promotion of complementary feeding); iron–folic acid supplementation for pregnant women; vitamin A supplementation for children; and hygienic disposal of children's stools. Scaling up this intervention package to full national coverage would require $82 million over the five-year period from 2018 to 2022. This investment would avert 4,249 deaths and 421,360 cases of stunting and save 23,713 DALYs.

The wide variation in nutrition outcomes across governorates suggests inefficiencies in the implementation of effective interventions that should be addressed. Geographic targeting of governorates and individuals differentially affected by poor nutrition outcomes both saves resources by reaching those most likely to be affected by interventions and is allocatively efficient by targeting those vulnerable populations most in need. In addition, it would be helpful to understand how nutrition spending is disbursed through the sectors and distributed to target populations. A number of inefficiencies can arise when there are multiple layers from disbursement to implementation. Further inefficiencies can arise if funds are tied to specific activities or delivery channels, but these approaches are not appropriate in all contexts. A balance must be found between securing funds for specific nutrition activities and allowing flexible spending for nutrition outcomes. Achieving that balance will depend largely on an ability to translate options and results through the delivery system to the targeted population.

Absorptive capacity is another potential area of inefficiency. It is not enough to disburse funds; the funds must be used appropriately. Lack of personnel, poor infrastructure, and weak supply chains are often large contributors to lack of absorptive capacity. On the supply side, additional resources are required to develop new capacity and strengthen the existing health system to address malnutrition. Egypt utilizes the Monitoring of Results Equity System (MORES) framework, which can allow, for example, an in-depth look at how effectively health centers are performing.

An important factor especially relevant to multisectoral programs such as nutrition is the ability to coordinate efforts across sectors. Coordinated efforts in programming can create significant efficiencies in sharing resources, delivery platforms, and messaging, and can improve the effectiveness of interventions. Integration of multisectoral efforts in sectoral plans and priorities is important to ensure that implementation is also efficiently achieved within sectors.

Currently, Egypt does not have a fully-costed nutrition action plan. However, the GoE is committed to developing such a plan. It will be important to have realistic cost estimates for achieving the goals of any plan developed, as well as disbursements aligned with those estimates. Without a thoughtful alignment of costs and impacts, disbursements will not align with needs and inefficiencies will result. Further alignment of nutrition policies and plans with overall health and other sector strategies is also vital to facilitating efficiencies within and across sectors.

Longer-term development and coordination are occurring through the Ministry of Planning, Monitoring and Administrative Reform in response to the Sustainable Development Goals (SDGs). Global nutrition strategies are integral to 10 of the 17 SDGs. Multisectoral nutrition planning should not be done in isolation; it should work in step with the Sustainable Development Strategy: Egypt Vision 2030.

SUMMARY OF FISCAL SPACE

Table 5.4 summarizes the prospect for creating fiscal space for nutrition in Egypt using the five pillars discussed in this chapter. Improved macroeconomic

TABLE 5.4 Fiscal space for nutrition in Egypt

FISCAL SPACE SOURCE	EXPLANATION	PROSPECT FOR FISCAL SPACE
Conducive macroeconomic conditions	Would increase the medium- and long-term GDP growth from improved productivity due to a reduction in stunting	Good
	Has potential for improved revenue generation	
Reprioritization of nutrition within the government budget	Would strengthen intrasectoral coordination	Limited
Increase in sector-specific resources	Would entail taxes earmarked for health (or nutrition), mandatory fee-bearing programs (such as insurance), or user fees for public health facilities	Limited
Nutrition-specific grants or foreign aid	Egypt is not heavily reliant on aid in nutrition.	Limited
Increased efficiency of the existing sector outlays	Would produce allocative and operational efficiency gains in delivering only the most cost-effective interventions in stunting reduction	Good

Source: World Bank assessment, based on guidelines laid out in Heller 2005.
Note: GDP = gross domestic product.

conditions in the long run as well as medium-run efficiency gains are two areas with good prospects of generating significant additional resources for nutrition.

In the long run, it is reasonable to expect significant economic growth from the greater productivity of Egypt's workforce stemming from the reduction in stunting. Lower levels of stunting and the resulting improved health will also reduce reliance on social programs and cut stunting-related health costs. Aside from economic growth, GoE revenue could also grow if tax revenue increases through an expanded tax base, new taxes, or more efficient tax collection.

Allocative and operational efficiency gains can be obtained in the medium run by focusing on delivery of the most cost-effective interventions in stunting reduction: IYCF (especially promotion of complementary feeding), iron–folic acid supplementation, vitamin A supplementation for children, and promotion of hygienic disposal of children's stools. These interventions are also those that can be scaled up quickly either with the existing capacity or with relatively small investments. This strategy is expected to translate into substantial economic benefits and return the highest economic benefits over the productive lives of the children who receive the interventions.

This discussion relies heavily on public information available for the health sector in Egypt. A complete analysis of fiscal space for nutrition that includes both health and the seven other represented sectors would require expanding the specifics in the pillars discussed here to include information that represents all nutrition spaces. This would include an assessment of the elasticity of nutrition spending with respect to GDP, which will require assessing in turn elasticity across sectors; an understanding of the share of nutrition expenditures in the budget and the disposition of all stakeholders toward expanding that share; an assessment of potential revenue sources in each of the ministries earmarked or connected to nutrition programs and outcomes; an examination of the effects of the law Regulating the Work of Associations and Other Institutions Working in the Field of Civil Work on donor participation in Egypt; and a thorough examination of the distribution channels for nutrition interventions and the willingness and ability of the relevant sectors and higher levels of the government of Egypt to administer the multisectoral efforts to combat malnutrition.

NOTES

1. Health and Population; Agriculture and Land Reclamation; Industry, Trade and Small Industries; Supply and Internal Trade; Social Solidarity; Local Development (representing governorates); Higher Education and Scientific Research; and Education.
2. See http://scalingupnutrition.org/share-learn/planning-and-implementation/tracking -nutrition-investments/ for a description of the three-step approach used by SUN countries.
3. Organisation for Economic Co-operation and Development/Development Assistance Committee Creditor Reporting System. OECD/DAC CRS database: https://stats.oecd.org /Index.aspx?DataSetCode=CRS1.
4. The Health Accounts Country Platform provides the System of Health Accounts (SHA) framework, tools, and templates. Data are publicly available through the WHO'S Global Health Expenditure Database (GHED). Information and data are available at http://www .who.int/health-accounts/en/.
5. http://www.oecd.org/tax/automatic-exchange/common-reporting-standard/.
6. The system also has the capacity to track development assistance from private donors, of which one, the Bill and Melinda Gates Foundation, currently participates.
7. http://stats.oecd.org/.
8. "Basic nutrition" includes direct feeding programs (maternal feeding, breastfeeding and weaning foods, child feeding, school feeding); determination of micronutrient deficiencies; provision of vitamin A, iodine, and iron; monitoring of nutritional status; nutrition and food hygiene education; and household food security.
9. A complete list of DAC and CRS codes can be found at http://www.oecd.org/dac/stats /dacandcrscodelists.htm.
10. Elasticity of 0.47 implies that a 1 percent increase in GDP is associated on average with a 0.47 percent increase in the government health expenditure.
11. World Bank, World Development Indicators (database), current health expenditure (percent of GDP) indicator SH.XPD.TOTL.ZS, https://data.worldbank.org/indicator/.

REFERENCES

D'Alimonte, M., S. Heung, and C. Hwang. 2016. *Tracking Funding for Nutrition: Improving How Aid for Nutrition Is Reported and Monitored.* Policy Brief, Results for Development (R4D), Washington, DC. https://www.r4d.org/wp-content/uploads/R4D_TrackingAid4Nutrition -final-1.pdf.

Bevan, David. 2005. "An Analytical Review of Aid Absorption: Recognizing and Avoiding Macroeconomic Hazards." Paper presented to Seminar on Foreign Aid and Microeconomic Management, Maputo, March 14–15.

Heller, P. 2005. "Back to Basics—Fiscal Space: What It Is and How to Get It." *Finance and Development* (International Monetary Fund) 42 (2). http://www.imf.org/external/pubs/ft /fandd/2005/06/basics.htm.

Heller, P. S., M. Katz, X. Debrun, T. Thomas, T. Koranchelian, and I. Adenauer. 2006. "Making Fiscal Space Happen: Managing Fiscal Policy in a World of Scaled-up Aid." Working Paper, International Monetary Fund, Washington, DC. http://www.imf.org/external/pubs/ft /wp/2006/wp06270.pdf.

Horton, S., and R. H. Steckel. 2013. "Malnutrition: Global Economic Losses Attributable to Malnutrition 1990–2000 and Projections to 2050." In *How Much Have Global Problems Cost the World? A Scorecard from 1900 to 2050*, edited by B. Lomborg, 247–72 Cambridge, U.K.: Cambridge University Press.

IMF (International Monetary Fund). 2016. World Revenue Longitudinal Data Set (WoRLD), https://data.world/imf/world-revenue-longitudinal-dat.

OECD (Organisation for Economic Co-operation and Development), Eurostat, and WHO (World Health Organization. 2011. *A System of Health Accounts. 2011 Edition.* Paris: OECD Publishing. http://www.who.int/nha/sha_revision/sha_2011_final1.pdf.

World Bank. 2018. "Middle East and North Africa." In *Global Economic Prospects, January 2018: Broad-Based Upturn, but for How Long?*, 117–156. Washington, DC: World Bank. http:// pubdocs.worldbank.org/en/124691512062603210/Global-Economic-Prospects-Jan-2018 -Middle-East-and-North-Africa-analysis.pdf.

APPENDIX A

Statistical Methods Applied to Analysis of the Determinants of Malnutrition among Egyptian Children

METHODS

The following describes how the determinants from each level of the UNICEF Conceptual Framework for the Determinants of Malnutrition were operationalized and the analytic approach taken.

Identifying the immediate determinants

Disease incidence. The Egypt Demographic and Health Survey (EDHS) provides information on recent incidence of infectious diseases among young children (MOHP, El-Zanaty and Associates, and ICF International 2015). In our analysis, we coded variables for the incidence of diarrhea and respiratory infection. For diarrhea, respondents were asked if the child had diarrhea in the two weeks preceding the survey. A response of "yes" was coded 1; 0 otherwise. For respiratory infection, respondents were asked if the child experienced a cough accompanied by short rapid breaths in the two weeks preceding the survey. A response of "yes" for both conditions was coded 1; 0 otherwise.

Identifying the underlying determinants

Feeding practices. Feeding practices were defined according to the established World Health Organization (WHO) standards for infant and young child feeding (IYCF) practices (WHO 2008). Specifically, it is recommended that children under 6 months of age be exclusively breastfed and that children 6–23 months old of age continue breastfeeding and have a minimum number of feedings of nutritionally diverse complementary foods. A nutritionally diverse diet must include foods from at least four of the seven basic food groups; (1) grains, roots, and tubers; (2) legumes and nuts; (3) dairy (milk, yogurt, cheese); (4) meat and fish; (5) eggs; (6) fruits and vegetables rich in vitamin A; and (7) other fruits and vegetables. Table A.1 summarizes the recommendations for dietary intake for children 0–23 months of age, along with how the relevant indicators were coded in our analyses.

TABLE A.1 Indicators for feeding practices

AGE GROUP	RECOMMENDATION	VARIABLE
Under 6 months old	Exclusively breastfed	Exclusively breastfed = 1 if breastfed in the 24 hours preceding the survey and had no other solid, semisolid, or soft foods or liquids; = 0 otherwise.
Breastfed, 6–8 months old	At least two feedings and diverse diet	Adequate feeding frequency = 1 if fed with solid, semisolid, or soft foods at least two times during the 24 hours preceding the survey; = 0 otherwise.
		Diverse diet = 1 if child consumed foods from four of the seven basic food groups in the 24 hours preceding the survey; = 0 otherwise.
Breastfed, 9–23 months old	At least three feedings and diverse diet	Adequate feeding frequency = 1 if fed with solid, semisolid, or soft foods at least three times during the 24 hours preceding the survey; = 0 otherwise.
		Diverse diet = 1 if child consumed foods from four of the seven basic food groups in the 24 hours preceding the survey; = 0 otherwise.
Nonbreastfed, 6–23 months old	At least four feedings and two feedings of milk and diverse diet (four of the six basic food groups, not counting dairy, the seventh)	Adequate feeding frequency = 1 if fed with solid, semisolid, or soft foods at least four times during the 24 hours preceding the survey; = 0 otherwise.
		Adequate milk feeding = 1 if child was fed with any combination of powdered/tinned/fresh milk, infant formula, and yogurt at least two times in the 24 hours preceding the survey; = 0 otherwise.
		Diverse diet = 1 if child consumed foods from four of the six basic food groups (excludes dairy from the standard seven) in the 24 hours preceding the survey; = 0 otherwise.

Care practices. Care practices for both the mother and infant are considered. Infant care practices included early initiation of breastfeeding and timely attendance at a postnatal checkup after birth. Early initiation of breastfeeding was dichotomized and coded 1 if the mother reported having breastfed the infant within one hour of delivery; 0 otherwise. Timely attendance at postnatal checkup was coded 1 if the mother responded that the child received a checkup from a skilled provider within two days of birth; 0 otherwise. Maternal care practices included attendance at antenatal care visits, delivery in a health facility, and timely maternal postnatal care. Antenatal care was dichotomized, with 1 representing four or more visits during the most recent pregnancy; 0 otherwise. Delivery in health facility was coded 1 for "yes"; 0 otherwise. Maternal postnatal checkup was coded 1 if the mother reported being examined by a skilled provider immediately or within two days of delivery; 0 otherwise.

Household environment. The adequacy of the household environment was assessed based on the availability of improved water source and improved sanitation facilities. Improved facilities for water and sanitation were defined according to standards established by the WHO/UNICEF Joint Monitoring Programme for Water Supply, Sanitation, and Hygiene (2017). Variables for improved sanitation facility were each coded 1 if they met the Joint Monitoring Programme (JMP) criteria; 0 otherwise.[1] Because nearly 86 percent of children lived in households with piped water, water source was dichotomized as 1 for piped source; 0 otherwise.

Health services. Access to and utilization of health services was proxied using child's immunization and vitamin A supplementation status. Completeness of immunization was defined based on guidelines for age-appropriate immunization from Egypt's Ministry of Health and Population (UNICEF 2015). Vitamin A status was based on a child receiving a vitamin A supplement in the six months preceding the survey.

Women's empowerment. Women's empowerment has been linked to positive child health and nutrition outcomes (Smith et al. 2003). We defined women's status based on a series of questions about participation in three decisions: on large household purchases, on visiting her family, and on seeking care for herself. Each of these were dichotomized into binary variables for analysis.

Identifying the basic determinants

Basic determinants were modeled using maternal education and household wealth quintile. Maternal education was coded into categorical responses for no education, completed primary or less, incomplete secondary, completed secondary, and higher education. Household wealth quintiles were based on the Demographic and Health Survey (DHS) classifications, with wealth quintile 1 comprising the poorest households and wealth quintile 5 comprising the richest households.

OTHER BACKGROUND CHARACTERISTICS

The regression models used in the analyses controlled for other maternal, child, and household background characteristics. These were maternal stature, maternal body mass index (BMI) status (thin, normal, overweight/obese), maternal age group (15–19, 20–24, 25–29, 30–34, 35 or older), child being a boy, child's birth order (1, 2, 3, 4, 5, or greater), the preceding birth interval (less than 24 months, 24–35 months, 35–47 months, 48 months or longer), mother's report of child's size at birth, and the number of children under 5 in the household.

STATISTICAL ANALYSIS

Analytic sample. The 2014 EDHS data set includes records on 15,848 children under 5. Included in the sample are 5,752 children (36 percent of 0–5 sample) 0–23 months of age with valid anthropometric measurements. Our analytic sample excluded children who were not usual residents of the sample household (328 cases) or not the youngest child living with the mother (231 cases). Our final analytic sample included 5,193 children 0–23 months of age.

Analyses. Analyses were conducted using the R statistical computing software version 3.3.2 and accompanying packages for complex survey analysis and data manipulation (Lumley 2004; Smith et al. 2003).[2] We used chi-square tests to assess the association between each variable and the odds of stunting. Variables from the bivariate analysis with p values of less than 0.30 were selected for inclusion in the subsequent multivariate models. We used multivariate logistic regression models to assess the association between the odds of stunting and the set of child, maternal, and household variables at the immediate, underlying, and basic levels of the UNICEF framework for determinants of malnutrition. We then fit three models. First, we fit a model (I) for all children 0–23 months of age, including all covariates except breastfeeding and complementary feeding variables. Second, we fit the same model for children 0–5 months of age with an additional variable for exclusive breastfeeding (model II). And third, we fit model (I) for children 6–23 months of age and included variables for complementary feeding practices such as feeding frequency and diet diversity (model III). We report odds ratios and 95 percent confidence intervals for the multivariate models. Covariates from the regression estimates with p values less than 0.05 were considered significant. We used survey weights and took account of clustering to adjust point estimates and standard errors for the complex sampling design of the DHS.

NOTES

1. The JMP classification for improved water source is as follows: piped water into the dwelling, public taps, boreholes/tube wells, protected wells and springs, rainwater, packaged water, delivered water (including tankers and small carts); improved sanitation facilities: flush and pour flush toilets connected to sewer, flush and pour flush toilets or latrines connected to septic tanks or pits, ventilated improved pit latrine, pit latrines with slabs, composting toilets.

2. Lumley, A. T. No date. "Survey: Analysis of Complex Survey Samples". R package version 3.32. https://rdrr.io/rforge/survey/; R Core Team, R: A Language and Environment for Statistical Computing. R Found Stat Comput. 2016; version 3:3503, doi:10.1007/978-3-540 -74686-7; H. Wickam, tidyverse: Easily Install and Load the "Tidyverse," R package version 1.2.1. 2017, https://cran.r-project.org/package=tidyverse; H. Wickham and E. Miller, Haven: Import and Export "SPSS," "Stata" and "SAS" Files. R package version 1.1.1. 2018, https:// cran.r-project.org/package=haven.

REFERENCES

Lumley, A. T. 2004. "Analysis of Complex Survey Samples." *Journal of Statistical Software* 9 (1): 1–19.

MOHP (Ministry of Health and Population), El-Zanaty and Associates, and ICF International. 2015. *Egypt Demographic and Health Survey 2014.* Cairo, Egypt and Rockville, MD: Ministry of Health and Population and ICF International. https://dhsprogram.com/pubs/pdf /FR302/FR302.pdf.

Smith, L. C., U. Ramakrishnan, A. Ndiaye, L. Haddad, and R. Martorell. 2003. *The Importance of Women's Status for Child Nutrition in Developing Countries.* Research Report 131, International Food Policy Research Institute, Washington, DC.

UNICEF (United Nations Children's Fund). 2015. "Immunization and Health." In *Children in Egypt: A Statistical Digest.* Cairo: UNICEF.

WHO (World Health Organization). 2008. *Indicators for Assessing Infant and Young Child Feeding Practices: Part 1—Definitions: Conclusions of a Consensus Meeting held 6–8 November 2007 in Washington DC, USA.* Geneva: WHO. http://apps.who.int/iris/bitstream/handle/10 665/43895/9789241596664_eng.pdf?sequence=1.

WHO (World Health Organization)/UNICEF (United Nations Children's Fund) Joint Monitoring Programme for Water Supply and Sanitation. 2017. *Progress on Drinking Water, Sanitation and Hygiene: 2017 Update and SDG Baselines.* Geneva. https://www.who .int/mediacentre/news/releases/2017/launch-version-report-jmp-water-sanitation -hygiene.pdf.

Distribution of Sample by Key Characteristics and Regression Analysis Results

TABLE B.1 Distribution of sample of children 0–23 months of age by child, maternal, and household characteristics

	NATIONAL (n = 5,193)	URBAN GOVERNORATES (n = 714)	RURAL UPPER EGYPT (n = 1,632)	URBAN UPPER EGYPT (n = 611)	RURAL LOWER EGYPT (n = 1,408)	URBAN LOWER EGYPT (n = 494)	RURAL FRONTIER GOVERNORATES (n = 102)	URBAN FRONTIER GOVERNORATES (n = 232)
Child characteristics								
Sex								
Male	52.5	49.9	51.5	57.0	52.1	55.5	51.9	53.1
Female	47.5	5.01	48.5	43.0	47.9	44.5	48.1	46.9
Age group (months)								
0–5	21.6	20.3	24.0	23.5	20.4	18.1	14.3	19.7
6–8	15.1	13.3	16.2	16.4	14.8	13.1	16.5	11.9
9–11	13.4	16.3	11.0	12.9	14.4	14.4	10.4	15.5
12–23	49.9	50.1	48.8	47.2	50.4	54.4	58.8	52.9
Birth order								
First	27.7	26.6	23.9	25.1	31.8	28.1	17.8	31.5
Second	28.6	32.4	25.4	28.5	29.2	32.9	26.4	36.3
Third	22.8	22.7	21.0	22.4	24.4	23.5	20.9	14.5
Fourth	12.5	14.0	14.0	14.4	10.7	11.0	13.7	9.0
Fifth or later	8.4	4.3	15.7	9.6	3.9	4.5	21.2	8.7
Birth size								
Large or very large	2.2	1.4	2.3	0.4	2.9	2.2	1.1	4.4
Average	80.9	85.9	80.5	85.2	79.1	79.2	92.2	72.3
Small or very small	16.9	12.7	17.2	14.4	18.0	18.6	6.7	23.3
Has all age-appropriate immunizations	82.6	85.0	80.8	82.4	83.3	82.7	78.0	85.9
Maternal characteristics								
Age group (years)								
15–19	4.8	2.2	5.8	3.2	5.4	3.7	5.5	2.5
20–24	28.3	16.6	31.1	23.5	32.5	18.9	20.7	31.2
25–29	34.2	36.2	32.0	30.7	35.0	40.1	38.6	32.9
30–34	20.7	25.4	20.0	25.4	18.0	24.3	19.9	20.1
35 or older	12.0	19.6	11.1	17.2	9.1	13.0	15.3	13.3
Education								
No education	16.3	10.3	27.9	13.0	11.5	6.7	35.8	11.4
Primary or less	8.7	8.5	10.9	7.5	7.8	6.7	14.7	7.5
Incomplete secondary	15.0	14.1	18.0	13.4	14.2	11.4	10.9	13.0

continued

TABLE B.1, *continued*

	NATIONAL (n = 5,193)	URBAN GOVERNORATES (n = 714)	RURAL UPPER EGYPT (n = 1,632)	URBAN UPPER EGYPT (n = 611)	RURAL LOWER EGYPT (n = 1,408)	URBAN LOWER EGYPT (n = 494)	RURAL FRONTIER GOVERNORATES (n = 102)	URBAN FRONTIER GOVERNORATES (n = 232)
Completed secondary	43.7	41.0	36.0	45.1	49.9	45.5	25.1	44.4
Higher education	16.3	26.1	7.2	21.0	16.6	29.7	13.5	23.7
Maternal characteristics								
Height								
<145 cm	0.7	0.3	1.2	0.6	0.4	0.2	2.3	0.1
≧145 cm	99.3	99.7	98.8	99.7	99.6	99.8	97.7	99.9
BMI								
Thin (BMI <18.5)	0.4	0.3	0.7	0.2	0.3	0.0	0.3	0.0
Normal (BMI ≧18.5 and <25)	23.8	23.0	29.1	19.4	23.2	13.5	30.9	28.4
Overweight or obese (BMI ≧25)	75.8	76.7	70.2	80.4	76.5	86.5	68.8	71.6
Attended at least four antenatal visits during last pregnancy	83.0	89.6	72.6	81.0	88.3	91.8	64.9	84.6
Had postnatal care checkup after last delivery	97.7	98.7	97.7	98.9	97.4	96.5	100.0	97.0
Delivered last child in health facility	88.2	95.2	79.0	90.9	91.0	97.5	76.0	90.1
Makes decisions about her own health care	80.2	85.9	76.0	87.0	79.3	85.0	69.2	80.1
Makes decisions about large household purchases	63.6	71.0	52.3	74.3	66.4	70.7	60.5	57.7
Makes decisions about visiting her family	71.9	82.2	64.2	79.8	71.6	79.1	64.8	70.0
Household characteristics								
Place of residence								
Urban	29.8	n.a.	n.a.	n.a.	n.a.	n.a.	n.a.	n.a.
Rural	70.2	n.a.	n.a.	n.a.	n.a.	n.a.	n.a.	n.a.
Wealth index								
Poorest	16.7	0.8	31.4	4.0	15.7	2.6	33.8	14.0
Second	18.8	0.8	35.4	3.6	18.1	1.9	31.3	5.0
Third	25.4	2.0	25.8	7.5	41.0	3.4	27.0	4.1
Fourth	22.8	31.6	7.4	39.5	25.2	36.4	7.9	27.6
Richest	16.3	64.8	0.0	45.4	0.0	55.7	0.0	49.3
Household has piped water into the dwelling	89.7	96.5	90.5	97.0	85.6	90.8	60.2	68.1
Household uses improved sanitation	88.9	99.5	92.7	98.4	78.1	99.2	99.3	100.0
Number of children under 5 in the household								
Less than three	87.5	91.6	81.5	90.5	89.6	92.7	72.0	89.4
Three or more	12.5	8.4	18.5	9.5	10.4	7.8	28.0	10.6

Note: BMI = body mass index; cm = centimeter; n = number; n.a. = not applicable.

TABLE B.2 Adjusted odds ratio of stunting for children 0–23 months of age in Egypt

	AGE GROUP		
	0–23 MONTHS	0–5 MONTHS	6–23 MONTHS
	ADJUSTED OR (95% CI)	ADJUSTED OR (95% CI)	ADJUSTED OR (95% CI)
Sex (reference: female)			
Male	1.47*** (1.22, 1.78)	2.01** (1.28, 3.16)	1.44*** (1.17, 1.78)
Child's size at birth (mother's report) (reference: average size)			
Large or very large	0.54 (0.25, 1.17)	1.74 (0.36, 8.47)	0.42* (0.18, 0.99)
Small or very small	1.25 (0.98, 1.60)	1.88* (1.06, 3.34)	1.16 (0.88, 1.52)
Early initiation of breastfeeding	0.75** (0.60, 0.93)	0.67 (0.38, 1.17)	0.77* (0.61, 0.98)
Adequate meal frequency			0.99 (0.80, 1.24)
Fed a diverse diet			1.13 (0.91, 1.41)
Currently breastfed			0.91 (0.69, 1.20)
Exclusively breastfed		0.93 (0.54, 1.60)	
Mother's education level (reference: completed secondary)			
No education	1.11 (0.82, 1.49)	1.24 (0.64, 2.40)	1.12 (0.80, 1.56)
At least some primary	1.34 (0.95, 1.90)	1.20 (0.52, 2.75)	1.37 (0.94, 2.02)
Incomplete secondary	1.35* (1.03, 1.77)	1.78 (0.95, 3.34)	1.25 (0.93, 1.70)
Completed secondary	1.07 (0.82, 1.41)	1.08 (0.55, 2.09)	1.06 (0.78, 1.44)
Higher	0.87 (0.71, 1.08)	0.81 (0.50, 1.31)	0.88 (0.69, 1.12)
Child received postnatal checkup	0.99 (0.76, 1.29)	0.63 (0.34, 1.17)	1.04 (0.77, 1.39)
Mother received postnatal checkup	1.68 (0.87, 3.23)	1.96 (0.41, 9.31)	1.63 (0.80, 3.35)
Woman participates in decisions on large household purchases	0.87 (0.69, 1.10)	0.78 (0.45, 1.33)	0.88 (0.68, 1.13)
Woman participates in decisions about visiting her family	1.02 (0.80, 1.30)	1.10 (0.60, 2.03)	1.04 (0.79, 1.36)
Wealth quintile (reference: poorest)			
Second	1.20 (0.88, 1.64)	0.52 (0.22, 1.23)	1.32 (0.93, 1.87)
Third	0.89 (0.64, 1.22)	1.03 (0.50, 2.14)	0.88 (0.61, 1.27)
Fourth	1.02 (0.70, 1.48)	2.48* (1.03, 5.99)	0.87 (0.57, 1.31)
Richest	1.17 (0.74, 1.87)	2.51 (0.77, 8.17)	1.03 (0.62, 1.72)
Household has improved toilet facility	1.05 (0.74, 1.49)	1.22 (0.53, 2.82)	1.02 (0.69, 1.52)
Region (reference: urban governorates)			
Rural Upper Egypt	1.48 (0.96, 2.30)	1.62 (0.54, 4.85)	1.55 (0.96, 2.50)
Urban Upper Egypt	1.74** (1.20, 2.51)	0.89 (0.37, 2.13)	2.04*** (1.35, 3.09)
Rural Lower Egypt	0.97 (0.64, 1.48)	0.91 (0.33, 2.51)	1.00 (0.63, 1.58)
Urban Lower Egypt	0.99 (0.67, 1.48)	0.40 (0.14, 1.12)	1.21 (0.78, 1.88)
Rural frontier governorates	0.86 (0.38, 1.98)	2.40 (0.30, 19.40)	0.77 (0.31, 1.93)
Urban frontier governorates	1.33 (0.80, 2.20)	0.57 (0.18, 1.78)	1.53 (0.87, 2.70)

Note: CI = confidence interval; OR = odds ratio.
*p < .05 **p < .01 ***p < .001.

TABLE B.3 Adjusted odds ratio of stunting for urban children 0–23 months in Egypt

	AGE GROUP		
	0–23 MONTHS	**0–5 MONTHS**	**6–23 MONTHS**
	ADJUSTED OR (95% CI)	**ADJUSTED OR (95% CI)**	**ADJUSTED OR (95% CI)**
Sex (reference: female)			
Male	1.51** (1.11, 2.06)	1.92 (0.90, 4.09)	1.47* (1.04, 2.07)
Child's size at birth (mother's report) (reference: average size)			
Large or very large	0.46 (0.09, 2.30)	0.05* (0.005, 0.64)	0.51 (0.09, 2.88)
Small or very small	0.98 (0.65, 1.48)	1.64 (0.58, 4.64)	0.91 (0.57, 1.46)
Early initiation of breastfeeding	1.08 (0.76, 1.53)	0.72 (0.31, 1.67)	1.24 (0.83, 1.84)
Adequate meal frequency			1.08 (0.75, 1.55)
Fed a diverse diet			1.07 (0.74, 1.53)
Currently breastfed			0.83 (0.53, 1.28)
Exclusively breastfed		0.76 (0.30, 1.97)	
Mother's education level (reference: completed secondary)			
No education	1.31 (0.73, 2.36)	0.51 (0.14, 1.88)	1.61 (0.86, 3.02)
At least some primary	0.81 (0.42, 1.59)	0.77 (0.18, 3.29)	0.74 (0.34, 1.60)
Incomplete secondary	1.15 (0.71, 1.86)	1.59 (0.47, 5.44)	1.07 (0.62, 1.84)
Higher	1.11 (0.78, 1.60)	1.33 (0.56, 3.18)	1.05 (0.70, 1.57)
Mother is overweight or obese	0.90 (0.62, 1.31)	0.45 (0.20, 1.00)	1.10 (0.70, 1.72)
Child received postnatal checkup	0.82 (0.53, 1.26)	0.21* (0.06, 0.75)	1.06 (0.67, 1.69)
Mother received postnatal checkup	3.61 (0.90, 14.38)	3.02 (0.28, 32.23)	4.58 (0.76, 27.66)
Mother participates in decisions on large household purchases	0.85 (0.58, 1.24)	1.93 (0.82, 4.53)	0.74 (0.48, 1.12)
Mother participates in decisions about visiting her family	1.19 (0.76, 1.86)	0.59 (0.20, 1.69)	1.34 (0.81, 2.21)
Household in top two wealth quintiles	1.17 (0.66, 2.08)	1.65 (0.41, 6.56)	1.13 (0.59, 2.16)

Note: CI = confidence level; OR = odds ratio.
*$p < 0.05$ **$p < 0.01$ ***$p < 0.001$.

TABLE B.4 Adjusted odds ratio of stunting for rural children 0–23 months in Egypt

	AGE GROUP		
	0–23 MONTHS	0–5 MONTHS	6–23 MONTHS
	ADJUSTED OR (95% CI)	ADJUSTED OR (95% CI)	ADJUSTED OR (95% CI)
Sex (reference female)			
Male	1.48** (1.17, 1.87)	2.06* (1.18, 3.61)	1.47** (1.13, 1.91)
Child's size at birth (mother's report) (reference: average size)			
Large or very large	0.50 (0.21, 1.24)	1.83 (0.29, 11.55)	0.35* (0.13, 0.95)
Small or very small	1.39* (1.03, 1.86)	1.95 (0.97, 3.96)	1.32 (0.95, 1.84)
Early initiation of breastfeeding	0.64** (0.48, 0.85)	0.64 (0.29, 1.43)	0.65** (0.48, 0.88)
Adequate meal frequency			0.92 (0.69, 1.22)
Fed a diverse diet			1.20 (0.91, 1.59)
Currently breastfed			0.95 (0.66, 1.36)
Exclusively breastfed		0.95 (0.47, 1.90)	
Mother's education level (reference: completed secondary)			
No education	1.08 (0.76, 1.53)	1.67 (0.77, 3.58)	1.01 (0.68, 1.49)
At least some primary	1.53* (1.02, 2.30)	1.50 (0.54, 4.22)	1.52 (0.97, 2.38)
Incomplete secondary	1.48* (1.07, 2.06)	2.06 (0.98, 4.33)	1.36 (0.95, 1.96)
Higher	1.02 (0.67, 1.55)	0.80 (0.28, 2.28)	1.07 (0.68, 1.69)
Mother is overweight or obese	0.83 (0.64, 1.07)	1.09 (0.60, 2.00)	0.79 (0.59, 1.05)
Child received postnatal checkup	1.09 (0.78, 1.52)	0.99 (0.48, 2.02)	1.06 (0.73, 1.54)
Mother received postnatal checkup	1.28 (0.61, 2.70)	1.70 (0.26, 10.95)	1.26 (0.56, 2.83)
Mother participates in decisions on large household purchases	0.88 (0.66, 1.17)	0.53 (0.28, 1.00)	0.96 (0.70, 1.31)
Mother participates in decisions about visiting her family	0.97 (0.72, 1.31)	1.27 (0.64, 2.50)	0.95 (0.68, 1.32)
Wealth quintile (reference: poorest)			
Second	1.15 (0.84, 1.57)	0.54 (0.23, 1.28)	1.25 (0.88, 1.77)
Third	0.76 (0.55, 1.05)	0.95 (0.47, 1.92)	0.74 (0.51, 1.06)
Fourth	0.81 (0.53, 1.22)	2.39 (0.98, 5.88)	0.63 (0.39, 1.01)
Household has improved toilet facility	1.23 (0.87, 1.74)	1.25 (0.55, 2.85)	1.22 (0.83, 1.80)

Note: CI = confidence level; OR = odds ratio.
*$p < 0.05$ **$p < 0.01$ ***$p < 0.001$.

Glossary

adiposity The quality or state of being fat.

anemia Defined as a hemoglobin concentration below a specified cutoff point that can change according to the age, gender, physiological status, smoking habits, and altitude at which the population being assessed lives. The World Health Organization (WHO) defines anemia in children under 5 years of age and pregnant women as a hemoglobin concentration of less than 110 grams per liter at sea level. A low hemoglobin concentration impairs the ability of red blood cells to supply oxygen to body tissues and is associated with an increased risk of maternal and child mortality. Anemia can be caused by an inadequate intake or poor absorption of iron, folate, vitamin B_{12}, and other nutrients, as well as infectious diseases (including malaria and hookworm infections) and genetic factors. Iron-deficiency anemia reduces the work capacity of individuals and entire populations, with serious consequences for an economy and national development. In addition, the negative consequences of iron-deficiency anemia on the cognitive and physical development of children and on physical performance—particularly on the work productivity of adults—are major concerns.

anthropometry Measurement of physical body characteristics, most commonly weight and height, but also circumference of body parts (head, arm, waist, etc.), as a tool for monitoring growth. Anthropometry is also used as a proxy indicator of nutritional status. Anthropometric indicators can point to malnutrition, but they do not provide evidence of deficiencies in specific macro- or micronutrients.

body mass index (BMI) A measure of relative weight given by weight in kilograms divided by height in square meters. In adults, both underweight (thinness) and overweight are measured using BMI.

colostrum The first breast milk secreted in the first few days after childbirth, often thick and yellow. Colostrum has many health and nutrition benefits: it contains antibodies and other proteins that help transfer immunity from the mother to child and protect the infant from infection; it contains growth factors to keep the intestines mature; and it is rich in vitamin A, vitamin K, and other nutrients.

complementary feeding The process of introducing age-appropriate, adequate, and safe solid or semisolid foods in addition to breast milk or a breast milk substitute when breast milk alone is no longer sufficient to meet the nutritional requirements of an infant. The target age range for complementary feeding is 6–23 months.

disability-adjusted life year (DALY) A measure equivalent to a year of healthy life lost from a health condition. The DALY, developed in 1993 by the World Bank, is a measure of the overall disease burden and combines the years of life lost from a disease and the years of life spent with disability from the disease. DALYs averted is a key measure used in health economics to evaluate and compare the cost-effectiveness of health programs and interventions. It captures the number of years of a person's life saved by a given intervention and adjusts it by the health status that person is expected to have during those years. Combined with cost data, DALYs allow one to estimate and compare the cost-effectiveness of scaling up nutrition interventions in different countries.

epigenetic modifications Changes in the expression of genes (rather than the genes themselves), which can stem from external and internal environmental exposures and influence physiological processes such as metabolism and the development of disease. Epigenetic modifications provide a potential link between maternal nutrition, early life environmental exposures, and susceptibility to disease.

food fortification Addition of micronutrients to food during or after processing.

infant and young child feeding (IYCF) Feeding of infants (under 12 months of age) and young children (12–23 months of age). The key interventions of IYCF include protection, promotion, and support of optimal breastfeeding practices (exclusive breastfeeding for the first six months and continued breastfeeding for two years or beyond) and support for and promotion of optimal complementary feeding practices (such as the timely introduction of complementary feeding). Issues of policy and legislation around the regulation of marketing infant formula and other breast milk substitutes are also addressed by these interventions.

Lives Saved Tool (LiST) An estimation tool that translates measured coverage changes into estimates of mortality reduction and cases of childhood stunting averted. LiST is used to estimate the impact of scaling up health and nutrition interventions on maternal, newborn, and child health, and stillbirths.

low birthweight (LBW) Weight of less than 2,500 grams at time of birth. LBW is a significant public health concern, with the birth of LBW infants 20 times more likely than that of heavier infants. It is associated with a greater likelihood of developing stunting and chronic diseases later in life. It includes preterm neonates (born before 37 weeks of gestation), small-for-gestational-age neonates at term, and the overlap between these two situations (preterm and small-for-gestational-age neonates).

macronutrients The fat, protein, and carbohydrates needed for a wide range of body functions and processes.

malnutrition A broad term commonly used as an alternative to *undernutrition* but that technically refers to any dysfunction of nutrition, including inadequate, excessive, or unbalanced nutrition.

metabolic syndrome A group of risk factors including abdominal obesity, dyslipidemia, hypertension, and impaired glucose tolerance.

micronutrients Essential vitamins and minerals required in miniscule amounts for the maintenance of essential body processes.

mid–upper arm circumference (MUAC) The circumference of the mid–upper arm as measured on a straight left arm midway between the tip of the shoulder and the tip of the elbow. This measure can be used to measure acute malnutrition and wasting in children 6–59 months of age.

nutrition-sensitive interventions Interventions that address the underlying determinants of malnutrition and development (such as food security and adequate resources) at the individual (especially maternal and caregiver), household, and community levels; access to health services and a safe and hygienic environment; and access to information about healthy food choices. These interventions incorporate specific nutrition goals and actions. Nutrition-sensitive programs can be used as delivery platforms for nutrition-specific interventions, which can increase their scale, coverage, and effectiveness.

nutrition-specific interventions Interventions that address the immediate determinants of malnutrition, including fetal and child nutrition and development or the nutritional status of older children and adults (adequate food and nutrient intake, feeding, caregiving and parenting practices, and burden of infectious disease).

obesogenic Factors tending to make individuals fat, such as environments that promote decreased physical activity or increased intake of energy-dense foods.

overnutrition Consumption of more calories than needed to maintain growth and health.

overweight/obesity For children under 5, overweight is measured as a child who has a weight for height more than two standard deviations higher than the median for a child of the same height and sex, according to the WHO Child Growth Standard. WHO has recommended classifications of overweight (BMI greater than or equal to 25) and obesity (BMI greater than or equal to 30) that are associated with an increased risk of some noncommunicable diseases. As a measure of relative body weight, BMI is easy to obtain. It is an acceptable proxy for fatness and has been directly related to health risks and death rates in many populations. At the population level, the prevalence of overweight/obesity derived from BMI cutoffs can be useful for developing and implementing policy actions and for facilitating prevention. BMI cutoffs for overweight and obesity can also be used as screening tools to identify high-risk individuals and for diagnostic purposes in combination with other clinical measurements and risk factors.

short stature Often measured in women of reproductive age and defined as height less than 145 centimeters. Women of short stature are at greater risk of obstetric complications because of a smaller pelvis. Small women are at greater risk of delivering an infant with low birthweight, which contributes to an intergenerational cycle of malnutrition because infants of low birthweight or retarded intrauterine growth tend to be smaller as adults.

stunting Often referred to as "chronic malnutrition" and measured as low height for age, stunting is the most common form of undernutrition. Among children under 5, stunting is reflected in low height for age (that is, a height more than two standard deviations below the median height of a child of the same age and sex, according to the WHO Child Growth Standard). The percentage of children with a low height for age (stunting) reflects the cumulative effects of undernutrition and infections since and even before birth. This measure can therefore be interpreted as an indication of poor environmental conditions or long-term restriction of a child's growth potential.

undernutrition A state of inadequate or unbalanced intake or absorption of the macro- and micronutrients needed for growth and maintenance of health, resulting in nutrition deficiency. Undernutrition covers a range of disorders, including growth failure and micronutrient deficiencies.

underweight Low weight for age. Among children under 5, underweight is reflected in a weight that is more than two standard deviations below the median weight of a child of the same age and sex, according to the WHO Growth Standard. The percentage of children who are underweight can include children who have both low weight for height and low height for age. Thus it is a composite indicator and can be difficult to interpret.

wasting Also known as acute malnutrition. Among children under 5, wasting can be measured using weight-for-height or mid–upper arm circumference. Using weight-for-height cutoffs, wasting is defined as a weight that is more than two standard deviations below the median weight of a child of the same height and sex. Using MUAC, acute malnutrition is defined as an MUAC of less than 125 millimeters or the presence of bilateral pitting edema. There are two levels of wasting severity: moderate acute malnutrition (MAM) and severe acute malnutrition (SAM). Wasting in children is a symptom of acute undernutrition, usually as a consequence of insufficient food intake or a high incidence of infectious diseases, especially diarrhea. Wasting in turn impairs the functioning of the immune system and can lead to greater susceptibility to infectious diseases, increased severity and duration of such diseases, and an increased risk of death.